Y. B. Mulhur.

Good luck and best wishes.

Ludothini.

February 1999.

A SAPPER'S WAR

Leonard Watkins

MINERVA PRESS

MONTREUX LONDON WASHINGTON

A SAPPER'S WAR
Copyright © Leonard Watkins 1996

All Rights Reserved

ISBN 1 85863 715 5

First Published 1996 by
MINERVA PRESS
195 Knightsbridge
London SW7 1RE

2nd Impression 1998

Printed in Great Britain for Minerva Press

A SAPPER'S WAR

*This book is dedicated to those men and women
who, in the words of Rupert Brooke, form some corner
of a foreign field which is forever England.*

*They gave their lives in order to stop the
power-greedy nations from conquering the world
and subjecting its peoples to slavery.*

And to

*Guy, my one year old grandson.
May it please the 'powers that be' to see that he and his
generation do not have to experience war and bloodshed.*

CHAPTER ONE

THE BEGINNING OF IT ALL

So this was the inside of a French brothel! Very dimly lit with high ceilings and walls mostly covered with drapes and curtains of various colours and materials, at least this was the impression gained through the drunken eyes and fuzzy mind of a twenty year old virgin soldier – Lance Corporal Royal Engineers to be exact.

My French companion and I were standing in what appeared to be a central hallway of a large dingy building with several corridors leading off into the darkness beyond. My newly found friend approached the very buxom 'Madame' of the brothel and held a rapid conversation with her in French, during which the words 'soldat Anglaise' were used several times, with the appropriate glances thrown in my direction.

The 'Madame' appeared, at last, satisfied with what was being said to her, gave a clap of her hands and a couple of shouts in a high pitched voice and, surprisingly, from odd corners there appeared girls of all shapes and sizes, some white, some black and some of varying degrees between the two.

They were slowly herded into a resemblance of a straight line - no comparison with the drill movement on the barrack square at Chatham of course - but then this was, after all, a totally different reason for forming a line.

On completion of this manoeuvre the 'Madame' turned to me, spoke rapidly for at least three minutes in fluent French, none of which I understood, but by her arm actions and gestures I was made to understand that I was to inspect 'the goods on show'. Never had an inspecting General been faced with such a task and never, in history before, I guess, had a L/Cpl RE been faced with (a) keeping 'Madame' under control (b) dealing with each girl in turn who was trying her best to catch my eye and at the same time show her wares to the best advantage and (c) trying to behave normally, to walk and talk straight when my body was not doing what my brain was telling it, if it was telling it anything at all.

I stood for several seconds in front of No.1 girl. From memory, she was rather a large country-type with a made-up face and dark hair. Without hesitation she reached forward, grabbed both my hands and placed them firmly on her breasts and uttered two French words, "Bon! Eh?" as her face lit into a pleasing smile. This action came as quite a shock to me because, as I said before, I was, at twenty, still a virgin soldier.

I realised that Madame was telling me the girl's name and was already moving to girl No. 2, so this told me in as many words 'Don't hang around, you are not here all night'.

As I stood in front of No. 2, another shock was in store, she reached down to the front bottom of her flimsy clothes and promptly lifted her hem to face level so revealing the whole of her front. I found myself gazing at a coffee coloured body of doubtful pedigree and most certainly something I had never gazed at before, a nude female! She reached for my hand, caressed it for a moment and then attempted to place it in an even more intimate place on her body than No. 1, and at the same time repeating the "Bon, eh? Trés bon, eh?"

By this time my brain was beginning to wake to reality and was sending out signals of alarm. What was I doing here? What was I doing in a country totally unfriendly to the British, and so liable to have my throat cut at any moment? Looking along the line of girls I judged that there were still about fifteen to be 'inspected' and wondered that if No. 1 and No. 2 had acted as they had done, what was still to come? So again I said to myself, 'How the hell did I get into this?' So, I had better start explaining to you.

Firstly I have entitled the book 'The Sapper's War' because that is exactly what it is; it covers the period from 1937-1946, so taking in the Second World War, and is all written from the 'lower ranks' point of view. The reader will appreciate that the

War from the Generals and Political Leaders points of view has been well documented on many occasions, but few people of 'the other ranks' have, either through lack of time or opportunity, bothered to set down their personal experiences for all to share.

Again, I must stress that all incidents are absolutely true to the best of my memory at age seventy one years, and are indeed verified by a rough diary kept by myself which sometimes was written under very adverse and trying conditions e.g.: a corner of a very wet and muddy slit trench with all sorts of things flying through the air above, or in the corner of some ruined farmhouse probably wrapped in an army blanket whilst desperately trying to dry out clothing which had been saturated by several days of rain, rain which had to be experienced to be appreciated. The diary just had to be written under these conditions and brought up to date every few days, because so many things were happening, that to think back over a week or so would probably distort what had really taken place.

There are so many versions of events and things that happened (or did not happen) written about today (1993/1994) that I am more than pleased to be able to 'put the record straight' from personal experience. You will find that I have been very blunt, even shocking on such things as (a) bullying of recruits (b) so-called male rape (c) cowardice (d) sadism etc., but I again repeat that all that happened is as I recorded it at the time.

Early 1937 was not a good time for this country, in fact, most of the world was suffering from extreme poverty and degradation but, as events turned out, a lot of this was hidden away by world leaders and politicians, and so was never really appreciated by the common man.

There were two very strong leaders of their countries in Europe who were to affect my life very much indeed (1) Hitler, leader of Nazi Germany and (2) Mussolini, leader of Fascist Italy. If this had been known at the time would it have made any difference? It is very doubtful because one had to grab any opportunity that was offered and progress from there.

I was born the youngest of a family of two boys and a girl in a small South Wales market town. My father was a male nurse at the local mental hospital. Prior to that he had been a haulier to a local building contractor and was the proud owner of two fine horses. His job was to haul building material and men to the various projects in a specified area. I say proud owner because two photographs taken of the 1910 'School Walks' in Brynmawr, when the New Griffin Hotel was being built show him in the background proudly sitting on his horse and cart. These postcards had been written on by him and sent to my Mother during their courting days. She was a cook to a family in Edgbaston, Birmingham, something which most working class girls did in those days and was called 'being in service'. Money was hard to come by in 1937, but Dad was very hard working and indeed very lucky to have full employment, because all around us, particularly in the valleys area of South Wales, hundreds of men were on the dole. The weekly wage from 'The Jug,' as the local mental hospital was called, was about £2.17 shillings a week. Today's inflation figures and decimalisation makes that an unbelievably low figure but Mother somehow made ends meet. There was the rent to pay on a two down three up cottage, and to help, indeed to keep the family in vegetables and fruit, father would work like a slave in the garden.

Of Mother I cannot give enough praise. Although small in stature, she worked very hard to bring up her family, cleaning, shopping, mending, cooking and the thousand and one things a good mother has to do on little money. Her cooking could not be faulted in any way and here her years of service obviously stood her in good stead. Kind and generous, she would go out of her way to be friendly to all who came into contact with her.

In order to help out with the family budget, my sister started work at fourteen in a local grocery shop, my brother apprenticed himself to a local baker (temporarily anyway) but eventually became a fully fledged postman, and I was running errands part-time, before leaving school, for the local high class tailor. My father, bless him, would sometimes walk with me on these errands – sometimes four miles each way – and after a day's work at 'The Jug', all for a couple of shillings a week. One thing I will always be grateful to Mr Potter the tailor for, is that he introduced me to some wonderful books. It opened a new world to me to read Conan Doyle, Micah Clarke, Rodney Stone etc. and eventually found there was not enough time in the day to do all the reading I wanted.

Another man to whom I shall be eternally grateful was my head teacher at Hereford Road (Boys) School, AV Pavord. A man of immense character, strong personal views on all subjects and whose knowledge of everything on land and sea was limitless, or so it appeared to my fourteen year old mind at the time. He treated us senior boys as men and in turn we responded by doing our utmost for ourselves and him. The cane or other forms of corporal punishment were, in contrast to all the other teachers, never used, and yet he had the best disciplined class in the school. Indirectly he was one of the causes of me following the career I did. He had taken us on a trip into the Wye Valley and at a pocket of rock high in the cliff face overlooking the river, he pointed out to us all the interesting landmarks which could be seen for some dozen or so miles around. The one remark which stuck in my mind was:

"See the smudge of buildings right in the distance where the Wye joins the Severn? That is the Army College where boys aged fourteen onwards are taught trades and professions of their choosing."

CHAPTER TWO

THE FUTURE TAKES SHAPE

Some months after this trip, my Mother received a letter from no less a person than Brigadier General Bruce Tulloch – a well-known dignitary in the district – requesting that she bring me to tea at his house one day when it was convenient.

Well the great day arrived and we walked the several miles to this huge stone house on the hill with its high walls and gravelled driveway. By the time we were ushered into the presence of Mrs Bruce Tulloch, I was completely mesmerised by the amount of marble and silver which seemed to be everywhere. She appeared to me as a strong but kindly personality, one who had spent years overseas (for instance) playing the part of the Colonel's Lady and dealing with servants and minor individuals with grace and ease.

Her first words floored me: "The General has been called away," and then she went on to explain just what the General had wanted to say to me.

He, apparently, was a strongly religious man and regularly attended St Mary's and Christ Church services whenever possible and he had noted me and 'my bearing' when I was singing or moving in procession with the choir. He had had words with both the vicar and curate of those respective churches and both had given me an excellent character reference (little did they know the material they were talking about)! The General thought that I was 'just the type' of boy who would benefit from learning a trade or profession at the Army Apprentice College, Chepstow, deciding afterwards whether or not to make the Army my career. Furthermore, he had already spoken to the Commandant of the College who had said that there would be 'an intake' of boys the next January and if I was agreeable and sat and passed the written examination I could be one of those privileged boys. Well, the tea and cucumber sandwiches were very good and Mother seemed delighted to be moving in those high circles.

Now I was faced with decision time. On the one side, entering a profession was out without the schooling necessary. Apprenticeship in a building firm (which father approved of) would have meant six months or even the first year running errands for the men on site, making tea, cleaning up every mess as it happened and being a general dogsbody to all and sundry. No thank you!

On the other side of the coin there waited what every boy (or nearly so) of fourteen dreamed of - unlimited sports facilities, soccer, cricket, rugby, hockey and even rifle shooting. A three year plus apprenticeship into a trade or profession. Daily school studies up to unlimited standards, depending on the student of course. No time wasting running around as tea boy, and, a big and, to be paid for it all the time I was learning and enjoying myself. All this within thirty miles of home, to which I could pop back every weekend when I was not playing soccer etc.

The choice was made without much hesitation. My 'Uncle' Reg took me to the barracks at Newport to sit the entrance examination, he got well and truly drunk (being an ex-navy man) while I was sweating it out, and I had to bring him home, something which involved practically carrying him on and off trains. A good man, who was recalled to the Navy when war broke out and killed within the first few weeks on a motor torpedo boat in the Channel.

Mother insisted that what remained of his body had to be brought home for burial, although she had to search desperately to get enough money together for that to happen.

Well the Maths, English and Intelligence tests were duly passed and I got my joining date as 21st January 1937 - aged fourteen and a few months.

Mother came with me by bus to Chepstow, and while I had twenty minutes to wait for the Beachley bus, her bus for the return journey left immediately. I can still see that handkerchief, and the tear-stained face looking at me as the bus pulled out. My heart was in my boots – Mother, what had I done?

Joining that Army School was not just a shock, but a whole series of shocks which my sheltered way of life, up until then, had not prepared me for.

The everyday life of a young Army recruit is something experienced by thousands of men, so those matters will not be dwelt upon, but a brief outline of things and happenings which I think were out of the ordinary should prove interesting and sometimes shocking reading, and here I repeat that everything that did happen occurred exactly as I remember it, all those years ago.

CHAPTER THREE

ARMY APPRENTICE COLLEGE, CHEPSTOW

In recent times I have watched TV programmes and read in the press about bullying and sexual misconduct in the Army, and seen strong denials by usually senior officers of these things ever taking place. It is realised by all thinking people, of course, that wherever groups of boys or men are confined to restricted areas for eating, living and sleeping such as the Services, Public Schools etc., such things as sexual misconduct do take place, whereas bullying is practically an everyday occurrence. The denials, trials, court-martials, take place in order to prove the innocence of that particular body, which must be seen to be whiter than white, but there is always the poor scapegoat who 'carries the can' for the 'crime' although it is being perpetrated by many others all the time.

The most miserable things were happening to me, such as being herded around like lost sheep, being shouted at in foul language, living in unheated army huts, being made to eat food that my Mother would have had nightmares about, being made to wear thick khaki shirts and trousers, which, after one day, rubbed your skin raw. Standing shivering, in mid January, on a windswept barrack square until you could stand no more, and, as happened to me and many others, falling flat on your face in a dead faint, coming around to find you had a smashed mouth and nose. All these things I could put down to Army discipline and Army life, and although it was proving to be very hard I was willing to accept them, knowing that eventually, as I grew out of the recruit stage, things would improve.

There were also things that made life practically unbearable, things which today, looking back, make me wonder why I didn't do more about it at the time, like complaining to what seemed an unapproachable officer or senior NCO. The thought did occur on many occasions that less than thirty miles away was a wonderful home, where all the love and affection I had missed recently would again be lavished upon me; that is, of course until the Redcaps came to pick me up.

The first experience of the so-called 'Administration of the Army' was the fact that a certain number of boys had entered Chepstow (as it was always referred to throughout the Army) on the same day and these had to be divided between the four Companies - A B C and D. A Coy had 60, B had 58, C had 60 odd and D (my lot) had 29. This wonderful piece of 'Admin.' was the cause of endless suffering and bullying. Every week each of these Groups (as they were called) had to produce, depending on the season, three teams to play against each other at soccer, rugby and either hockey or cricket. There is no way that 3 teams of 11 men could be had out of 29, so we were always either men short or had to accept 'bodies' that were not required by the other sides. Our defeats at soccer averaged 12 nil, rugby 50 points etc., etc. and as the Army Authorities took 'ability at sport' very seriously, we were soon in trouble. We became the laughing stock and the butt of jokes from all those wonderful teams of fifty or sixty strong. In turn we were called by the 'Admin.' people, lazy, useless and a collective lot of scroungers. Please imagine the feelings of those men of 39D Company.

It is with very sad and mixed feelings that I have, over the past 50 years, turned the pages in the School Chapel of the Book of Remembrance and there, for all to see are the names of the men who died for their country. Of all the Groups that passed through that school, 39D had the most decorations and, in proportion, gave more lives than any other Group. Such wonderful boys, sacrificed in a totally unnecessary way as Charlie Shaw, Jock Drongin (my mate), 'Dukie' Stanley, Frank Palmer, 'Tich' Mouser, Bob Bullen, my other friend whose headstone I traced many years later to the British Military Cemetery in Medjez-El-Bab. His date of death was October 1943 (22 years old) and yet the campaign ended six months before that. I wrote to the RE Records and various Sapper organisations for some explanation, because buried with Bob were a dozen or so other Sappers of various ranks. No one could tell me why, so I must assume that a huge explosion took place on that day.

The incident that happened next still stands out vividly in my memory and can never be erased. Earlier I spoke about leading a sheltered life and how this new way of life was causing shock after shock until, I think, the breaking point had arrived. It is told exactly as I remember it happening at the time, following the sequence of events.

My Group shared two miserably cold army huts and a washroom, open ended, with four toilets and a row of basins with cold water, no hot. In my room slept sixteen boys and a senior boy (of about 18) in a closed-in bunk, who was in charge of the discipline of the room. Among these sixteen boys were two boys from a senior group, who, I understand, had failed some exams or other and had been relegated in order to start their training again, by name 'Monka' Marsh and Rosy Waddington. 'Monka' could be best described as an ape-like creature, strong, rough, slow minded and had earned the name 'Monka' from appearance. Rosy Waddington was totally different, flabby, fat, giggly and went by the name of 'Rosy' because of an almost Bunter-type figure.

There was little furniture to share between sixteen, just one table and two forms. All wooden and scrubbed white every night by whosoever the 'roster' detailed that week. A description of the forms would be – because it features in the story – three or four wooden battens, planed smooth, supported by metal legs and held upright by metal bracing from underneath the centre to the base of the legs. Because of lack of furniture, every boy sat on his bed of an evening doing his personal chores, and there were plenty of those, boots to 'bone' and polish, brass to polish etc., etc. Each boy had a kit box to keep all personal things in such as writing materials, books, magazines etc.

On this particular evening 'Monka' announced in a loud voice that someone had pinched his stamps, and that he was going to search everybody's kit until he found them. Thinking back on this I wonder why an alarm bell had not rung in my mind sooner, because, for several days prior to this, 'Monka' had been more than friendly towards me, putting his arm around me or attempting to stroke my backside at every opportunity - naturally, I resisted most strongly and almost came to blows on one occasion. Looking back now on my early photographs of those school days, I can imagine that, with my curly fair hair, blue eyes and freckles, I did have a somewhat pretty appearance and it was this that attracted Monka and his animal desires.

They worked their way around the room going from kit box to kit box and finding nothing until, that is, he came to my box. On lifting the lid, there, for everyone to see were two stamps, obviously, to my mind planted there by Monka. About this there was no doubt because I wrote only one letter a week to Mother who always sent me a stamp, knowing how little money we got, inside the local weekly paper with her letter.

He immediately shouted,

"Thief, thief!! Come on boys strip him off!"

This, believing Monka, a crowd of the boys did, under firm protest from me and under his directions proceeded to carry me, naked, to the freezing cold washroom. One of the forms was produced and I was forced to lie face down on it with a dozen boys holding both legs and arms. By twisting my head I could see that Monka had now appeared. The appearance shook everyone and they all had second thoughts about what they were helping to do. He was naked with the look on his face of one who had lost control of all sense. He had an erect penis in his hand and was masturbating frantically, his whole objective being to ram this into my backside. There was no way in the world that I was going to allow this to happen and struggled furiously. As I broke free, he reached a climax and dribbled on to my backside. He then disappeared from view through the washroom to the sound of Rosy shouting, "Scrub him off, scrub him off!!"

This was carried out with the use of buckets of ice cold water and a bass broom.

As harrowing as this incident was to my young and clean mind, I knew that I could overcome it because I was innocent of stealing his stamps and what's more could prove it. After washing properly, (we had no shower or bath), I wrapped up as warm as possible, went to bed and lay awake for hours, thinking about what action to take next, knowing now that I had been branded a thief.

A thief in the Army, or any collection of men, is someone to be despised by all and sundry. It meant that no kit was safe from him, and everything had to be locked away at all times. In addition to this, he was usually a sneak as well, one who would go running to his senior at the first chance with 'tales out of school'. My first protest should have been through the boy of 18, an A/T Cpl who, as I said previously, was responsible for the discipline of that room, and then up the chain of command as high as I could go. But, thinking long and carefully about it as I had done all night, I realised that firstly, he would get into trouble for allowing this to happen - where had he been? Then there were the boys, who, believing 'Monka', had aided and abetted him.

Then, most of all, there was dear Mother, through whom I knew that I could prove her weekly stamp was sent to me without fail every week. To think of her in a trial or Court Martial giving evidence after listening to all the sordid details of what had happened to me was just beyond all possibility. She could not have survived it.

In no way was I going to be branded a thief. When reveille sounded and everyone was stirring it was a matter of going over to Monka's bed and demanding in as loud a voice as I could muster - what was he going to do about what had happened? Why had he lied about the stamps? Why had he involved the boys in his dirty work etc., etc.? He avoided me, grabbed his towel and made his way to the washroom, followed closely by me demanding to know the answers to those questions again and again in a loud voice, which was overheard by everyone within earshot. This 'campaign' of mine was closely followed up at every opportunity, even on the 'square'. If Sgt. Reeves would fall us out for a short break, the same answers would be demanded from a position directly in front of Monka.

At last people were taking notice and when Sgt. Reeves asked: "What's to do?" the reply he got was,

"Just a personal quarrel."

My best chance of proving my innocence would of course be when the mail arrived with the stamp inside. Never was there such a long week and by now he was beginning to issue threats, such as,

"If you keep on, I'll knock the shit out of you," etc., etc. His skin had been penetrated!

Friday arrived at last and with it, my paper from home. Several of the boys were around the table, and they were asked to watch while Charlie Shaw opened the paper, and there, as I knew it would be, was the most beautiful stamp in the world a 2d King George VI, I think, attached by a piece of perforated stamp paper to the top of Mum's letter. The truth was there for all to see including Monka, who was now asked by several voices - why? Why had he done this to Watkins? He immediately blamed Rosy -

"It was his idea to plant the stamps," and flew across the room and smacked him full in the face. His assumed rage was terrible and he repeatedly rained blows to the face until dragged away. 'Rosy' was blubbering and the whole story, hatched by both but under Monka's directions, came out.

When the reasons for not reporting the whole incident came out it was decided that I wasn't such a bad sort after all!

Again I repeat, this is an incident which could have happened in any walk of life where boys or men live together, and most certainly helped to make and shape character.

Initial training consisted of three weeks on 'the square', under Sgt. Reeves, a typical 'old sweat' of many years standing whose coarse wit caused many a titter in the ranks, followed by a rollicking. A sample might be:

"If you don't hold your head upright, boy, I'll take you in the corner and do you."

No rifles were issued – we were only boys – just foot and cane drill. These three weeks were broken up by spells in the classroom, and what a relief they were.

An examination had to be passed, in several months time, called the Army 2nd Class Certificate. It was for English, Maths and Map Reading and proved quite reasonable under the careful tuition of one, 'Drag' Elders – a warrant officer in the Education Corps whose total height, when in a temper, was about 5' 1". There were also several periods during the week of 'gym', a sweat shop where time was passed skip jumping, climbing wall bars, breaking one's neck over a high horse or trying to climb over unassailable beams. It must have done something for me because after about a year of it, the 'gang of lads' at home on the river bank could easily be beaten at running, jumping etc.

Even at this early stage, a great feeling of friendship was beginning to manifest itself amongst the boys. Monka and Rosy had been posted and we settled down to making a good thing out of what appeared to be bad. 'Passing Out' parade, for instance, was at the end of the first three weeks square bashing and, according to the old sweats, was something to be dreaded because one had to be 'bulled' up to the eye brows, with all the dignitaries, from the Commandant downwards to inspect you. When the great day came, it came and went as an almost enjoyable experience. Some of the boys' fathers were time serving and had taught their offspring the (Army) words to our marches. For instance when the school band struck up Colonel Bogey - words everyone knew, and the slow march, the name of which I have long forgotten, but known to us as:- 'Somebody shit on the doorstep, Mother she said it was me' etc., etc. was quietly sung in the ranks and, unbeknown to the hierarchy, a great time was had by all.

Bullying was an everyday occurrence and was systematically carried out on scruffs, thieves, sneaks and even for religious reasons.

One of the main causes for what is called collective bullying would be instigated by the instructor who would say, for instance, such and such a boy is really scruffy and if you cannot teach him to improve by the time 'Passing Out' comes along, there will be no weekend passes for anyone.

As for religious reasons, a lad in our Group was Jewish, named Epstein. He, although a cheerful type, became the butt of a whole lot of bullying particularly from the senior boys.

Enough has been said about early training and we now progress to 'Workshops'. Shocks galore again.

I had been accepted as a stone mason, not first choice by any means. I would have much preferred one of the 'clean' trades such as electrician, fitter, etc., but here we were, filling the only vacancies available at that time.

Here I was to meet the character who would affect my life in a most unlikely and unwanted way - 'Bill' W.

He was a fairly tall, stringy man, dour and miserable with a grim face until he thought that he could get a laugh at the expense of some miserable apprentice, like me, with no risk of retaliation.

He misjudged me from day one and thought that here were easy pickings for his cruel and sadistic behaviour.

After a few months of bricklaying only, under decent military instruction, we were handed over to the master mason 'Bill', for his instructions in the complicated art of stone carving and laying. The intricacies of which were to amaze us with its many and varied names and forms of laying etc.

Not to dwell too long on this spell of learning, this way of life was, nevertheless, very hard indeed. Out in all weathers, lifting and chiselling huge lumps of stone, mixing concrete etc. On one occasion several senior boys and myself were detailed to unload a lorry full of 1cwt bags of cement. My age was just fifteen and as each bag was dumped unceremoniously on to the shoulder of each boy, I felt my knees buckling under the weight. Five tons of twenty bags to the ton, for five boys, twenty bags each to be carried about thirty yards each time. It was impossible to straighten one's back for weeks afterwards, apart from being doused in a layer of thick cement. Baths were available only after sports day, when the bath house attendant would unlock a line of grubby deep shower basins where one had to curl into a ball in order to get covered by the water. So the cement had to be washed off afterwards in cold water.

Over and above all this was 'Bill'. He took great delight in using sarcasm in the extreme and creating situations where the unlucky recipient of his tongue would be embarrassed nearly beyond endurance. For instance, after two years or so of cutting and laying stone, a trade test had to be passed. This usually consisted of cutting and laying an ashlar wall containing a window and door opening within a set period of time. Speed was essential, therefore, and sometimes a mortar joint was not filled 100%. This attracted 'Bill' like a magnet and he would stand on the other side of the wall pretending to be able to see through the joint. The first the poor victim learned that things were not what they should be, was a loud 'Cooeee' from the other side of the wall. The cooeee was always followed by the words – 'I can see you!'

This stupid performance by a supposedly intelligent adult was repeated several times in an ever increasing loud voice, until everyone within earshot had stopped whatever they were doing and stood watching, while Bill, pretended to peer through the offending joint, then straightened his knees and leered at the poor victim over the top of the wall. Imagine the embarrassment caused to the young lad, who dared not answer back in fear of the consequences. Although Bill was a civilian, he had all the powers that be behind him as far as insubordination was concerned. It was felt, and discussed amongst the boys later, that one day 'Bill' would have those words rammed down his throat. These comments were usually followed by: 'When I'm a bit older and bigger'!

It really was a hard life; poor accommodation, poor food, bullying by senior boys, sadistic NCOs screaming abuse at the slightest misdemeanour and on top of it all, 'Bill'. One day someone would give him as good as he was dishing out. Little did I know, at that time, that it would be me and that as a result of just a few words, my future would be changed.

Not to depart from the sequence of events, another favourite practice of 'Bill's' must first be described. This again was cruelly designed to cause maximum embarrassment to the poor victim.

During the course of the day, lectures would be given by 'Bill' on the theory side of the trade. Sometimes these were given in the classroom or the corner of the Masons' shop – a huge building of bolted angle iron and corrugated sheeting – stone cold in winter, red hot in summer. 'Bill' had a small office in the corner from where he could see all that was happening. In various parts of this large building would be groups of bricklayers under their instructors and several groups of masons of various ages, all of course under 'Bill'. During these periods of lectures, questions would be asked by 'Bill', and amazingly always answered by the senior boys quickly and without much thought. It took several months experience to realise that it was fatal practice to answer:

"I don't know, Sir." That word 'Sir' was always used when addressing 'Bill', but we liked to think that it was spelt 'Cur'.

If an innocent had answered truthfully to a question,

"I don't know Sir". 'Bill' was immediately in his element and would repeat,

"I don't know, Sir?" and then in an even louder voice, "He doesn't bloody well know!" Please imagine the situation when the peace of the workshop is being disturbed by this leering, intelligent man, who by now had progressed on to such profanities as:

"When your nose is covered with blood on your wedding night", and other such evil expressions, "will you say to yourself, "I don't know?"

Naturally by now all eyes were on the victim, but secretly everybody was hoping – "I wish he would shut up and stop making such a fool of himself."

By now it will be evident what sort of man 'Bill' really was. To us miserable apprentices it appeared that 'Bill' was trying his best to make our lives as unpleasant as he possibly could. We could only dream of the day that 'Bill' would be answered back in the same manner as he was using to his victims.

During the day 'Bill' would sometimes disappear, for periods of half an hour or so, and it didn't take our spies long to report that 'Bill' was having a cup of tea with his friend 'Snake eye' Johnson - a Warrant Officer Class One who was overall superior of all the building trades and had an office in the 'chippies' shop some sixty yards away from the masons. 'Snake-eye' Johnston was a sleazy, devious character hated by one and all. This office was central to the 'chippies' shop and raised some ten or twelve feet above the floor, surrounded by glass so that he could watch all that went on below. Naturally when 'Bill' was away on these trips, discipline in the mason's shop tended to relax a little. One small pastime was for a group of boys to compete with each other in trying to stick, by throwing, our trowels into a mortar 'spot' board, which had a central mark on it and was carefully propped on end. On this occasion, either 'Snake-eye' was out or the tea wasn't available, because 'Bill' came back early. As he came through the door he saw the group of boys enjoying their only pastime, and decided that someone would have to be punished.

I will never forget the words he uttered, nor my reply:

"Watkins! You little bastard etc., etc., etc.!"

Now before telling you my next action, it must be explained that it was an unwritten law amongst the thousand-odd boys in the school that the word bastard was never used as a profanity.

Probably every other swear word in the book was used but never, never, bastard.

The reply given to this evil mouthful by 'Bill' was, in a calm and I hoped, loud voice:

"Woolerton, if I am a little bastard, then you are a bigger bastard etc., etc., etc.!"

The scene was one of shocked silence; 'Bill' performed a little dance, then his face began to darken. At first we all hoped that he would burst a blood vessel or at the very least have a heart attack, but he recovered and shouted at the top of his voice for Sgt. Charlton to come immediately.

Now Sgt. 'Bob' Charlton was one of the bricklayer instructors whom I met long after the war again when serving as a Quartermaster to the T.A. at Swansea.

He remembered the incident well and a long discussion followed about that 'intelligent adult', 'Bill'!

But Sgt. Charlton had no choice but to march me under 'Bill's' shouted directions, up to 'Snake-eye's' office, there to stand at the foot of the stairs while 'Bill' explained to 'Snake-eye' what an evil person he had waiting downstairs! The discussion continued for sometime, then the culprit was wheeled 'before the presence' and told what a bad boy he was talking to dear old Mr Woolerton like that.

The following days passed very slowly while waiting for the punishment for the 'crime' to be announced.

When it did come, the shock was almost unbearable. Those two evil men had hatched between them a scheme which was to affect me for years to come, so much so that I seriously considered running away from it all and even involved my parents in trying to change my trade. It was to be relegated six months. For someone not involved in that type of life this would mean very little, but to me it meant, (a) saying goodbye to all the friends that I had lived with for several years. This was a terrible thing because the great day was coming when we would all say goodbye to Chepstow and join the Corps of Royal Engineers at Chatham to start our 'man's' service and future career; (b) join a completely new Group of boys whom, although I knew by sight had never been really associated with; and (c) serve an extra six months under 'Bill'!

An application was sent in to see the Officer Commanding 'D' Coy demanding the reasons for this severe punishment, one by name 'Pod' Rees, Major RE, a sloppy individual of poor standing in the boys' eyes. To my punished mind the thought that only one individual was being punished, when several others were involved in the crime was beyond comprehension, but of that matter, of course, I said nothing.

The reasons given were,

"You were insolent to your instructor. You were playing about in workshop time," and, "You are the leader of boys who misbehave."

These reasons were absolute nonsense and the CO was told so in an outburst which showed just how I felt about it all.

"Give me fourteen days scrubbing floors or shovelling coal instead of relegation – please!"

"March him out, Sgt. Major," was the answer.

It was a black day and one that caused endless heart-ache, because by now a feeling of true comradeship had developed between the boys of 39D. We felt that the world was against us and therefore together we were against the world.

A word must be said here of the Sgt. Major in charge of 'D' Company who was of an Irish Rgt. with a broad Irish accent, which was extremely hard to understand, but to make matters far worse he had a harelip. To disguise this he had developed a very fast method of speaking. In other words, no one knew what he was talking about, so it was decided that, because his messages were matters of discipline and probably important, we would have to select key words from his speeches, put them together afterwards and then try to carry out his instruction. Needless to say, his speeches were translated time and again incorrectly and we would receive 'rollickings' for 'doing what we ought not to have done'.

At this point I decided that 39D was my Group and therefore 39D would have my company at all times except when attending Workshops, School, Gyms etc., then my company was required with 40D, who when full acquaintance was established, turned out to be a fine set of boys.

Several other incidents are worth recording of those Chepstow days. One or two involved bullying which in some ways affected my later life, so I suppose that they are the important ones.

This is to do with a character called 'Codseye'. Why 'Codseye'? It was never really known but it was rumoured that several years before there had been Provost Sgt. in the camp who was a 'Codseye' so this name caught on. He was from a senior group to me, therefore bigger and stronger, a very good school boxer and a known bully.

On Friday afternoons, all A/T NCOs were required for lectures and therefore the march 'down to workshops' was supervised by senior boys, detailed for the chore. On this particular Friday it was our turn for the short straw, and we drew 'Codseye'. Now the usual Friday afternoon was little more than a disciplined stroll, the boys quietly chatting to each other. Not so with 'Codseye' in charge. He wanted arms swung to 'shoulder height' and no talking, etc. This, of course was strongly resented and on arrival at the Workshop he was told in no uncertain manner by the majority of the sufferers, including me, "What the hell did he think he was on," and, "are you after promotion?"

That evening, 'Codseye' showed what a bully he really was. For, strolling quite happily back from the Dining Hall after tea, on turning the corner of the hut, I was struck full in the mouth by a very hard fist - stars! And red mists! And on coming around two front teeth loose, a badly bruised mouth and very sore nose. By this time 'Codseye' and a bulky friend were disappearing into the distance. The words of Robert Service came to mind.

"The thought awoke to kill, to kill and it filled you through and through."

The vow was made then and there that one day my turn would come.

The following morning the area of my face which had received the blow was a mess, so it was decided that a visit to the Medical Officer and Dentist had to be made. Sick parade had to be experienced to be believed and consisted of packing all 'small kit', that is washing, shaving, cleaning kit etc. in case (the Standing Order said) you were to be admitted to hospital. To ensure that this order was obeyed, this kit was usually inspected and checked by the on-duty Sgt. Woe betide anyone who defaulted. The real reason of course was to deter people who were not really ill: those on sick parade were always considered to be scroungers.

The Medical Inspection (MI) Room was a large part of an Army hut, divided into two. The Medical Officer (M.O.) used the smallest part as a treatment room and was always accompanied by his right hand man 'Bert'. Now 'Bert' was the sick room orderly who carried out the M.O.'s wishes, such as 'hot poultice on this boil', or 'drops in this boy's left ear', etc. All these instructions were given over the top of a dividing curtain, and it appeared to us that 'Bert' took great delight in making the poultice as hot as possible, or the gargle etc. evil tasting to the point where you were almost sick when using it. 'Bert' would do anything for his 'Lord and Master' the M.O., because he had a 'cushy' job, when jobs were hard to come by, and was obviously an ex-service man. The M.O. was, to us, on a level with God himself, a Lt. Col. in the Medical Corps, tall, white-haired and aged about 110.

The waiting room was large and bare with forms all around for the waiting patients to sit on and read, a book was essential, because you waited your turn for hours on end. It was always full, and perhaps the chance would come to meet old 'Bill so and so who you hadn't seen since the year before last'. Hence a lot of chatting.

Until, that is, Larry Shield (the M.O.) decided that enough was enough and would say: "Mr..." whatever 'Bert's' surname was, "go and stop that noise out there!"

'Bert' had a very simple method of doing this, he would quickly open the door and anyone he saw talking would be booked for a dose of 'white'.

He would then announce in a loud voice: "Anyone seen talking again will have a dose of 'green'."

This would create absolute silence, because, as a senior boy explained in a whisper, a dose of 'white' was an evil smelling liquid which guaranteed to keep you on the toilet seat for at least two days, while a dose of 'green' was a mixture, provided by 'Bert', of castor oil and an evil smelling green liquid of such high viscosity it needed swallowing in one hard lump. This was a three day job accompanied by stomach pains. Hence, noses in books in the waiting room!

"Fighting eh!?" was the M.O.'s greeting to me.

"No sir, walked into a door, sir!"

A doubtful look then a feel of a very sore nose then, "Nothing broken, come and see me next week, in the meantime see the dentist at 15:00 hrs today."

The 'sick report' said M&D, which translated, meant Medicine and Duty, so after the dentist, who by the way arranged for two false teeth on a small plate clipped to the other teeth, it was back to normal duty for me.

In no way was 'Codseye' going to get away with it. That night I tapped on the door of the A/T RSM of the school. A word of explanation here.

If as a boy you were good at Workshops, School, Sports etc., you could earn promotion to A/T Cpl, A/T Sgt., A/T CSM or even A/T RSM, A/T being Apprentice Tradesman - the lowest form of animal life outside a zoo. The remainder speak for themselves and were obtained mostly by 'the old Army game' of 'kidology'. It was mostly prestige that was carried by these ranks, although there were some small privileges to go with them. The rank was dropped on leaving

'Chep' and, amazingly enough, they seldom did well in the Corps for promotion. Well as you can see the A/T RSM was a God like figure to me and was in the now senior group, the same as 'Codseye'.

There followed this conversation: "Good God! What have you done to your face Watkins?"

"Walked into a door! But I have really come to see you to referee a fight between me and your 'Codseye'.

He realised immediately what had happened and, looking me over and guessed my weight to be about three stone less than 'Codseye' said,

"God, man alive, he will kill you!"

"That's as it maybe, but I still want the fight!"

"Right, when you have had your face fixed, I will fix the fight!"

You will have gathered that the senior Group, – which, by the way was always called 'The Draft' and woe betide any recruit if he didn't know just who the draft was when asked – left the school after three years training, and as they did so a new Group would be taken in to start training. It was getting into May 1939 and 38 Group would be leaving in June for Chatham and their future in the Corps. The Dentist was very slow getting my new teeth fixed and whenever Fletcher and I came into contact he would study my face and then shake his head. Enough said!

It was an unwritten law in the school that a day or so prior to the departure of 'The Draft' they would run around the rooms, long before reveille, tip everyone out of bed and make a general nuisance of themselves. Sometimes, like 39, they would do something that would be talked about in the school for ever and a day. More of that later.

On this particular morning I remember flying out of bed and landing with a crash on a very hard floor. Yes, 38 Group were doing their rounds while it was still dark, and would then depart never to be seen again!

As was stated earlier, this fellow 'Codseye' was to come into my life again, on more than one occasion.

The first being several years later. The war had been going sometime. I was fairly new to a Field Company RE in a place called Fordingbridge, Hampshire.

To cut a long story; along with four other chaps we were selected as junior NCOs, provided that is, we passed a three week cadre course. This type of course taught you to become an NCO and, of course, tested you at the end to see if you were of 'sufficient material' etc.

A truck delivered us to Minsted Manor in the New Forest, a building of, from memory, high ceilings, and mostly large rooms, with a number of Army huts within the grounds. It had been 'taken over for the duration' by the Army and was now HQ for 215, our Field Park Company.

Report to so and so office, was the instruction, and enter one at a time, your Sgt. in charge of the course would be receiving you. On the door it said 'Knock and Wait'. I did this and when told to enter did so with some trepidation.

Unbelievably the Sgt. with his head bent over the desk, all those miles away from Chepstow, was 'Codseye'! Without looking up growled,

"Name?" When he heard the reply, Watkins, he glanced to his right, where a typed list of some three dozen names was lying and ticked off the name.

He then looked up to speak, but silence ensued for at least thirty seconds then:

"Well, well, look what God has sent me! If you think that after three weeks, under my tuition, you will pass as an NCO."

The following day he made a point of sorting me out with words to the effect that because I was a regular soldier I was to set an example to the other conscripts and woe betide me if I didn't set a good one!

As a result of this I was expected to be the leader at PT. The best shot. First at cross-country running. The smartest at drill etc., etc.

It was plain from the start that 'Codseye' would probably give me a lousy report and so no hope of promotion, but fortunately the young officer who was the overall organiser of the course had been watching us closely, and also marked-up the written exam papers on completion. Surprise! Surprise! Number 1 of the lot!

Two weeks later promotion to the dizzy heights of L/Cpl followed and my troubles had started again. But enough of that, there are a few more months to serve at Chepstow yet.

Melvin, was a name that was also to influence my life in a big way during later years.

A/T CSM Melvin to be exact. Sometime after the 'Codseye incident' he made the surprising remark to me that:

"You're the bloke who was cheeky to our Codseye and caused all that trouble! Keep out of my way or I'll fix you!"

From that day on he took great delight in such stupid remarks as

"Watkins, hold your head up!", "Watkins swing your arms higher!" "Watkins stop nattering on parade etc. etc.!" This, of course, was some sort of campaign to try to get me to retaliate as in the 'Codseye' incident. Self control was strictly adhered to, however, and it was a beautiful day when his Group, 'The Draft' departed from Chepstow. Never? to be seen again!

Some ten years later, after the war of course, and in the course of my career as a senior NCO there came a posting to No. 10 Trades Training Rgt. RE at Chatham, Kent, as of all things, a stone-mason instructor – shades of 'Bill' Woolerton!

Again to cut the story short, it soon came to my attention that in the nearby School of Military Engineering there were some wonderful courses available for Quantity Surveyors, Clerks of Works and in types of surveying and engineering. The Clerk of Works Course was really a first class course, being fourteen months of intensive study of all aspects of the building trade. By good fortune I had already taken the Ordinary National Certificate in building, which stood me in good stead when applying for the course. Other qualifications required were:

> Army 1st Class Certificate
> Qualified in a recognised building trade for ten years minimum.
> Clean record etc., etc.

Applications and interviews followed, then three months waiting and, great joy, acceptance. This was obviously a great chance, on completion of Army service, to take this up as a career in 'Civvy Street'.

The great day came. Report to North School Classroom One for a 'Pre-Course' lecture.

The most awful of shocks came when the Officer Commanding North School introduced the four Army instructors, the senior of whom was Warrant Officer Class I Melvin!!

After the lecture he queried me:

"What have you done since leaving Chep? Where did you get to in the war? Have you met any of the other lads in recent years, etc.?" And then, "You won't get through this course while I am senior instructor!"

The bottom had dropped out of my world again!

Course procedure was several weeks of builders' maths, and then several weeks of each and every trade and aspect of building. Each period was followed by a stiff examination and, if a standard of 50% overall was not maintained, the shirker was off the course. Needless to say numerous chaps fell by the wayside.

In the ensuing months, Melvin did his best to carry out his threat and eventually, by devious means, succeeded.

It was heartbreak time; all those months of study with the prospect of an excellent career to follow, only to be forced back to the old army daily grind of duty.

Yet this inspired great determination to try again, and three or four years of very intensive study, until the reward of the Higher National Certificate in Building and the Institute of Clerk of Works (Civil) were achieved.

Application and interview followed with acceptance on the cards.

Sure enough, within two months, the sweat of a new Course had started, but this time with decent honest instructors. Success was achieved and Melvin was never heard of again, although rumour had it that he had emigrated to Australia, and later died of one of those 'down-under' diseases - RIP.

One or two more incidents are worth recording before leaving 'Chep'. I mentioned before that 'The Draft' usually carried out some feat or other before leaving, such as tipping everyone in Camp out of bed etc.

39 Group was determined to make a lasting name, so a plot was hatched to raid the Married Quarters and tip out of bed all the NCOs who had been hard ones during our spell at 'Chep'. An excellent map was produced of the layout of the 'targets' and one very dark night (AM) we rendezvoused and set off the three or four miles to the Staff Quarters.

Things went tragically wrong because, by some unknown means, the Provost staff (led by Sgt. Witte – 'Dim-wit' of course) had broken our code and were waiting for us, on either side of the one road from the Camp. Their chief armament appeared to be hockey sticks and so a running battle ensued. Our main concern was not to be recognised: much trouble would follow.

Fortunately that night we were dressed in balaclavas or 'cap-comforters', so there was little chance of recognition. The scrap, while it lasted, was pretty fierce, bearing in mind the fitness of these seventeen year olds after lots of PT and sport. Plenty of bruises and one broken leg were our net gain but the injuries on the police side, judging by the briefing afterwards, were horrendous!

Arriving safely back to bed, it came as a bad shock to find my 'bed card' missing. This was the identifying card in one's locker (wardrobe) giving full details of the owner. I had 'had it'!

Footsteps sounded outside, a leap into bed fully clothed, which achieved little and a voice, as the bed-clothes were ripped off, said one word, "Guardroom!"

In explanation, while most of the Provost Staff were setting the ambush, the remainder were checking for empty beds and removing all the absentees' 'bed-cards'.

The scene on arrival at the Guardroom was like a pantomime; dozens of A/Ts in all sorts of weird dress, some with black faces, standing in a heap with more arriving every minute.

When 'Dim wit' was satisfied, after a card check, he called everyone to attention and announced in a very cruel voice,

"Your Company Commanders have been sent for, and you are all for the high-jump!"

Here it was, 4am, and 'Pod' Pees had been ordered out of his bed to deal with this 'rebellion'! Woe is me!

To cut a long story short - many a harsh word was spoken, none in praise of our act, and we all were 'awarded' ten days 'Jankers' (CB). 'Dim-wit' took great delight in having so many floor scrubbers, brass polishers, and sweepers under his care at one time.

Many years later there were lots of stories that 'went the rounds' about 'Dim-wit' but were never substantiated, so we'll leave well alone.

The other 'achievement' by 39 Group, and I take credit for this, was to climb, in total darkness, a very high chimney which was being built for the 'Workshop' boiler house. The theory was to drape a sheet of cardboard, suitably painted, on a loop of cord over the chimney. It worked perfectly and settled about ¾ away up the chimney where it was almost impossible to cut down.

The other stunt was to drape the Administration Block, where all the high and mighty worked, with the 'Siegfried Line'. This consisted of lots of dirty and 'holey' socks and underclothes, grudgingly contributed by dozens of lads. No retribution came from the last two stunts and so 39 Group were to be seen walking with a swagger for days afterwards.

Looking back at those last months at Chepstow, it is astonishing to think that here was a glorious chance for the British Army to train its personnel in the business of mine warfare, booby trap clearance etc., but no! Just normal duties! How right the critics were proved who claimed 'that the Army was totally unprepared for war'.

There are, as you can guess, hundreds more stories to be related about Chepstow but time and space does not permit here, so enough about the Sapper at peace, let us move on to the Sapper at War.

CHAPTER FOUR

TRAINING BATTALION ROYAL ENGINEERS

July 1940 arrived with a posting to No. 1 Training Battalion Royal Engineers. Chatham Depot had been extended, because of the war, and now consisted of various Training Battalions scattered about the country.

Seven bright young lads of eighteen left Chepstow that morning, each wondering what the future had in store, particularly now the war had started in which we were bound, as regular soldiers, to be involved. It was a beautiful day and we, thankfully, were shaking off the sights and sounds of Chepstow for ever.

It was virtually an all day journey; bus to Chepstow Station, train to Newport, Newport to Paddington, Paddington to Victoria, Victoria to Folkestone, Folkestone to Shorecliffe by bus. There it was, a barrack square surrounded by a large number of huts on three sides; the fourth side was bordered by the road to Folkestone. Outside the huts were acres of fields used for training purposes.

All the remainder of the personnel, who made up the 'War Party', were recruits conscripted from the London area. Most of them were old enough to be our fathers but, looking back, probably averaged about 35 years of age.

For the first three weeks it was endless square bashing, rifle shooting, route marching etc., at the end of which the selection of 'Star' men was made. L Watkins was the name printed 'On Orders' and the recollection of the presentation by the local General Commanding still causes me some embarrassment. Regular soldiers were allowed to keep their 'service dress' with peaked cap etc. for 'walking out' and ceremonial parades. At that time the order for hair cuts was 'cut short back and sides, with no more than two inches on top'! My hair was always thick and curly and its length was maintained by carefully tucking all the top bits under the peaked cap. There was no way that image was to be destroyed! Or so I kidded myself.

On the presentation morning, the Battalion with wives, sweethearts etc. were drawn up on three sides of the square, with the General and his minions on a small dais in front. The drill was to march out in front of the dear old boy, salute smartly, wait for his words etc., salute, then march back to the ranks, band playing appropriate tunes. The first part was achieved no bother and the General did his stuff then, how unkind God can be, a gust of wind took my cap off, the locks came tumbling down, a gasp, quite audible, went up and I 'scuttled' back to my place in the ranks. The sounds of footsteps approaching and then the words of the dreaded 'Party' Sgt./Major were heard "Star man! We *are* going to visit the barbers tomorrow aren't we?"

When tomorrow came, a visit to the barber's shop was somehow more important than breakfast or dinner. Nothing more was said of the incident and it died a natural death although there were one or two 'friendly' remarks made by senior NCO's such as:

"Fancy trying to tuck that lot under your cap!" and,

"If you had let me know my Mum would have loaned you a hat pin!" etc., etc.

The silliness of our training amounted to sheer stupidity at times, with lots of physical practice and lectures which dated from the last war and would, undoubtedly, never be used. For instance there was lots of talk 'going the rounds' about the new Bailey Bridge now in production. A bridge, which everyone forecast, we would be using in the front line in order to get the Army quickly over rivers etc.

It was rumoured to fit together like a Meccano set and was strong and very quick to erect. No lectures were given about it and no pictures shown but eighteen months later we had to build one in the dark and under enemy fire! And dozens more to follow.

Much of our time was spent building the old fashioned pontoon and folding boat bridges, that were seldom used on active service.

Knots and lashings, lifting gear, forming anchors, use of pickets etc. were all taught and examined but seldom used.

Why not teach the latest technology in mines and booby traps, both our own and those of the enemy; that way a lot of lives could probably have been saved?

Another incident shows how silly certain aspects of Army discipline were. The 'Party' was undertaking rifle shooting on Hythe ranges, a very well laid out range in which any stray shots went out to sea. All firing was done from slit trenches instead of the normal lying down position. Suddenly a whole lot of JU87 (Stukas) came diving out of the clouds to attack the airfield close to the range, I think it was called Lymme (or similar) airfield. As each Stuka dropped its bombs and flew out to sea it skimmed within feet of our heads.

"No firing! No firing!" the Sgt. could be heard shouting.

The thought came 'How stupid, when probably dozens of people are being killed on the airfield, besides damage to planes and buildings: we are sitting here with loaded rifles and being told to leave the dear Stukas alone!'

It was too much to bear and so when the next one came over I shouted very loudly,

"Rapid fire!"

Everyone within earshot was delighted to do so, and a wall of fire went up at this plane. Unfortunately we could not see the result of this shooting because by now a load of planes were skimming out to sea and our AA (Bofors) guns had woken up, so it was complete chaos! As far as Army discipline was concerned, however, it was soon established who had shouted 'fire', and a discussion between the 'leaders' followed.

After some time, and still on the ranges, came the ominous announcement,

"You will hear more about this later."

When the time came to leave the Training Battalion in November the punishment manifested itself. The name Watkins was not included in the list of names for the next cadre class, something which the 'star' man automatically qualified for and, of course, on successful completion of which the first stripe was awarded. When enquiries were made as to 'why not included?' the answer received was, you are eighteen and therefore too young to take charge of men of 38 and upwards. Stuff and nonsense!

Some two years later when the Company had been under heavy air attack over a long period, the Colonel R.E. (CRE) issued a directive. All fire from low flying enemy aircraft would be returned from personnel on the ground, preferably as a squad or body of troops because this would give a spread of shots. A sum of £10 would be awarded to all personnel of a successful squad. Furthermore, we were also drilled in the number of degrees to aim off when aircraft was crossing our front or coming at an angle.

Because Shorcliffe was on the coast of Kent there was, naturally, a great deal of aircraft activity going on above, but fortunately, apart from a few dozen cartridge cases 'pinging' on to the barrack square, the barracks went untouched.

It was vastly different when for the next period of training (September '40) we were 'sent on detachment'. This involved occupying a number of houses - mostly sleeping on the garage floors - around a public house called 'The Valiant Sailor'. It is still there because it was seen and described in detail to my wife when we were travelling to France last year, on the coast road between Dover and Folkestone. This area became known as 'Hell Fire Corner' because, during this period, there was always intense air activity or cross channel shelling taking place.

Shortly after arrival the duties were detailed. Mine consisted of three separate duties:-

Duty 1:   Lewis gun was sited in a hedgerow about thirty yards from the pub; this was to be manned four hours at a time, and all enemy aircraft within range were to be fired at. Needless to say, this type of gun had not been seen before by any members of the Party. Plans were made and eventually a demonstration given. The magazine held 100 rounds and could do devastating damage in untrained hands.

Plenty of practice followed because, as was quickly established, the German fighters carried one or two bombs and when returning from escorting bombers over England, they were determined not to take their bombs back home and so would paste any suitable target. After a spell of this it was found that a 100 round magazine was used up in minutes.

To make matters a lot worse the high level bombers would also drop what they had left over, but of course these were well out of range of the Lewis Gun.

Duty 2:   Man the telephone switchboard in the 'Valiant Sailor' for a shift of four hours. Needless to say this was a marvellous duty, apart from all the aircraft activity. The landlady, bless her, always kept us supplied with beer and sandwiches. Another activity the German fighters took great delight in was shooting all the barrage balloons in the area down. It was quite spectacular; most balloons had a life of two or three days at the most.

A small airfield called, I think, Hawkhinge, was situated just inland from 'The Sailor'. This earned great and regular attention from fighters and Stukas alike. It was said that because the airfield had lost so many planes through this bombing that they decided to fool 'Jerry' by placing wooden planes around. Rumours had it that several days later, the Germans dropped a lot of wooden bombs on the place. But nothing was confirmed!

Duty 3:   This one was almost unbelievable! "You are to stand on this cliff edge, with a rifle and bayonet, at night, on a four hour shift, and keep your eyes down on the English Channel. Every hour there will be a set of green flares fired into the sky from two boats known as the 'Dover Patrol'. If the flares are red ones you will immediately run to that small hut over there, lift the field telephone receiver, crank the handle several times and shout in a loud voice. 'They are coming! They are coming!' and replace the receiver.

It had to be assumed who 'they' were and, of course, no one would explain who you were telling that 'they' were coming.

What is more incredible still, was the fact that when, next morning, there was a discussion taking place along the lines: "Fancy! We are the first contact between our forces and those Nazi Hordes invading our country!" a statement was made by a L/Cpl. to the effect that the door of the hut we were told to run to was always kept locked! Next morning a check was made of this statement and proved to be true. Apparently the Sgt. kept it locked in case someone stole the telephone! Headlines: Britain lost the war because the Sgt. was down town boozing!

As September wore on, so the air activity increased and eventually we were spending most of our days in slit trenches. Then came a black day - the first heavy daylight raid on London. The German bombers could be seen as they left the French coast, hundreds of them, and surrounded by fighters on all sides. The effect of these low flying aircraft directly overhead was shattering, especially to the conscripts of the Party, all of whom came from the London area. When the news came in that evening that London had received a very heavy daylight raid, pandemonium reigned amongst our conscripted War Party.

By midnight the only able-bodied men left to man the defence against the 'Nazi Hordes' were the few ex-Chepstow boys; the rest had made a bee-line for London to see how their families were after the bombing raid. Everyone felt sympathy for them, and within two days they were all back 'in the fold'. Lectures on military discipline and loyalty followed, but fortunately, no punishment was meted out.

The cliff edge was about 100 yards from our luxurious accommodation (two blankets and one ground sheet) on the garage floor, and whenever any action in the channel was taking place, such as dive bombing convoys etc., and you felt brave enough to watch, a spectacular view could be had of the Stukas diving past you and dropping their bombs on the ships below. The ships were firing back and, of course, were soon joined by the shore batteries and one small Lewis gun; one can imagine the absolute chaos taking place!

One day things changed dramatically. There were these huge spouts of water close to the ships, reaching ten times the height of them, just like the bombs falling, but no Stukas, no 'ack, ack' and certainly no Lewis gun from the hedge. The ships were hugging the English coast and well spread out, obviously to avoid these huge water spouts. Then it registered – we were watching the very first shelling of a Channel convoy from some twenty miles away. Every few minutes a salvo of shells would land with a terrible roar, but somehow the ships survived, at least all the time we were watching. Above the French coast a line of black dots could be seen, probably about a dozen of them. The 'experts' said 'observation balloons to watch the shell strikes'. Probably so, but when this shelling occurred on practically a daily basis, where were our fighters to shoot those sitting ducks down, in the same way as the Messerschmitts enjoyed shooting down our barrage balloons?

For the people brave enough to still live in 'Hell Fire Corner' there now began a period of absolute terror and misery: cross Channel shelling. This was done with huge calibre guns and would continue for hours on end, and over a period of days. Accuracy was out of the question; it was purely done for the terror effect.

If you can imagine an express train, the one that roars through the station, passing overhead or landing close by with a huge eruption then you have some idea. Please remember that people were dying and being maimed by these 'monsters'.

Before long Britain had established several of our own batteries, and so the famous 'cross Channel duels' started. Once again chaos reigned!

One spectacular daylight air raid on Folkestone will always be remembered. Just how many died or were injured during that raid we will probably never know; the figures were always kept secret then, 'bad for morale and all that you know!' and as far as is known, were never published.

The roar of German aircraft diving low overhead took me from the switchboard to the front of 'The Sailor'. There was a perfect view, looking to the right, of Folkestone being bombed by a stream of Junkers 87B (STUKAS) and 88s. Their bombing, against very little opposition, seemed to continue for ages. At the height (or depth) of it, a huge gas holder took off from the ground amidst lots of flames, and appeared to float for several hundred yards before coming to rest. Our hearts went out to the people of Folkestone. To think that this madman could bring so much slaughter to an innocent people, people whose last wish was to wage war! It was after this raid that most of our thoughts turned to getting the training finished and doing our bit to get this enemy finished!

It was now early October '40 and the spell of 'detachment' completed. The move back to Shorcliffe was, in a way, welcomed because, all of a sudden, the bombs and bullets were no longer flying about. Several more hectic weeks of training followed, then came the time to split up the Party and join the respective Units from which your war would be fought. It could be almost anywhere in the world and in any type of Unit. Would it be Assault Engr. Field Park Coy: Field Coy: Training Depot or whatever?

Together with seven others I was to join a Field Company at Fordingbridge, Hampshire.

CHAPTER FIVE

FIELD COMPANY - TRAINING FOR WAR

On arrival at Fordingbridge, which was at that time, a collection of houses and shops, mostly strung out along the road from Salisbury to the Ringwood/Bournemouth area, the Company appeared to have commandeered several of the larger buildings in the town and surrounding areas.

One or two regular soldiers, such as the C.O. Sgt. Major and a Section Sgt. appeared to form the 'backbone' of the 'Coy'. The remainder were all conscripted, some of them much against their will. The areas they were drawn from, were Sussex, Kent, Hampshire and London, and a good set of lads; most of them were, with a few exceptions of course. Age group varied considerably, especially later on with replacements, but at this stage was anything from 22 to 42. A great many of them were good tradesmen indeed, and the remainder appeared to have good knowledge of the construction industry. The overall impression was one of a good average intelligence and a friendly spirit to all and sundry. The friendships (and petty jealousy) between ranks, was at first hard to understand, being a regular soldier, but when given some thought and realising that these chaps had been called up together, done their training, drilling, fieldworks etc. together, then one or two of them were selected to be NCOs with power over their fellow men, this feeling could be easily understood. Now integrated into this lot had to be eight regular soldiers of eighteen years of age, who were boys really, cheeky and full of their own importance. There was a lot to learn!

On arrival the directive was - 'Report to the Riverside Café'. That sounded like a good start, but it turned out to be Coy: H/Q with a fair sized area to the rear where almost all the Coy: could be paraded.

The café area was modern and large enough to feed most of the Coy: at one sitting. It also housed the Coy: dances, whenever they could be organised.

The Coy: was divided into 3 sections and H/Q, each section being divided into Sub-sections of 12 men with a L/Sgt. or Cpl. in charge, aided and abetted by a L/Cpl. All sections were scattered within a radius of two miles and could (in theory) be formed up as a Company quite quickly.

We duly arrived at the 'Riverside' and a quick meal was conjured up from somewhere within the depths of the building. During the meal the 2nd-in-command of the Coy: came in to 'have a chat', a Capt. Williams who people referred to as 'The Ringer'. It was at a later time that the reason for this name was divulged.

A look of amazement crossed his face when every man stood up on his appearance into the room. This changed to delight when he realised just how much respect these regulars were giving him, but to cut a long story again the gist of his talk was:- "We have requested you regular soldiers from the training Battalion to help to form the backbone of the Coy: we are desperately short of NCOs etc., etc." He was to learn! So were we!

My posting along with 'Ginger' Dalton was to 3 Section, at that time housed in 'The Mill'. A derelict ramshackle place fit only for rats, cats and No. 3 Section.

Here, we must go back to the last week in the Training Battalion. It was decided that as we would probably never see each other again, we would have a drinking session to end all drinking sessions, and it really was!

It started the lunch time before departure and continued through afternoon, evening and most of the night until, I believe, no-one was left standing. At 'our local' in Folkestone some bright individual suggested that instead of settling down to steady drinking.

"Let's work our way along all these interesting bottles on the top shelf!"

Why, why was everyone agreeable? There was never a harder lesson learned in so short a time!

One moment the contents of the glass was a very agreeable and expensive brandy, the next a rather thick scented green liquid.

Many days later it was agreed that the top shelf had been 'conquered' and at least one half of the next shelf down, but there all sensible recollection finished. My head (and stomach) told its own story for a full week afterwards!

The first week of training with the new Unit was interesting, but not carried out with much enthusiasm because of the after effects of the drinking bout. In a dazed condition the Section Sgt. could be heard describing various types of scaffolding as used by 'The Engineers', but when questions were asked, the replies given were also from the same deranged mind. They say that the first impression of a person is very important, if this is the case then there wasn't a very high opinion formed of the two regulars from the elite Training Battalion. But as the days progressed and the 'fog' cleared so things began to take shape.

About this time Southern Command received a new commander, someone we had never heard of, Lt. Gen. Bernard Law Montgomery by name. His reputation soon spread and before long he had called all senior officers to HQ for pep talks on the way he wanted the 'Command' to 'take shape'.

One of the first things was:-

Every man will run a minimum distance of five miles every week. The run would be supervised by an officer, and every man in the Unit would take part; this included all officers, NCOs, cooks, cleaners, bottle washers, drivers and batmen. This order caused a great deal of consternation amongst the conscripts because, judging on appearances, the only running some had done was ten yards for a bus. The order was welcomed by the 'Regulars' because being extremely young and fit, they were soon leading 'the field' each week by some distance.

Shortly after this, regular physical training was started. This became an almost a daily event and, for reasons already given, was enjoyed by the 'Regulars'. 'Monty' was already beginning to make his presence felt. Years later our paths crossed again when he jumped down from his staff car at the height of the battle for the river Sangro in Italy, handed over a quantity of 'Players' cigarettes, a luxury indeed, and said, "Share them amongst the men," and was gone from whence he came.

The war at home was now taking a nasty turn indeed. It was late 1940, Hitler had lost the 'Battle of Britain' and had now decided to terror bomb our cities by night. The first target was Coventry. This was an appalling slaughter for which Hitler would pay dearly in later years. One of the next targets was Southampton and, being only a few miles in a straight line from 'The Mill', provided both a horrifying and spectacular sight.

The next morning the order was given, "You as a RE Company will proceed to Southampton and will clear all unexploded bombs and devices, make safe all buildings damaged in the air-raid, fill in bomb craters."

The order was acted on promptly and we duly arrived in Southampton to find a scene of carnage, chaos and destruction. The whole of the centre of the city was just about totally destroyed: what were modern shops and stores were just heaps of rubble or tottering shells ready to collapse, the main streets were all cratered and ripped up, gas mains were on fire, water spouted from fractured mains, people were digging in the rubble for those buried. What a terror weapon the bomb was proving to be. This really was an introduction to war at the receiving end of man's inhumanity to man, and unfortunately one that was to be repeated many, many times.

Where to begin? A very wise, but very inexperienced young officer like everyone else, quickly decided to split into Sub-sections, and to give help where required but, if possible, to give priority to recovering survivors, shutting off fractured gas mains and trying to control water breaks.

The casualty figures for this raid were never given to us but must have been very high indeed. The smell of death was everywhere.

After a few days of this chaos, things began to sort themselves out, and the Company settled down to a programme of securing unsafe buildings and filling in bomb craters. The 'drill' for this was usually a steel wire rope around a key point, linked up to a bulldozer, which would then pull away the bottom floor. It was heartbreaking, being a mason, to see some of those beautiful buildings in ruins. Some of them were multi-storey and of recent construction. Many tales were told at the end of the day of heartbreaking and amusing incidents.

One such story was to do with 'Plummers', the outfitting and clothes store. It was in the process of being 'made safe' when the General Manager appeared on the scene and indicated to the demolition party that 'somewhere below this pile of rubble' was the Store safe containing the week's takings, which was absolutely full of money. He also indicated that there would be a reward paid, "if the safe was recovered intact". The incentive was created and work commenced, at first by hand, then aided by a small bulldozer. After many hours of toil the safe was duly recovered, looking slightly battered, but serviceable, and duly handed over to the manager. The opening ceremony was watched by dozens of eyes, full of expectancy and no doubt belonging to itchy palms. The key and wheel were turned with some effort, a crowbar invited to help along and the door wrenched open. There for all to see, stacked from the base to the top, were thousands of pounds, but all burnt to a cinder! Just as soon as they were touched by the manager they collapsed and came floating or tumbling out. Several other tales were also told, for example, one which affected just about everyone in Fordingbridge and district, and caused many a smile.

One of the Sub-sections were demolishing an ex-amusement arcade when they came across a whole lot of burnt out 'one arm bandits'. Inside the machines were columns of pennies, all burnt and fused together. A penny seemed to be worth much more then than now being of good size, good quality copper etc. The pennies were duly lifted from their place of rest and carefully transported back to Fordingbridge where this very industrious intelligent and far-seeing Sub-section worked long into the night, separating, cleaning and polishing the heads of and tails of Kings George V and VI.

For many months afterwards, even up to the day the Company left in 1942, it was guaranteed that any change one received in pubs, shops, cinema, canteen etc. in the whole district, would include highly polished coppers.

The amount of stores 'recovered' after their owners had written them off as unserviceable was truly amazing. Tinned fruit and cream with the occasional glass of best brandy seemed to be on the daily menu!

With the task of Southampton behind the Company it was back to training. It was very much routine and soul destroying. Daily lectures were given on everyday weapons, gas warfare (perhaps an essential!) mines, explosives, bridges, etc., of which, as it proved later, very little was put into practice, as it had been superseded by newer materials and methods.

Occasionally, a fortnight's 'Bridging Camp' would be held on the Thames at Wallingford. These were a disaster and always dreaded by the 'other ranks'.

These were always held in mid winter: frozen cold taps, strip washes in the open, living under canvas, bridging with antiquated equipment, and usually rain or snow, these are the memories of those camps. If you try shaving under a cold tap, in the open with the temperature never above freezing, and a 'North Easterly' blowing you will appreciate the situation!

During one of these holiday camps the C.O. gave a friendly talk on war time conditions and how interesting it would be to simulate those conditions by bridging at night.

This was embarked upon and from about 22:00hrs, when it appeared to be a cold, but dry night, the first pontoon was in position and everyone had thoughts of at least a half day in Wallingford the following day.

Then it started to rain, which rapidly turned into very cold sleet and soon found its way down the neck, through the trousers and boots, and everywhere else that rain penetrates after a period of exposure.

But the C.O. (who was an intelligent, military minded, sarcastic, blunt to the point sort of man) can tell the story much better:

"It is now 03:00 hrs and I am calling this 'exercise' off as from now, you will all parade, when I will address you, at 09:00hrs tomorrow."

09:00hrs duly arrived and a very sorry collection of 'soldiers' assembled on the muddy saturated 'parade ground'.

Over to the C.O. who as stated previously, was an intelligent but extremely military minded type.

"Gentlemen! Last night we held an exercise which was to have simulated war time conditions, with the enemy very close to, or even holding, the far bank of the river. The first pontoon was launched into position and things were going along very smoothly and quietly. All the stores appeared to be laid out in position and I was delighted with the progress made.

"Then it started to rain! The rain turned to sleet and soon people were taking a soaking and frankly, I was quite surprised at first how smoothly everyone carried on with their tasks.

"Then, suddenly, we reached the 'F-----g' stage! and from that moment on it was f--- this, and f--- that and where is the f-----g cable, etc., etc. until I could stand it no more, so the exercise was called off!

"Tonight gentlemen, we will do the same exercise again and whether it rains, snows, or the river Thames freezes over, the job will be done quietly, smoothly and with no sound above a whisper or else the task will be repeated on the following night and if necessary on consecutive nights until it is done properly!"

That night the sky was clear and very cold, but no rain! The Thames was bridged in record time and not a sound was heard except for the dear old Sgt. Major whispering to his 'loved ones' 'please do this' and 'please do that!'

Before leaving dear old Fordingbridge there is one more incident that is worth mentioning.

With the invasion of England, by that German madman, still on the cards, it was decided, in 1941, that all sources of fuel which might help the German cause would have to be prepared for destruction. On the Southampton water inlet was, and still is today thank goodness, a huge oil refinery at Fawley owned by American and British interests. The large oil storage tanks, similar to gas holders, covered a good many acres of ground and numbered in their hundreds.

The orders were "prepare all tanks for demolition". As will be appreciated by those of any knowledge at all of demolition at this scale and magnitude, this was a tall order indeed.

After much thought the decision was that an explosive charge had to be used for each tank's destruction but, at the same time it also had to set the oil on fire so that the destruction was complete. Each tank had also to be wired in such a manner that all leads ran to a central position and connected to one main switch. What a headache!

Our stay was quite a lengthy and enjoyable one. Billeted in a large country manor in Beaulieu on the edge of the New Forest, our feet were soon 'under the table,' because the local girls appeared desperately short of young male company.

The Company football team was also more than holding its own in the local football league.

The decision was to use 'Foo' gas, which came in forty gallon drums and was a highly volatile gas which burst into flame on exposure to air. Each storage tank had one of these drums, dug in at 45° angle, secured yards away from the tank. The area of drum exposed above ground was sealed by sandbags, the front edge facing the tank left clear and on which was planted one slab of gun cotton, fully primed apart from the

No. 33 detonator which was held at a central position. The theory was that when 'invasion started' was signalled, the detonator would be positioned and the switch used!

What destruction that would have been and what a sight too, with all those tanks in flames simultaneously. It was also 100% certain that whoever placed the detonator in position and threw the switch would lose their life!

One word here on friendship. While still here at Beaulieu the writer, having completed the aforementioned Cadre Course, received his first stripe, the other recipient being close friend and ex-Chep boy 'Ginger' Dalton.

There was a Junior Guard Commander duty to be performed on the next Sunday and of course it was to be either 'Ginger' or myself with me being the loser. Celebrations were held on the Saturday night and a number of 'our lads' finished up at the local whist drive and dance. Cutting the story short again, the 'Belle of the Ball' was escorted home by the writer and a basis for firm friendship was established.

The day following could not be used for dates because of this Guard duty so arrangements were made for 'later in the week'. Imagine the surprise on the Sunday afternoon when one of the chaps on guard said,

"There's a beautiful young lady at the gate asking for you by name!"

It turned out that while horse riding that morning, she had been thrown, broken one arm and badly damaged the shoulder of the other and –

"Would I walk her the several miles home because she had been desperate to see me, but now her arms were aching terribly!" What a position to be in; either lose your beautiful new girlfriend or get 'a friend' to stand in for me! The second alternative was decided upon and after some persuasion Ginger agreed to stand in for several hours while the other duty was performed.

Mission completed under two hours flat and, feeling quite happy about life in general, returned to the 'Manor' ready to resume guard duties.

Total chaos! One hour ago the C.O. (no less) had arrived and had found no guard or Junior Guard Commander on duty! On discovering this situation, and without any hesitation whatsoever, he had turned out all personnel from the 'Manor' and had them paraded on the front driveway and was proceeding to lecture them in a very forthright manner about the lackadaisical way and sloppy manner we all approached our duties with, when up the drive, with a contented smile on his face strolled the culprit.

The greeting still rings in all the recipients' ears, that is, those within a 100 yds radius, and will not be repeated here!

A dozen or more men were promptly dispatched to search the village for 'Ginger' who was found after not much searching in the local pub half 'blotto' in his celebration.

"I didn't think anyone would bother us on a Sunday afternoon!" was his only comment.

Needless to say we were both 'on a fizzer' in the morning and, in front of no less a person than the C.O. himself. We both thought that his face was still red from the day before, or was it his natural colour?

This paragraph is far too short to account the words spoken by that 'intelligent and military minded man' nevertheless some phrases still ring in the writer's ears such as:-

"If we were on active service I would ensure that you would both be shot at dawn!"

Without further ado, both culprits were stripped of that hard earned stripe and sent from the room with four ears full of fleas.

It was in later years that it was realised that this little escapade would be duly recorded and would affect promotion.

Shortly after this the C.O. was replaced by a younger man. 'Why? Was the Company going on 'active service?' was the question asked by one and all.

Several weeks later an 'order' was published requesting volunteers for the 'Paras' or RE Airborne. 'Ginger' was one of the first volunteers and within weeks was posted along with several of the other 'boys', never to be seen again, so it seemed at the time, but...

Some 15 years later, and so a long time after the war, the writer was stationed at the School of Military Engineering, Chatham, carrying out the duties of a Military Clerk of Works. Very enjoyable it was too, and, of course, was ideal preparation for 'Civvy street', when suddenly, but for only a short time thank goodness, that peaceful life was shattered by no less a person that 'Ginger' Dalton.

'Married Qtrs.' were available at Chatham and a very comfortable one was occupied by the writer and his wife. One day an invitation was issued, and accepted, to see an air display at nearby Rochester airport. Imagine the shock to see Sgt. Major 'Ginger' Dalton dropping out of the sky on the end of a parachute. Yes it was indeed him, so contact was made and an invitation to the 'Mess' was issued.

By sheer coincidence the Annual Ball was to be on the following night and after several hours at the bar 'Ginger' was ready to show the world how to dance, but, as was well remembered from the Fordingbridge days, he always did have two left feet. It was after some persuasion that my wife, who by the way was dressed in her finest regalia, agreed to the next dance with him. The waltz started well enough, but after one circuit 'Ginger' decided to hot it up with his latest jitter-bug steps, much to the concern of the RSM. and PMC. It wasn't very long before he was flat on his face with my wife spread-eagled too! With the dignity due to his rank he was carried off the floor and for some reason, never understood, my wife was inconsolable for several days and asked several times, "How did you make friends with such a man?"

He departed several days later, and, to my knowledge, hasn't been heard of since.

A year rolled by and by some misinterpretation of my records, a L/Cpl. stripe again arrived on the sleeve. The Company must have been desperately short of NCOs!

A posting followed to a new Section on the Isle of Wight. The outstanding memory of that spell, beside meeting new friends of course, was that while crossing the Southampton water by ferry, my peak cap, my beautiful peak cap, the one I had for years and had shaped by cutting the peak and 'propping' the front to resemble a 'guards' cap, the one that had hidden my mop then let me down at the 'Starman' ceremony, was caught by a gust of wind again and lost to the waters of the Solent for ever more! Heart broken! It was beret after that, a common head dress!

As 1942 wore on the order came our way to prepare for a long move by road. Was this it? Were we on our way overseas? After much speculation and guesswork we were on our way. Road convoy north and finished the journey on the west coast of Scotland between Ayr and Troon, at a small village called Monkton, a wasteland of sand dunes and unholy weather with the wind continually driving in from the Atlantic. A desolate spot indeed and so far from civilisation that any local population appeared to have migrated long ago, at least, no one came our way during our few weeks stay.

Several combined 'exercises' were carried out by the Company with a British 'Commando' unit, No 4 or 6, time has erased the number, who we were to meet again in action and under vastly different circumstances. Lots of the men that we became friendly with were either killed, wounded or taken prisoner.

The Commando camp was right out on the headland at Troon and so they suffered the same atrocious conditions as ourselves, continuous gales blowing in from the Atlantic with nowhere to hide. Most of the 'exercises' turned out to be both disgusting and degrading and, no doubt, could have caused serious illness if they had been allowed to continue. It was only a minor mutiny by the troops that saved the day. The reason for this was firstly that all personnel were paraded in full battle order, which, to the uninitiated, means all the equipment required in battle: a pack, rifle and bayonet, steel helmet, pouches (ammunition), respiration equipment, gas cape (rolled), jack-knife, anklets (web) and issued boots. A very heavy and cumbersome load especially when you and the equipment are soaking wet! The first hint we had of what was to come was when we were asked, "Are there any non swimmers?" then, "Are there any strong swimmers?" When these two bodies of men were sorted out, arrangements were made that every non-swimmer would be accompanied by a strong swimmer. What was to come? There followed a march to the beach and embarkation on to boats which, from memory, held about a dozen men. The boats were then taken out to sea, during which journey considerable attention was given to the depth of the water by 'plumbing' with an oar. Realisation dawned!

"Everybody over the side and make your way back to the shore! You are just out of your depth so when you hit the water get cracking!"

The wise people realised immediately that their best chance of survival was to start swimming before the packs and equipment were filled with water. This they did and survived but, by God, the water was cold and rough! Just imagine, beside the equipment worn there was also a rifle across the top of the pack! The task was almost impossible and only the very fit, which fortunately the writer was that time, (God how long ago!) made it, exhausted, to the beach. All other people were left clinging to the side of their boats or were being pulled ashore by the 'strong' swimmers.

What a disaster! Whoever gave that order (irrespective of rank!) should have been court-martialled and punished severely. Not enough thought or planning was put into the idea, and fatal accidents could have resulted. It was mentioned before that serious illness could have followed, and that was no idle statement because, after reaching the beach totally exhausted and gasping for life giving air after choking on several lungs full of water, it was realised that not only did every man smell vile but pieces and blobs of human excrement were clinging to his wet uniform, had entered his pack and had even filled his ammunition pouches and army boots.

The reaction to this was of some men being violently sick, others dashing along the beach and throwing themselves into a cleaner stretch of water, and others stripping off completely and jumping into cleaner water. All this upheaval had been caused by lack of planning in the first instance, and not bothering to find out just where the sewage pipe from Prestwick Airport and surrounding areas discharged into the sea. We had been dropped at the very point of discharge.

All equipment and clothing polluted by this incident should have been destroyed immediately but, true to the policy of the British Army, time off was given to every man so that his equipment would be thoroughly scrubbed clean, his rifle and boots cleaned, polished and inspected, while all uniforms were sent to a special cleaning centre in Ayr.

Much more publicity should have been given to this incident and as mentioned before, somebody's 'head should have rolled' but no, everything was hushed up. It was very fortunate for all concerned that no serious illness resulted.

The next move for the Company was to a very nice and friendly town some fifteen miles from Glasgow called Kirkintilloch. This proved to be almost a rest camp after Monkton, that is, except for the gruelling route marches over what the men referred to as 'The Scottish Highlands', some fairly rugged and steep mountains not too far distant. 'Could these have been the Grampians?' was the question asked.

The townsfolk here turned out to be very friendly indeed, and anyone who failed to get his feet 'under the table' was either totally stupid or aloof to the 'local peasants'. On route marches cups of tea and sandwiches always appeared whenever a rest was taken. Travel on public transport, if in uniform was always free. Many broken hearts were left behind, and travelled with us, when the Company finally left for Liverpool during October 1942.

One incident is worth relating before leaving Scotland altogether, and really was an 'eye opener', because it was the first experience of 'our transatlantic cousins', who, from here on in will be referred to as Yanks. It was found that the American troops did not object to this, and in the same way did not expect us to object to the term 'Limey', although at times it was used, or appeared to be, in a sarcastic manner.

A Sub-section of the Company (mine) was detailed to collect stores from Prestwick Airport, and whilst this chore was going on a large American lorry was seen well and truly bogged down in a mud filled ditch.

The driver accepted our offer of help, but he told us to 'wait a bit for his buddy who was fetching a Jeep'. To us this was puzzling because, we asked, what use could a Jeep possibly be – a small light vehicle almost a car in size – against the weight of an army truck and a mud filled ditch? All praise to the Yanks for something almost impossible to credit. The Jeep arrived with four men, reversed on to the truck, connected up a winch rope and, said the driver, "Would you fellas pile on to the Jeep and cling wherever you can?"

This was done making a total of nineteen men on the Jeep! Then the miracle happened. At first the Jeep was pulled back by the weight of truck and mud, but when the driver engaged the 4-wheel drive, up came the truck like a 'hippo' from the mud hole! All hats off to the Yanks for ingenuity!

CHAPTER SIX

EMBARKATION FOR WHERE?

At Liverpool we boarded what appeared to be quite a large ocean going liner, which had been converted into a troopship for 'the duration'. She was the 'Otranto', a 20,000 ton rolling, heavy box floating on very rough seas, and a target for enemy attention, as we soon found out, which was to become our home for a good many weeks.

The first shock came when it became apparent that only half the Company was aboard, the other half being on a sister ship, all the other troops on both ships were American Rangers, the equivalent of British Commandos. There were many hundreds of these on both ships and the realisation dawned on us that because these were crack assault troops, we were embarking on an invasion of some kind. Was it to be Europe?

The next shock came when an announcement was made that we had been 'selected' to land ahead of the Yanks in order to clear the beaches of mines and booby traps. Thanks very much!

After several days of taking on troops and general settling-in, the 'Otranto' left Liverpool and followed the coast up to the Clyde. The observant people on board saw that the boat had a large number of assault boats in various positions around the ship. From the Clyde we moved to one of the large Scottish Lochs and started an exercise which turned out to be a full scale rehearsal of what was to come.

Firstly it was announced over the tannoy system that so and so section of so and so deck were to proceed to the so and so 'sally-port'. On arrival we were greeted by scrambling nets slung over the side and this Field Coy: RE was expected to scramble down, in full kit, to the assault boats waiting below. This we achieved with some difficulty, all the time thinking two things, if this were the real thing we would be first ashore and therefore the first to catch anything thrown by the enemy, and secondly, the open sea would not be nearly so calm as this Scottish Loch! It was totally dark and some confusion seemed to be reigning judging by the amount of shouting and swearing going on. All this should have been dead quiet on the enemy's doorstep!

The boat set off at last and although nothing could be seen of any surrounding boats they most certainly could be heard. By some good fortune we found land, the ramp lowered, and a charge followed up the beach for some fifty yards, there to sit and wait the coming of the Yanks. A radio message was sent back to the ship to say that the beach had been cleared of all mines and booby traps. The result of this message was total chaos; whistles blew, lights flashed, men shouted until a fair comparison could be made to the noise at Highbury when Arsenal scored!

Why on earth had the 'powers that be' not practised us in this type of landing exercise before now? Time and time again instead of mucking about like we had been doing (the Limeys anyway) for several years?

The eventual result was that the exercise was declared fairly successful, apart from the several boats that had got lost between ship and shore, and the one or two boats which dropped men when they were still out of their depth, and apparently put them ashore on the wrong beaches. It was to be hoped that the real thing would prove more of a success than that! We were to find out very soon.

CHAPTER SEVEN

THE JOURNEY

The Otranto left the Clyde on the 13th October 1942 and at some distance into the Irish Sea was joined by quite a few other ships of various shape and size. Before many days had passed it became apparent that we were part of a very large convoy with ships stretching to every horizon, and to complete the picture, dozens of destroyers and other battle wagons circling and shepherding the convoy.

After several days of heading due west we were met by a convoy of mixed shipping, including war ships, heading due east. This, of course, was a prearranged rendezvous with a very large contingent of Yankee troops straight from their training bases in America. One previously large convoy had now turned into one of gigantic proportions. For several days we appeared to be going in a large circle, one day west the next day east, then west again until at last enquiries were made of the crew, by those interested enough as to 'just what is happening?'

The answer received was not very pleasant: "We are circling and zigzagging because a pack of U-boats have been located in the area and the convoy leaders have been told to take any action necessary."

What a haul for those U-boats if we had been located, and what a disaster for the Allied cause! The Otranto was just about the biggest ship there and, loaded with troops as she was, would have made a prime target. We were now about centrally placed in the Atlantic, so what hope for survivors?

After about thirty odd days out in the Atlantic (it was November 8th when land was first seen) the convoy was joined by a force of capital ships, known as 'H Force' from Gibraltar. This included the aircraft carrier 'Ark Royal', battleships

'Nelson', 'Rodney' and several cruisers. Now we knew that something big was afoot.

That evening a long lecture was given to the Company along the following lines: "The convoy you are travelling in is the greatest force of seaborne troops in world history. You are to take part in 'Operation Torch' which is the invasion by American and British troops of French North Africa, that is Algeria and Morocco, and later Tunisia. You, Royal Engineers, will land first ahead of the American Rangers and clear the beaches of all mines, booby traps and obstructions. The beaches are all sandy and maybe in some places Somerfield track will have to be laid in order to get the vehicles ashore. All ranks will now be issued with stars and stripes arm bands. These will be worn on both arms until further notice. Any questions?"

Well, of course, there were thousands.

"Why do we have to pretend to be American?"

"Because recently, when Hitler occupied the whole of France, (previously he had only held the northern half) the French sailed out of Toulon and headed for Morocco. This did not please British Naval Command because of the fear that they would fall into German hands: including a few capital ships, they were the cream of the French navy. Winston Churchill requested the French fleet to sail to Portsmouth. This they refused to do and after much talk and threatening the fleet was given a certain time to come from Oran to Portsmouth. This they again refused to do, and consequently they were bombarded by the British fleet, thereby losing many men (estimated in hundreds) and all their ships. This is the worst thing the British have done to the French since Waterloo and therefore, at the moment, the French attitude to the British is one of hatred. Please have your armbands in place when you land!"

"What are our objectives?"

"The overall picture is to land a large force behind the German and Italian armies, facing Montgomery in the Western Desert and to advance into Tunisia until Rommel is defeated!"

Apparently the immediate objective on landing was the capture of a small French airfield at Maison Blanc, just inland from our landing beach at Sidi Ferruch and when secured we were to move into the area of Algiers.

Before describing the landings it is worth describing the relationship between ourselves and the Yanks, bearing in mind that this was the very first time that either had met. The first and lasting impression formed of the Yanks was one of friendliness and generosity. Generally overweight, they were much better equipped, very much better fed and got at least double the money for doing the same job. If they looked for the same treatment from us they must have been very disappointed.

Another point worth noting was the fact that the majority of the Company were fairly young and single and had no matrimonial troubles left behind in UK, but the older married men often worried about leaving their wives at home when there were so many Yanks around - all 'on the loose' and loaded with money! As was proved many times over after the war, their fears had had some foundations. This feeling caused some friction but it was generally kept out of sight.

The first difference of note was, that after several days at sea, the Yanks had formed 'crap' schools. This is where several fellas would squat in a rough circle and throw the dice. Hundreds of pounds (and that's no exaggeration) would change hands on the results of a dice throw. These groups were to be found in every corner of the ship. Any space that could accommodate a 'school' would be occupied. If you kept watching for a while you could see and hear men talking to the dice in their hands as they shook, in all sorts of endearing tones! and in each position in front of the player would be stacks of pound notes and fivers. One of the reasons for the excess of money was, of course, they were just leaving the UK where they had been paid in sterling and all they wanted to do then was to change it to dollars!

Words about a troopship, written by Harry Beard in late 1940; no one with any experience will disagree!

She carried prisoners before
to the Antipodes; we go to war:
But here they pack us as they packed the foe,
eighty in this fouled-aired space below.
Bear us quickly to our journey's end,
we have our FREEDOM to defend!

CHAPTER EIGHT

THE LANDING AND ?

November 8th 1942 dawned with bright sunshine and clear skies, so different to 'Blighty' in November.

Overnight a large part of the convoy had passed through the Straits of Gibraltar and were now anchored off the coast of Algeria. The peaceful sight that met the eye was truly unbelievable and straight from the best holiday guide books. Golden sands with a background of green hills and whitewashed buildings, with here and there a small mosque, made up the panorama.

The convoy was probably about ½ to ¾ miles off shore and soon the call came to use the scramble nets. The Med was calm and little difficulty was met in reaching the flat decks of the LCAs. It came as a surprise to find just how much the flat bottomed boats rolled and pitched in the short journey to the beach. All the time nothing happened to shatter the peace and tranquillity of the scene, and here some praise must be given to the naval chap in charge of the boat because when the ramp was dropped, hardly a foot got wet before hitting 'terra firma'. Well, it wasn't quite firm, rather a soft sand which boded trouble for any wheeled vehicles which tempted to land in that area.

No mines, obstacles or booby traps of any kind were found and soon the Company were 100 yards up the beach, backs to the high sea wall and actually making a 'Brew'. The first on land for more than three weeks.

It was at this point that the signal was given 'beach clear', and the scene changed immediately. Suddenly there were hundreds of Assault Boats leaving the ships and, as if from nowhere, people with all types of movie cameras were amongst us and above us on the sea wall. They had come to record 'The Allied Invasion of North Africa!'

The scene was really laughable. There were these crack Yankee Rangers and Marines being made to charge up the beach, and told to make it look 'for real', whilst the representatives of the British Army were sitting against the sea wall and, by this time, drinking tea. The tea itself was alright for a quick brew but not kind on the taste buds. It was the type already mixed with sugar and milk and came out of the tin in a mixed powder.

But back to the charging Yanks! While the cameras were at their heights and rolling away, a quick thinking British photographer saw the chance to take a picture of the true situation.

It was published back home in, I think, the Illustrated London News. My parents, on seeing the picture, realised the situation, and, working out from the time taken after leaving the Clyde that the Company were involved, cut it out and passed it on. It raised quite a laugh amongst the Company, and today is still a treasured possession.

Shortly after this 'possession of the beach', the first German aircraft were heard flying very high overhead; obviously reconnaissance planes putting the enemy in the picture. Away to our right, on a prominent headland, some gun fire could be heard and it was assumed that 'the Frogs' were making a bit of a stand. That was the only disturbance during the whole landing.

Landings had also been made at Casablanca and Oran. This appeared to be very much a military error in landing troops so far west, when a landing in force, in Tunisia itself would have prevented the desperate action by the Germans of pouring in thousands of troops to hold the areas around Tunis and Bizerta. This mistake caused the loss of many lives and total misery for the Allied Armies for months ahead.

After hanging around for several days we were now reformed as a full Company. Clearly no one in command knew what to do next but, 'ours was just to do and die and not to ask the reason why'.

On the 11th November the Company was marched some twelve to fifteen miles to a small town called Biemandrie and billeted in the local school. The locals were mostly Arab and appeared to be very friendly but, it was soon found out, the reason for this friendliness was to be able to 'scrounge', or steal anything they possibly could from the troops. Occasionally some French civilians could be seen, but appeared to be quite unfriendly, so it was left there! Nobody bothered much, except those few who wanted to try out their schoolboy French.

This place Biemandrie was some fifteen miles from Algiers and no-one appeared to know what was happening, so the days were spent in kit cleaning, parades and lectures. In the meantime rumours started to come in that the Germans were landing troops near Tunis. But no one appeared worried!

On the 14th a move was made to an Arab town called Sidi Mouser, a little nearer Algiers, but still far enough away to be kept in the dark, with no one knowing what was happening.

Three more valuable days passed doing nothing and then at last things began to happen, but so slowly it was painful to be involved in such stupidity.

On the 17th the Company was marched to the rail depot in Algiers and while hanging around there for hours was 'put in the picture' as to what was happening. Then came the 'official' news and lecture.

"The Germans have been pouring troops by sea and air into the area around Tunis and Bizerta. There are several good airfields there and the best use is being made of them by using Ju 52's and giant ME-323 transport planes. They are reported to be flying several hundred sorties a day, so by the time Allied forces reach the area they will have built up a considerable army."

Question from an NCO:

"Then why are we kicking our heels around here doing nothing? And why have we landed in Algiers and not Tunis where all these German landings could have been prevented?"

A shout of total agreement from all who listened, then, reply by an embarrassed officer.

"Higher Command know what they are doing, they probably could not negotiate an agreement to land in Tunisia as they did with the French in Algeria and Morocco!"

A loud 'balls!' came somewhere from the captive audience to add to the embarrassment and then,

"Have the Germans then negotiated with the French for a landing in Tunisia?"

No possible reply to that of course! instead,

"This Field Company RE has been selected to form part of the 'Blade Force' and in order to strike for Tunis as fast as possible, we have commandeered a French train and you will board immediately. 'Blade Force' is made up of the tanks and armoured cars of the 17th/21st Lancers, some motorised infantry and yourselves."

The train was duly boarded by mixed British and Yankee troops and slowly lumbered off along the North African coast. A glance at a map will show just how many hundred miles there were to go and with a train travelling at no more than walking pace, there was no way that our coming would stop the German landings. They would have time to bring the whole German army over and take them back again!

The farce continued. The train itself consisted of a long line of goods trucks, on the sides of which was painted, in French, so many men, or so many horses. Into my truck were packed forty men, which gave you room for nothing except to stand in an upright position. Conditions were so bad that a lot of men climbed on to the roof to get room and fresh air. There was little danger from this because, as stated, the train only crawled along. Then we reached the Atlas Mountains, a line of snow covered rocky peaks through which the French had blasted the railway some years before. As you will realise, the temperature now dropped to below zero, and conditions became very bad. The troops were not equipped for winter travelling and on top of this there were no toilets available. The journey started on the 17th November and continued (slowly) by night and day through the nights of 17th, 18th and 19th arriving on the 20th. Whatever small stations the train stopped at to pick up water etc., had no toilet provisions and it became a familiar sight to see people running, at these stops, to attend to the call of nature, some with trousers around ankles and, because of the urgency involved, all sense of dignity forsaken.

When the train eventually stopped at a town called Souk-Ahras, we were amazed to find that the Tunisian frontier had not yet been reached, we were still in Algeria! Apparently this was as far as the French driver was prepared to go.

After much debating at this station by our Commanders and the French officials, it was decided to stay overnight and catch a different train tomorrow which would take us to the 'forward area'!

A march of all personnel in the Company was organised to an old French farm overlooking the town, where 'HQ' slept in the farm and all other bodies slept where they could in fields and barns around. The first spell of living rough had arrived and this is where my story starts, at the point when I said to myself, 'What the hell am I doing here?'

It was getting towards evening time with just enough daylight to seek out a clean and dry spot for the night. There were no blankets available as yet, so there was no alternative but to sleep with one's clothes on, because surprisingly enough for Africa the nights were bitterly cold. When everyone had just about settled down, all personnel were called together for a lecture on the latest situation. This only added to the stupidity of the situation.

"The Germans continue to pour troops into Tunisia and at the moment we have no means of stopping them except by air and naval attack. The good news is that the 1st Parachute Brigade has captured both Bone and Souk-el-Arba airfields, but sadly at the moment have no support from ground troops."

How sad when here still kicking about in Algeria were the tanks and guns of the 17th /21st Lancers?

Next message, "By the way, although the lights down
below of Souk Ahras look inviting, we are in a country which
is totally unfriendly to British Troops and therefore is strictly
out of bounds to all ranks!"

Well ever since those early days at Chepstow, it was found
that 'beating the system' was the most enjoyable thing to do, so
it was over the fields and into town as soon as the opportunity
arose.

It was several miles walking, but downhill all the way so it
wasn't too bad. Little thought was given to the journey home,
because the train of thought was concentration on 1) a nice little
French café with an appetising menu, or even bacon and eggs
would do after living so long on tinned food; and 2) a glass or
two of the local brew or even a few French Cognacs.

With apologies I must here slip into the 1st person 'mode'
because of the personal things that happened to me alone, so
making an alternative use of grammar very difficult. Please
bear with me.

To me the town, if you could call it that, seemed pretty dead
with broken down houses and shops, all in need of repair, dirty
streets, a very obnoxious smell hanging over it, and here and
there a grubby Arab shuffling along in the, what were by now,
dark alleyways.

After walking through the place several times I established
quite quickly that nowhere was a café or restaurant open – not
even fish and chips! In fact the only place with life in it was a
large, squalid looking bar which I suppose would have, by
stretching the imagination, passed for a pub back home.

Through the window it could be seen that its one and only
room was occupied by, as they say in books, a very motley
crowd indeed. A lot of people in uniform, which I guessed,
was the French Foreign Legion, quite a few French Army
people, and amazingly, a dozen or so French Naval people.
The rest were in all types of civilian garb, some of whom
appeared unwashed and greasy. All were standing or sitting in

72

small groups chatting closely, like all pub goers do, particularly the French.

The thought occurred that on a number of occasions we had been warned that these people were unfriendly to the British. What chance would I have on my own? What if those French sailors had lost mates when the British navy had sunk their ships? etc., etc.

I remembered then that the Yankee armbands were still being worn so nothing ventured nothing gained and opened the main door and walked in.

Dead silence greeted this complete stranger from another planet, probably the first British soldier that any of them had ever seen. Then came, "American? American?" from several voices. Taking the 'bull by the horns' the question was ignored and instead in a loud voice I asked if anyone there spoke English? If the reply was no, then I was in trouble, because the American idea would soon be exposed. Fortunately a civilian at the bar came forward speaking perfect English.

Then came the brain wave.

"Please explain to everyone that I am part of a very large American and British force, who have landed in your country in order to get rid of all the Germans, along with Gen. Montgomery, from North Africa! (cheers!)."

Now came the masterpiece.

"We need you Frenchmen to help us to do this, and have therefore brought with us lots of arms and ammunition for you. Vive la France! Viva Anglaise! Viva La General Giraud and General Juin!"

The latter names were pretty good thinking because they were the two French generals who were organising the French armies in North Africa.

Total chaos broke out, and by now of course they realised that I was British. A babble of questions followed.

"How many troops are you? Where exactly have you landed? Where are you going? When do we get our arms?"

Before I could start explaining to them, I had become a very popular man indeed, the drinks were already being lined up on the bar. Unfortunately it was a very strong spirit, and this appeared to be the only drink available to them, to which a small quantity of water was added so making it white, almost milky in appearance. If I had drunk one half of what was offered that night, the gutters of Souk Ahras would still be harbouring one British L/Cpl. Sometime later an explanation of that particular drink was given to me.

"Its 50% pure alcohol."

Nuff said!

After endeavouring to answer all the questions asked, I also explained to them that British paratroopers had captured Bone and Souk-el-Arba airfield and were now advancing on Tunis. This brought further cheers and became the subject of all their conversations.

By this time the strong spirit was beginning to have its effect and a little nag in the head was telling me,

"If you become senseless drunk, the least that you might suffer will be robbery, or even, in company like this, a cut throat. Also, how do you find your way 'home'? No one here knows where!"

By good fortune my English speaking friend stuck to me and promised to set me in the right direction etc., etc. From then on it was easy going on the spirit, but when the time arrived to leave, I found I was being kissed by the French Navy, Army, Foreign Legion and anyone else who could get through the crowd. Just how many times 'It's a Long Way to Tipperary' was sung I lost count!

My friend (name forgotten) and I found ourselves in the street almost incapable of standing and not giving a damn if there were fifty Germans just up the road. So we arrived at the French Brothel!

It was here that after the early introductions by him, he disappeared from sight, never to be seen again.

74

Really, at that moment, nobody was concerned whether he was alive or dead, my hands were full, as of those of an inspecting general with a long line of 'inspections' to get through. The choice was eventually made of a small Arab girl, probably in her late teens but it was hard to tell with a foggy mind and unsafe legs.

Madame appeared to be short of time at this point and hustled us both down a dimly lit corridor, keys rattling and jabbering away in French. To say it was depressing would be an understatement. Stone flagged floors, damp smell, and on each side of the corridor were cells - open fronted except for doors similar to prison cells, i.e.: full length bars from floor to ceiling. The last cell was reached and unlocked, client and call girl shepherded inside and the door locked behind. A rapid burst of French followed and Madame was gone!

The cell floor was rough stone flags with a six inch, in height, raised platform on the far side, this was covered in very rough and very dirty coconut (coir) matting. Doubts were beginning to flood through the fuzzy brain and when this young female backed up to the platform, raised her gown up to her chin, sat down and rolled up on to her shoulders with her legs either side of her face, I was frankly seeing things that I had never seen before. She was muttering away in French (or Arabic) and obviously grumbling about the time being taken over an everyday job to her. She was probably also complaining about the rough matting that her shoulders were resting on and who could blame her!

The thought occurred that no woman should have to behave like this and I chickened out! She appeared to be angry but some consolation showed on her face when she was given a shilling English coin with the explanation that it was silver and 'worth a bit'.

Madame was promptly called, 'Au Revoirs' exchanged and promises given for 'demain' along with a half dozen 'comrade.' My exit was made quickly and thankfully with virginity intact!

Out into the smelly street, which was completely deserted, because by now we were well into the night. My only clues to 'home' were that it was uphill, and several miles away then realisation dawned that I was a lost foreigner in a hostile land without even a smattering of the language!

It was shortly after this that the greatest coincidence in my life happened. Thinking back on it, it was probably life saving too.

The road back appeared steeper than the inward journey, so an alternative route was tried from scratch but after walking some miles it proved to be the wrong one - one young soldier was well and truly lost in the middle of North Africa.

Not giving up yet, the next plan was to 'kip' by the roadside until daylight, then get my bearings and 'bull' my way out of the consequences! Then right in the far distance there came the sound of voices singing and very slowly getting nearer. English voices? Never! But they were, and singing typical British army songs. In between the very drunken songs came some discussion on what to sing next. My hair stood on end; here was the voice of a Chepstow boy from the same group as myself named Scott. His voice was easily recognisable because 'Scottie' had been born and bred in India (his Father was a regular soldier) and the accent was unmistakable.

What a marvellous coincidence, but imagine the shock to him when a voice shouted out of the darkness 'Scottie!'

Dead silence ensued, then,

"Who the hell is that?"

Needless to say we fell around each others necks and instead of three drunken soldiers walking (staggering) through the African night there were four!

Questions and explanations followed with me sleeping the rest of the night on the concrete floor of a French barracks which they had commandeered. Before sleep was allowed, a bottle of good French brandy was dispatched by the four of us which turned the concrete floor into a feather bed, or nearly so!

Early next morning my Company had to be found and means of slipping in quietly without discovery. A brilliant idea was thought up, they (Scottie & co) had commandeered a French water truck, and knowing my Company would soon be requiring water for breakfast and ablutions, I persuaded 'Scottie' to accompany me with a full truck over to 'my place'. This was done without much difficulty and to the loud shouts of 'come and get it!' Figures came from everywhere with 'dixies', bottles and cans and took their fill. 'Bob' the section officer appeared delighted that one of his chaps had the ingenuity to go out early morning and commandeer water for the Company. It was goodbye and thanks to 'Scottie', never to be seen again! I wonder if he is still alive? If so, 'Scottie', please get in touch. Your voice, singing on that mountain, was the sweetest noise ever heard.

CHAPTER NINE

SLOW PROGRESS

The urgency of the military situation did not appear to be appreciated by anyone in Command. The Paratroops were way ahead of any ground forces, with what appeared to be very little effort to help them. The Company at that time, (and this situation occurred very regularly, that whenever a Division was hard pressed or in trouble, this Company would come under their command to help out) were under the Command of 78 Div., and all they wanted from us was the maintenance of the main road running forward into Tunisia.

No enemy had been seen or heard at that moment, because of course, we were many miles from where we were needed. Our sister Company did have some excitement by being attacked by German fighters (Messerschmitts), and unfortunately had several people killed.

After kicking about here for several days, the Company boarded one of those wonderful French luxurious trains again and, this time, crossed the Tunisian border and finished up in a small French town called Guardimou.

The Company divided into Sections here with No 1 (mine) sleeping rough, down by the river (I believe it was the Medjerda which seemed to wander all over this part of Africa). The job was to build a ford so that two crossings of the river would be established, the 'A' route or 'Up' route which was via the existing bridge and the 'B' or 'Down' route in the ford which would be for all traffic coming back from the 'forward area'.

It was explained that the ford was only a temporary measure and that a large convoy of Bailey Bridge equipment was now on its way up from Algiers.

It was now almost three weeks since the Algiers landing and still very little traffic was going forward on this main route to

Tunis. Occasionally a convoy of British or American tanks would cross the bridge. It was surprising to see the British tanks using transporters and yet the Yanks travelling on their own engines. Most of these were the General Grant type whose main feature was the off-centre gun. Another unusual difference was the use of hard rubber tracks instead of the heavy metal type. They were kinder on our roads but the considered opinion was,

"They will never reach Tunis because their engines will be burnt out long before." Perhaps there was some truth in this because they never were a success and were soon replaced by Shermans.

Late one afternoon a few days later I decided to try my luck in bartering for eggs from the local Arabs. This was easily achieved because they had plenty of eggs and nothing else, whereas we had plenty of tinned food and nothing else, so fresh eggs were indeed a luxury. The town itself was a collection of houses built around the railway station with the poor Arabs living outside this area.

After some very successful swapping of eggs for tins I was returning through town and so passing the station when the Germans decided that Guardimou should not possess a station anymore. Out of the darkness came swooping a group of JU 88's determined to bomb and machine gun anything they found.

Now unfortunately for me, after gaining a few dozen eggs, I had nowhere to carry them except to pile them up in my tin hat; in no way could I put it on and I certainly wasn't going to lose the eggs. Imagine the situation: down would come whistling a couple of bombs, followed by a hurried dive into the gutter and a balancing act with the eggs of which any circus performer would have been proud. The bombs weren't too bad, but on the way down the front gunner was having a go and on the way up, tail-end Charlie was enjoying himself.

Suddenly it was all peaceful again, although I understood later that a lot of the 'Arabs' were killed because they did not have the sense to shelter. I wondered afterwards, where was the French population? Not one was to be seen before or after.

The reason for the end of the bombing soon became obvious as they climbed and wheeled away. High up on the main mountain road from Souk Ahras appeared the Bailey Bridge convoy, and although they were driving with shielded lights were still visible to the Junkers. What sitting ducks they were, with no defence, and a good many bombs found their target and afterwards repeated runs with both gunners using up all their ammunition. Needless to say, we never did get our Bailey equipment, the convoy was shattered and a good many casualties inflicted.

Work on the ford had to carry on, of course, because no Bailey parts were now available to us, and it was while working here that German aircraft again tried to interfere with the everyday affairs of the Section. They dropped quite a few bombs early morning and machine gunned all around! Where were those damned Spitfires? Never saw one when it was needed, and we were supposed to have air superiority! Two of the Arabs were killed and quite a few wounded, but fortunately only one of our fellows wounded.

It was now the 1st of December 1942 and preparations were afoot to 'move up the line'. This entailed packing all the Section stores and equipment and loading them, and us, into the cattle trucks again, in a now partly wrecked station.

The train, whether it was the driver or 'red tape' caused it, refused to move and so a very cold night was passed standing in cattle trucks praying for the dawn, not the Germans, to come.

On reading through my writings, the words of John Jarmain, also written during the North African campaign, recur time and again.

They were not at tables written
With placid curtains drawn
But by candlelight begotten
Of the dusk and dawn.

They had no peace at their creation
No twilight hush of wings;
Only the tremble of bombs, the guns' commotion,
And destructive things.

CHAPTER TEN

UP FRONT

At last came the dawn and we were on our way. That night we arrived at Souk-el-Arba where again, the night was spent staying in cattle trucks. It was a larger town than what we had been used to and on the outskirts were a complex of airfields and landing strips. On these stood a number of fighters and Yankee light bombers.

The Germans knew, of course, of these airfields and promptly paid them attention by carrying out some heavy raids. Their method of breaking up troop concentrations by night was to fly over with heavy bombers which would drop canisters of anti-personnel bombs timed to explode a short distance above the heads of the troops. These were known to us as 'Butterfly Bombs' and were a particularly nasty weapon carefully designed to inflict as many casualties as possible.

The method used was for the aircraft to drop one or two which, after the plane had cleared, would burst open by use of an explosive charge. Inside the canister were dozens of these 'Butterfly Bombs', so called because the central metal container of explosive and shrapnel had a pair of 'wings' wrapped around them. On release these 'wings' would start turning while carrying the charge below them on a wire. It depended on the number of turns caused by the 'wings' for the bomb to explode, so they could be set to explode at any height. The pilot would be given his height and then it was left to the bomb. What an ingenious way of carrying out maximum destruction!

Sometimes the pilot would get the height wrong and the 'Butterflies' would explode too high or reach the ground before the number of turns required was reached. These were highly dangerous because when touched they would immediately explode and kill anybody nearby.

When troops, that is men experienced by serving some time in the forward area, heard these heavy aircraft overhead by night, they could be seen listening carefully for the loud 'pop' of the exploding canister. When this was heard it was immediately necessary to take cover of some kind with shelter of some sort over one's head. A slit trench was not very effective because of the down blast from the 'Butterflies', and so if one was fairly static for sometime, the use of sleepers or similar was sought as trench cover.

Our first taste of these was now at Souk-el-Arba, but very fortunately we were still in the station building and so were able to dive for cover. No casualties, but the 'forward area' was getting much nearer!

It was about now, early in December, that our trucks arrived from Algiers. They were greeted with a great show of pleasure because, as we thought, that was the last of those damned cattle trucks.

In reality it was a mixed blessing, because no sooner were we on the road to the front when very ominously painted signs started to appear on the road side, such as, 'Watch the Sky' or 'Is There a Spotter on the Cab?' or a burnt out truck on the roadside, and there were many, with a sign saying 'This truck did not have a roof spotter'. What it all meant was that the German airforce was patrolling these roads, and, as we soon found out, had complete control of the air space, with not a Spitfire to be seen. 'Why?' was the question asked so many times, after men had died from these strafings.

Travelling in convoy by daylight became impossible, because it brought the Messerschmitts down like hornets, and if your truck was unlucky, and without a 'Spotter' on top, the personnel travelling inside it did not stand a chance. Time and again we watched these '109s' come screaming in at zero feet, during the campaign. Each carried one or two small bombs which at first they would drop on or near the truck and then dive repeatedly, firing their forward fixed machine guns. It was estimated that each plane had about eight guns all 'zeroed' to hit a point at about two hundred yards in front of the aircraft. Anything in that area would be, without doubt, blown to pieces. Men would scream in terror when these devils were diving in, because once these planes were 'spotted' and the driver halted by repeated bangs on the roof, if you weren't more than fifty yards from the truck by the time the first bomb struck, you did not stand a chance. Sometimes these planes in addition to their machine guns, carried two 20mm canon. These were devastating to ground troops because they carried an explosive nose which, on contact, would explode and create havoc. You can imagine the damage caused by rapid fire of these together with some of their machine guns.

This type of attack, by German aircraft, we soon discovered to be our greatest danger.

As time passed it was found that there were some means of protection, of sorts, from the things that were sent over to kill you, but from aircraft there was little protection and, I would say without hesitation, these were the cause of most of the casualties in the campaign.

Then, a little later came the Stukas. Later on there will be descriptions of attacks personally experienced. They have been called many things by the experts such as 'long range artillery', but the description that fits them most is 'Terror Weapon'. If you have experienced, and lived through an attack by these monsters you will know the feeling of stark fear and terror! Designed to fly and dive slowly to their target they would arrive overhead 'in a cloud', and led by their leader would dive slowly on to their target. In addition to their terrorising noise, they were fitted with sirens which created a deafening wailing sound. The potential 'recipient' on the ground thought that his last moment had come, and it usually had, because the bombs could be dropped with great accuracy by a skilled pilot who aimed his aircraft at a target, and when pulling away knew that the bombs would continue on that alignment.

The most effective way, we read, of stopping these monsters, was with fighter aircraft who treated them as 'sitting ducks' on account of their slow speed. We had none of these of course and the only alternative for the Sappers was the Bren gun and small arms. But these proved ineffective because when you were in the target area and you had these screaming nightmares coming at you, the only thought was self preservation, by getting into the ground just as deep as you could. In some situations this 'drill' became almost a daily, and sometimes an hourly occurrence. A very hard lesson learned, never to be forgotten was that 'Fear is the first law of survival'.

To the troops on the ground the repeated questions asked were always the same "Where is our airforce?" and, "Where are the AA guns protecting our roads?"

It was here on the road between Souk-el-Arba and Souk-el-Khemis that we had our first experience of American troops under fire and it must be said that, under these circumstances they were magnificent!

Lots of stories were going around at that time about the Yanks being 'green to warfare' and that they were inferior to both British and German infantry, but my personal experience over the next few days made lies of these stories.

These particular Yanks were camping in the open fields and had taken over quite a large area and formed dumps with their ammunition and stores, with trucks spread out and all under camouflage.

Here it must be pointed out that this system was totally different to the British Army who would strive to get all their equipment, trucks and all, under trees or whatever cover was going. This was a lesson which was learned very early and which paid dividends time and again.

It wasn't very long before 'Jerry' found those Yanks, and over came the usual cloud of Stukas. There again I repeat, my hat came off to those Yanks. As the Stukas dived, a terrific and accurate barrage was put up from guns hidden around the perimeter. This had the effect of diverting the planes off their target and very little damage was done!

Unfortunately these attacks were continued over the next several days, with the Stukas dividing up and selecting various targets, so smothering the gunfire.

The casualties mounted as a result of these attacks and the 'Yanks' were forced to move back.

One of our young officers had a brilliant idea following this move. It was so simple and yet so effective.

Several dozen of us were 'volunteered' to go into this vacated area, collect all the rubbish left behind, and there were mountains of it, such as spare tyres, drums of oil etc. - gather it into heaps and set fire to it. It worked perfectly, and before long, over came the Stukas. There was no hesitation on their part and soon the bombs were raining down all over the area. What a waste of precious fuel, time and bombs!

It was never discovered if the act was repeated because it was time to move on! My praise to that young officer!

This move confirmed what had been said about camouflage. The whole Company was 'housed' in a very large wood on the outskirts of Beja, a town which turned out to be an important road and rail centre and became the objective for a strong breakthrough by German Panzers later in the campaign.

It was 'front line' positions now and eyes and ears had to be kept open for all sorts of things whizzing about with the idea of destroying anything they hit.

Life at this time was very sweet and you did all you could to keep it, but it was also very wet and grim. The rain was torrential and continuous with no respite.

The official issue of a ground sheet which could be used as a 'poncho' was a farce: in no way was it made of waterproofed material, and neither did it allow for Battle Order to be worn, because there was no allowance for a small pack on the back. So you either tried to wear it over your back and shoulders, which left you bare from the waist down or slung your pack on the side, as in Marching Order. Either way was unsatisfactory and one was soon soaked. To the designers of clothing for the British Army, no marks at all for this item.

There was, however, one piece of equipment which was never intended as a waterproof cape and it proved a real life saver – the anti-gas cape. Strongly treated with anti-liquid gas chemicals it also proved to be very waterproof, came down over the knees, had sleeves and room enough to wear a pack on the back and was carefully camouflaged. So full marks to the designers of the anti-gas cape, but thank God it never had to be used for what it was designed - Mustard and Lewisite gases. When not in use they could be rolled up and worn on top of the pack. So with the respirator worn on the chest and gas cape on the back the British soldier was well equipped for gas warfare.

It was found after being 'up front' a little while that the respirator, worn in this position, kept your body several inches above ground level when you had to 'dive' to avoid any nonsense coming from Jerry. This just did not correspond to your action of trying to dig into the ground with your fingernails, so they were soon abandoned, but kept handy 'somewhere in your kit'.

One more word in praise of the gas cape. It was sometime later when I saw a whole lot of German troops and at first thought they were our own because most of these were wearing gas capes in the rain. Probably still from the stores left behind at Dunkirk, but it just proved how valuable that cape was to front line troops.

After several days of being saturated in the woods it was decided to find a building in Beja with the roof still intact.

This was found after several changes of mind and duly occupied. Beja itself was receiving some attention from the German guns but no casualties were reported from the Company.

CHAPTER ELEVEN

MEDJEZ-EL-BAB

A scruffy little Arab/French town astride the River Medjerda with an all important bridge connecting the two parts of the town, and more importantly carrying the main road to Tunis, some thirty km away.

The Germans at this time held the ground to the east of Tunis and Bizerta, thence running South to Medjez and forming a corridor some twenty to thirty miles wide and parallel to the coast down as far as the Gulf of Gabes, and on to Tripolitania. This ground, as was now discovered, was held by very strong forces indeed.

The day after moving into Beja a reconnaissance party, myself included, was sent into the Medjez area to size up the situation from the Sapper viewpoint. Answers were required on how to deal with requests coming in from Infantry commanders about minefields which were killing their troops, and several more on bridges.

Apparently there was to be a 'push' coming off within the next few days on a Divisional 'front', with the objective of clearing the Medjez area and 'Long Stop' hill to the north-west. This was a very important hill which commanded the use of the Tunis Road.

Several 'probes' had already been made to ascertain the German strength and this had caused them to 'blow' the main bridge, to prevent its use by British Troops and to sew the whole area with minefields.

Now the Sappers were being called on more and more. The Infantry were suffering many casualties from anti-personnel mines and every armoured thrust seemed to come up against German teller mines. At first the Pioneers of the Infantry attempted to lift the mines, but suffered more casualties than before, because a lot of the mines were booby trapped purposely to prevent them from being lifted. So, as usual, it was 'send for the Sappers!'

Dealing with mines and booby traps was the most fearsome job of all, but as the present chapter is concerned with the happenings at Medjez-El-Bab, a point will be made of describing mine warfare later.

The British attack across the Medjerda, after several hiccups, was highly successful and 'Jerry' retreated some distance towards Matuer, a very strongly held position for which the Hampshires showed great courage and fighting ability at a later date.

Medjez was free of Germans, but the main bridge was blown and had to be built in a hurry because, as will be appreciated, the forward infantry would soon be desperate for ammunition and supplies.

It was decided that the Divisional Engineers would construct the bridge, but because, by necessity, this would allow only a single vehicle to cross at a time, it was decided to construct a ford alongside the bridge.

This was a brilliant idea when you considered the amount of traffic that was queuing up to get over, and of course, the empty trucks coming back after discharging their load.

But, and it was a big but! The river was wide and deep, something like the Wye at Chepstow, with a muddy bottom. So there were problems for my Section. Firstly, approach and exit roads needed to be created, off the main road and clear of bridge traffic. Secondly, there had to be enough graded hardcore to form a solid surface and high enough for trucks to cross without getting their engines wet!

Method used, 1) Commandeer every tipper truck in North Africa (or nearly so); 2) Round up ten thousand (or nearly so) 'Arabs' from Medjez, feed them a tin of bully and a few cigarettes a day; 3) Clear every bombed building for miles around for bricks and rubble to use as a base; and 4) Find a quarry with a good supply of graded chippings for surface work.

All these things were achieved and some sort of a ford began
to take shape, but then Jerry decided to take a hand. He knew,
obviously, that the river would have to be bridged and, of
course, exactly where that crossing was being made. A few of
his shells and mortar bombs began to get too close for comfort;
and then out of the blue came the Stukas.

There appeared to be only a few casualties among the
Arabs, but suddenly our labour force was reduced from ten
thousand to about fifty! These were either stone deaf and blind
or they had decided that they would die of hunger in any case if
no ration of bully was received, and who can blame them?

The ford was duly completed and traffic began to move at
last. The greatest hold up (and all 1st and 8th Army men will
appreciate this) were the Indian drivers! Either they were too
scared to cross our very 'well constructed ford' or drove off the
side of it with dire consequences. The winch trucks were kept
working overtime and many new swear words came to light
when it was found that most of the Indians did not speak
English, but more of that later.

'Medjez' became a ding-dong battle after that, with the
Germans well and truly dug in in strength and well within
artillery range of the town.

The Divisional Engineers were being employed elsewhere
and, because the Germans were occasionally attacking towards
Medjez, it was decided to wire up the bridge for demolition.

There were numerous smaller road and rail bridges in the
area, so the Company found itself split into very small groups
in order to prepare them all for demolition. This will give you
some idea of modern mobile warfare. Every bridge, and every
road culvert, would become obstacles for delaying advance
when blown.

To illustrate the importance of this, during the Italian
Campaign, the Germans blew, or cut, every single length of
railway line throughout the length of Italy.

Three of the prepared bridges came very close to falling into
German hands and so were duly blown. Whether the Germans

realised exactly what was happening or by sheer coincidence, the demolition party were well and truly 'strafed' by ME109s, for their trouble.

The main bridge in Medjez became the task (because of our good looks I suppose) of our Sub-section, twelve men and myself.

We concentrated on demolition of the bankseats more than the bridge itself because, we thought, if we had any worry at all, the Bailey could be dismantled.

Jerry took a keen interest in our welfare and sent the Stukas over several times, but unbelievably their accuracy was diabolical. We learned afterwards, from the Official Reports, that he had twenty squadrons of Stukas in the Bizerta/Tunis area, but some of these were under training (thank God).

We suffered, during these raids, one casualty only and that one was totally unnecessary. The story of that will be related in the 'French' chapter.

For many years after the war I wondered just what happened to all the thousands of tons of rubble dumped in the Medjerda, and I made a point of going back to see in 1989!

Of the ford there was no sign but a magnificent arched bridge was now the centrepiece of Medjez-El-Bab!

Another 'incident of war' is worth mentioning here before pressing on. A small detachment of the Section had the job of preparing a small bridge for demolition just north of Medjez, it was a rail bridge and a few men were detailed.

All went well until a large convoy of Yanks appeared on the scene, and asked our chaps,

"Where's this Goddam shooting range around here?" Which translated, probably means 'Where are the Germans?'

They were obviously 'green' troops straight from the States, and were duly warned that Jerry wasn't very far ahead.

The convoy was of mixed vehicles consisting of tanks (Grants), troop carrying trucks, jeeps and motorcycles, with the 'Yanks' riding at ease outside the tanks.

They travelled on down the road and must have found their 'shooting range' because the fireworks soon started with lots of bangs and tracers flying. All noise died after a while and the following night passed very quietly indeed.

The following morning, three of the boys were cooking breakfast ('Compo' rations, more about them later) in the (deserted) cottage close by, 'Dad' W was on the bridge shift when he called out,

"The Yanks are coming back!"

Joe M described to me later what happened next.

"As I looked up through the window I saw that the leading tank had for some reason persuaded 'Dad' to climb up on to the tank. This was indeed puzzling but the truth dawned on me when one of the 'Yanks' leaned over the bridge rail with a 'Tommy' gun in his hand and shouted, 'Come out English with your hands high!' They were German troops who, having captured the Yankee convoy lock, stock and barrel, dressed in their uniforms and headed into the Allied lines determined to cause as much havoc as possible.

"The three of us dived through the opposite window and managed to escape by running and crouching below the railway embankment into a culvert. We assumed that the Germans held their fire in order not to give the game away, but poor old 'Dad' W had had it!

"We heard reports later that as they got nearer to Medjez they also picked up a 'Redcap' Sgt. on traffic duty. After that they seemed to have disappeared altogether because we heard no more, but sometime later in the month an official order was published warning all troops to be alert for German troops dressed in Allied uniforms."

CHAPTER TWELVE

EATING AND SLEEPING

A chapter on these subjects has been included because this book is about the everyday life of the Sapper in peace and war. They are subjects which are never covered in books written by the strategists and generals and yet they make all the difference in winning or losing a war. Didn't Napoleon say something to that effect?

Many people have asked about these things during conversation, which shows just how little information has been published.

Early in the North African campaign, nights were nearly always spent in farms or empty houses when in the 'forward area', but, of course, very often it had to be slit trenches or the nearest convenient ditch.

During the winter period the two latter places were out of the question unless it was for life saving reasons, which it very often was, because of the torrential and never ending rain. You can take my word for it – a slit trench full of cold muddy water is no place to rest one's weary head.

The concrete or dirt floors of the farms or houses were not too comfortable either because the only bedding one had was the proverbial ground sheet and two blankets, but at least one was (hopefully) in the dry. It always amazed me just how quickly the British Sapper got himself off the ground to sleep. If, for instance, you were not enduring direct shell fire, and word passed around that you would be staying in that particular place for several days, from nowhere appeared timber frames (rectangular) covered in hessian (canvas) and standing on four legs. These were wonderful pieces of furniture and made very good beds but unfortunately were rather cumbersome to carry around when on the move and so the usual order when packing to move was, and I can still hear it now, "No beds on the trucks!" It was heartbreaking to watch those beautiful things burn!

Of course there were always ways and means of taking them – remember it was almost like life saving to sleep up off the mud – one of which was to bribe one of the truck drivers, say the ration truck, to pack it away out of sight in his 'wagon'. A 'going rate' was established after a few moves.

A stretcher was the answer to my Sapper prayer. Every Subsection had to carry one because we were usually out on detachment from the Section, and therefore if there were no RAMC chaps around we would have to get our own casualties to the 'Forward Dressing Station'.

For this purpose it proved itself very valuable indeed but it also provided me with a luxurious bed. As the Sub-section NCO (twelve men plus one) it was common sense for me to take charge of it and ensure that it moved from place to place with us. It was rather narrow and one had to lie straight but it was very gratifying to know that one could sleep (Jerry permitting) with a peaceful mind, knowing that you were up off the mud (four metal legs) and that your 'bed' would be travelling with you whenever duty called!

It was about now that we were issued with one of the most wonderful pieces of equipment ever designed for the British Army, and again I take my hat off to whosoever was responsible for the issue. The two man bivouac!

It was, of a necessity, very low off the ground which forced you to crawl to get inside, was camouflaged, water proofed and proved a God-send time and again. Six plus one, for the NCO, were issued to each Sub-section, and most of the chaps immediately saw the best method of providing comfort with safety.

This was to dig a slit trench first, wide enough for two usually, but stretcher width for me, then erect the 'bivvy' over it. This gave you headroom to stand up and safety from what those Germans were up to. Speaking personally, a paraffin

94

lamp had been 'obtained' from French North African Railways, and proved absolute luxury for writing letters home etc.

The main thing to watch with this trenching method was to 'channel' on the outside of the 'bivvy' in order to divert the rain water. Many times was the cry heard in the middle of the night

"My b----- trench is full of water!" or, "I'm soaked, this b----- tent must be leaking!"

Lots of stories have been told about the rations of bully beef and biscuits of the First World War, but for this one much thought had been put into feeding the troops.

This was by 'Compo' rations. They came packed in a wooden box containing food supplies for seven men one day or one man, of course, for seven days. Not only was there food but other necessities such as cigarettes, chocolate and toilet paper were included. Seven cigarettes per man per day, but of course if there were two or three non smokers in your Sub-section, the smokers were lucky. The toilet paper proved to be totally inadequate because it numbered exactly three sheets per man per day, the implication being that a healthy soldier carried out this physical function of nature once per day - shiny green apples from local fruit fields had not been catered for in the ration pack design. When complaints were made to the long suffering Quartermaster (who always had a ready answer) about the serious lack of toilet paper, his classic answer was, "Three pieces per day is sufficient for any soldier when used properly. One up one down and one for polishing!"

Later on the rumour circulated that officers had five pieces. I wonder why?

The tinned food was carefully designed to provide breakfast, main meal and sweet. Breakfast was usually a choice of, and this depended on the type of box supplied, soya link sausage or rolled tinned bacon. Main meal, stew, spam or bully with either rice pudding or sliced peaches. Of course there was the inevitable biscuit too, dry and very hard but still edible. Tea came as a mixed powder of tea, sugar and milk, all that was required was boiling water, this was obtained by filling a biscuit tin with sand and soaking it with petrol; it was surprising just how quickly a dixie of water would boil. It was 94 days before bread was tasted, and proved the most wonderful thing ever tasted.

These 'Compo' rations were excellent, but a deficiency of fresh fruit and vegetables soon became apparent. Some poor souls developed what were called 'Desert Sores'. These were a horrible type of open boil which were for ever weeping and sticky, so making the wearing of clothing and equipment almost unbearable.

Some little time after the North African campaign finished we had to cross the Med to South Italy in an American crewed Landing Ship Tank. This was a flat bottomed boat, in order to allow it to get well up the beach in an assault landing, and you can imagine how this caused her to pitch and roll in the slightest swell. This swell played havoc with everyone's stomach because in twelve months we had all become 'land-lubbers' again, and to cap it all we were suddenly on Yankee rations!

This needs some explanation. The British soldier's mess kit consisted of two rectangular aluminium tins about 8"x5"x3" deep, with one slightly smaller than the other so to fit inside. The smaller half was usually used to drink tea from, that is if the unfortunate soul had not 'obtained' an enamel mug during his service, they never were an official issue.

The cause of the stomach shock was 1st day breakfast, men queuing in front of a line of Yankee cooks to receive food in held out mess tins. First cook places in the tin one very hot bubbly greasy 'flapjack'. Second cook, a spoonful of very sweet maple sugar. Third cook, a spoonful of diced beetroot! and so on to the end of the line. All marvellous food for stomachs used to the richness of it all, but not to these stomachs, and the inevitable happened.

Decks were being hosed down several times a day, that is whenever the pile of horizontal groaning bodies could be shifted. Dry land was never so welcome!

CHAPTER THIRTEEN

OUR ALLIES THE FRENCH

In an alliance of several nations, things sometimes happen which are the cause of friction between them, but by using some diplomacy and tact these things can always be 'ironed out'. For instance, several occasions spring to mind where the Yanks were blaming the British, or vice versa for not doing (or doing) something or other, in the heat of the moment, but after discussing the 'whys and wherefores' friendship was usually restored.

Not so with the French. From the moment that the Allied landings took place in North Africa they went out of their way to show their dislike, more especially to the British. Was it Waterloo? Was it the Dunkirk Evacuation? We, the soldiers on the ground, could not understand their attitude. Was it the fact that we had landed in their colonial territory of North Africa, so causing the Allemande (Germans) to also land and cause tremendous destruction? The impression created by the First World War was one of general comradeship between British and French, or was it?

The incident at Souk Ahras must have been a 'one off', when a welcome was given to a British Soldier. It was probably the promise of a supply of arms being given to the French, and the compliment to the French soldier by asking him to help us to get rid of the 'Boche'.

The most noticeable early incidents concerned the surly attitude of the average 'Frog'. He would never attempt to speak to you or invite you into his house or farm. This, it is stressed, only happened some miles from 'the front', because in the forward areas no civilians were to be found, unless they were service personnel.

To enable you to appreciate their true attitude I will record some of the memories which have 'stuck'.

It was on the bridge at Medjez, very much a front line town at that time, with the Germans trying really hard to re-take it. Sub-section One (mine) was doing the maintenance of the bridge, which really meant sorting out the traffic. You can imagine a thousand vehicles, some very heavy, waiting to cross a narrow 'low class' Bailey with the occasional shell pitching close by and the Stuka pilots 'doing their training' on their obvious target. Some vehicles were just too much (such as the loaded tank transporter) for the bridge. These were made to off-load and drive (or winch) their load over separately. The delay caused the air to turn blue with swear words of several nationalities because everyone was desperately anxious to get over and out of the target area.

In the middle of all this, one Stuka group made a determined attack on the bridge, which caused all personnel to dive for cover. One of our tall (and very fast chaps when stuff was flying about) was Lofty P – and he was seen when 'leading the field' to take a dive over the parapet. This, of course, was proof that everybody and anybody will take any action necessary to save one's life. The bridge at this point was spanning the centre arches of the existing stone bridge so poor Lofty fell about twenty feet on to solid ground.

The Stukas were much more accurate this time and hit the bridge but only damaged it, while lots of bomb splinters actually came up through the decking. Shortly afterwards, when peace had returned, we climbed down to find 'Lofty', who was lying in a heap with obviously both legs broken and some internal injury judging from his groans.

Our ever ready stretcher was produced and 'Lofty' carried to the nearest medical dressing station. Unfortunately this turned out to be French, but the nursing 'Sister' in charge indicated that we were to gently place him on one of these beds. She appeared to show understanding and efficiency, so 'Lofty' was left with the promise of a return visit just as soon as possible.

The next day the position at the bridge worsened and a 'stand-by to blow' the bridge was issued. This meant a German attack was imminent and was probably the reason for the Stukas of the previous day.

After two days the 'flap' was off and the chance came to visit 'Lofty'. Shock of shocks, poor lad was lying almost as we had left him three days before, except for as he told us, having been fed a few bowls of soup. This was a terrible crime and many words of anger were directed at the 'Sister', and when the French 'Doctor' came in to see what all the noise was about, it was all I could do to prevent 'Lofty's' mate from thumping him on the nose!

Lofty was very carefully placed again on the stretcher and taken to the British Dressing Station on the Beja road, where the Medical Officer (Major RAMC) made a thorough examination. Afterwards he called me aside and very angrily demanded to know,

"Where the hell has this man been since breaking his legs?" After explanations given, more swear words followed and then, "You realise that gangrene has set in and one leg will have to be amputated and it will be touch and go on the other."

We heard some days later that one leg had been amputated and treatment was being given to the other, together with several broken ribs. What a totally unnecessary accident with the 'Frogs' absolutely refusing to help at all. It makes me wonder just how they would have treated a wounded German prisoner of war?

One of the other incidents which readily comes to mind was what happened to an everyday, common or garden 'Arab'. More of 'the Arab' later, but this particular Arab showed us just what the 'Frog' was really like.

We had 'bivvied' in a large olive grove just in front of Beja. Our trucks were out of sight and the trees just grew enough cover to hide the 'bivvys' from the ever present German fighters. On this occasion something must have attracted them on the road below because down they came like hornets. The whole area was sprayed with bullets and cannon fire, with the subsequent casualties. The nearest casualty to me was a little elderly Arab who had been harvesting a few of his olives. It was obvious that he had been hit by two or three bullets and was still alive but unconscious. Using our stretcher and the Section 15cwt truck, he was carefully put on the truck and driven to the French hospital in the town.

When the French doctor saw us arrive he pointed to a bed and said a few words which were not understood. Then he saw that the stretcher case was an Arab and his attitude changed to what looked like anger. Pointing to a door he made us understand that there he wanted him taken. We complied but were horrified to find ourselves in a mortuary. The doctor indicated a slab on which to leave him.

Once again a French doctor almost had his nose flattened, and the Arab was soon stretchered out and carried to the British Dressing Station. The only questions asked by the nurse in charge (female) was,

"Working with you was he?"

Well a 'no' here could have cost a man's life, so it was a white lie, and before we had left, two British soldiers were cutting his rags of clothing off. We never had a chance to follow up the case but were happy with the thought that everything possible would have been done for him.

'Smoky S' was one of our dispatch riders of note and did a very good job when no radio contact was possible. Some of his motor bike rides would take him to dangerous areas looking for the odd Sub-section holed up in the rocks!

He was a country loving chap, always ready for a quick laugh, and seldom a word out of place, so we became firm friends.

On this particular occasion of the story he had to pass through the French Sections to reach a Divisional Sapper unit. On his return to the Company he was hot and bothered, and looking very flustered indeed! His story when asked was:

"On a number of occasions I was flagged down by 'Frogs' who wanted to see my papers and asked where was I going? Why was I going? etc., etc., until I really had enough of it. Then it happened! A bunch of 'Frogs' were making quite a noise sitting by the roadside, and, unusually for them, called me over. What I saw horrified me; they had a pot of boiling water on a fire into which they were dipping in turn, two live chickens. Every time they pulled a chicken out, a handful of feathers was plucked from the live bird. The poor birds were in agony and I saw red. In no way could I stop myself from kicking their pot off the fire and telling them in good English just what cruel bastards they were and if they did it again I would shoot the bloody lot of them. How I walked away alive I don't know but I expect that there are a few 'Frogs' tonight wondering why the British are so stupid!"

These are just a few cases that readily come to mind without too much diving into the recesses. Only recently, in the early nineties, whilst motoring through Europe and crossing France, Holland, Belgium and into Germany and Denmark, it was very noticeable that at all Customs Posts, one look at the British Registration was enough to be waved through, that is until the French Customs played their game. Firstly you were kept waiting for no apparent reason, then a 'lady' appeared armed with a riding crop, with which she indicated that she wanted the boot opened. On compliance she very disdainfully started to turn things over with the riding crop. No word spoken but after another wait, a new 'Frog' appeared and grudgingly said "Cross!"

Why are they like this? Was she a daughter of one of the 'Frogs' who had his cooking pot kicked over all those years ago?

Here endeth the lesson on 'Frogs'.

CHAPTER FOURTEEN

THE 'WOG,' THE NATIVE ARAB

As you probably know the term 'Wog' comes from the British practice in Egypt years ago of stamping any natives' papers, working for Britain, <u>W</u>orking <u>O</u>n <u>G</u>overnment Service. These papers made him an official worker and so he could draw his money on the strength of them.

Now the Egyptian 'wog' was well known throughout the British Army. He was a beggar, thief, liar and would steal your false teeth if you slept with your mouth open. It was a known fact that without the British Army presence in Egypt over the years, half the 'Wog' population would not have survived.

Now was the Algerian and Tunisian 'Arab' any different? That is something to be found out but only by experience.

The impression given by the French 'Arabs', under their colonial rulers, was one of poverty, degradation and of a people only just tolerated by their Masters.

You did not see a lot of the women but the men, on an average, were dressed in rags, were uneducated and always appeared dirty. The better class Arab wore a long cloak with a hood with wide sleeves, almost down to the floor. It was made of a coarse blanket-like material which, although very rough, must have kept him cool in those very hot days of mid summer.

His living quarters were usually a mud hut with thatched roof and straw covered floor within the fields of the farm (French) where he worked. In the town the houses belonged to the French and the Arabs appeared to live wherever they could.

In the 'forward areas' the 'Frogs' seemed to have disappeared from the danger areas, but there always appeared to be the odd Arab about, who seemed to be looking after the place when the 'master was away'.

These people were in touch with each other over distances of miles, and very soon the British soldier on the ground picked up the method. The first call was always the same, and it is spelt as it sounded! *AHOYMOHAMMED!* This would be answered from way in the distance, and very often it was followed by other words, the spelling of which will not be attempted, but all were long drawn out, almost a yodel!

Talking to the front line infantry some time later, and particularly the 'Paras' they were quite adamant in saying that if the Germans were in listening distance of these Arabs when hollering, the one this end would be shot because it was suspected that he was passing on information on strengths of troops etc.

Some time later when attending a service with the 'Paras', it was well after the war, I was dumbfounded to see across their colours, in gold letters the word *AHOYMOHAMMED!*

When queried on this, the reply received was, "Oh this is the shout we are taught to give when jumping from the aircraft!"

In so many ways the Arab was so different to us, and one of the incidents which remain for ever in mind to illustrate this was:

One day as usual in the 'forward area' the German fighters were giving us a pasting with small calibre bombs and machine-gun fire. There were several 'Arabs' about, one of which was a small boy of about six years who unfortunately was blown up into a tree and died instantly. His father, on seeing this, took up a squatting position under the tree and began to pull his hair out in clumps. He actually had handfuls of hair in both hands. Then he started to bite each finger at a time and really did bite until they bled. It is to be hoped that you have learnt a little, from this chapter, about the Tunisian 'Wog', who of course is not a 'wog' at all but a native Tunisian.

CHAPTER FIFTEEN

MINES AND MINE WARFARE

The Sapper, or in the German army, The Pioneer, had a very important role to play when in the front line situation. A whole lot of his work was decided by whether the army was in retreat or advancing.

In retreat his job was to cause as much delay as possible by laying minefields, demolishing bridges, cutting railway lines, blowing up roads etc., etc. But in advance, the role was reversed and of the two, the latter was much more the dangerous job. This came about by the fact that a retreating army could lay booby traps of all types to catch the unwary Sapper. The Germans were particularly good at this and used some diabolical methods, at least by our standards, of which you will learn. These caused many an unnecessary death or disfigurement among the people clearing the obstruction.

Every army produced its own type of mines, some varied widely but others were obvious copies. A word here on the very brave Sappers who would, when a new type of mine was found, make it their job to strip it down to see what made it tick. Many were killed doing this deadly but necessary job, but doubtless they saved many more lives by their sacrifice.

It is recalled that one particular friend, when a new or different type of mine was found, would not rest until he had stripped it down. This would include the primer and detonator (ignition set) too, which were usually very complicated and were set to different pressures or delay times. Jack B was one of the many chaps killed doing this job.

Most mines were designed to stop the advance of a tank or tanks by blowing off a track, or in some cases destroying it almost completely. The most famous and well known of these was the German Teller mine. It was developed and improved upon over the years, with the ones in Africa, in common use, being the Mark IV.

It consisted, and most of them were nearly all the same shape, of a metal case about the size of a good 'healthy cow pat' but about three inches in depth. A carrying handle was on one side, and in the top, a recess into which fitted the ignition set. A plate of varying size (depending on the mark) then fitted over this. These were laid just below the surface of the ground but well out of sight. Normally they would not explode under the weight of an average man but no-one really experimented to find out the truth of this theory.

A good detector would easily locate it and it would then be neutralised and lifted, but and it is a *very big but* - the German mind devised several ways of preventing this, the first being two small threaded sockets, one on the side and the other underneath. Into these sockets there threaded what was called a 'pull' igniter which, when the mine was lifted and because they were connected, either to an anchor point or another mine or mines, would cause everything to explode. Lots of fatalities occurred this way, especially under such conditions as, rain, mud, speed, fear and tiredness, causing the wire to go undetected.

The other favourite way of killing off the British Sapper, or infantry man, was the anti-personnel mine. The type most frequently used was the 'S' mine, or sometimes called flower pot mine.

This again was an invention of the diabolical German mind and consisted of a metal cylinder the size of the largest tin of peas. Down through the centre of this was a delayed igniter which fired a propellant charge in the main base of the mine which then caused an inner cylinder (a smaller tin of peas) to rise into the air about four to six feet before exploding, so firing ball bearings over a wide area and killing or wounding all personnel within range.

These 'S', or Shrapnel mines, would be scattered throughout the minefield and were very hard to detect because the igniter system consisted of three thin metal prongs protruding above ground level, and if these were laid in grass or similar, were virtually invisible.

Several other types were later produced by the German mind, all ingenious and diabolical, such as the Holzmine, or as it was better known, the Box Mine. This was made entirely of wood (plastic later), with no metal at all, so making it impossible to pick up with a metal detector.

A smaller version followed later called a 'Schu' mine. This had just enough explosives to shatter a man's leg, and many casualties were caused before the cause of this explosion was recognised.

The British were much more 'Geneva conventional' with their mines, which in a way, was a mixed blessing because in a war where the front line areas were always changing hands, the Sapper very often found himself lifting his own mines, which, had they been booby trapped as the Germans were, would have caused many more casualties.

The main anti-tank mine was modified many times and towards the end of the war resembled the Teller mine, but the one most used in Africa and Middle East was the Mark V.

This in shape and size resembled a medium size saucepan with a heavy type igniter set fitting into a recess in the top centre. Resting over the top and on the igniter was a four legged 'spider' which was held in position by lugs on the side of the body.

The design was good and simple to lay so speeding up the process of laying a field which sometimes 'saved the day'.

The anti-personnel mine was usually a Shrapnel mine which, when exploded, would scatter shrapnel over a wide area. The favourite position for fixing these was about head height to a post or fence and they were detonated by a trip wire. Many a German patrol when operating (as usual) in the dark were caught out by these.

The other mine which proved very successful in most conditions was the Hawkins Grenade. Successful because it could be used (more later) for personnel or tank warfare and could be clipped to a Sapper's belt so making it available in quantity when required. The danger in carrying this mine was very real indeed, because it was activated by an acid filled glass tube detonator.

This danger was first exposed very vividly, and unnecessarily, during the attempt to capture one of the airfields near Tunis in November '42.

During the raid a line of Sappers, including two personal friends, were directed to climb the rugged ground up to the airstrip. Each carried an armed Hawkins on his belt; the leading man slipped, so exploding all grenades. There were no survivors.

Usually a minefield was laid as a belt varying from about ten yards upwards in depth and of any width. These, as in the German case would usually consist of 'Tellers' placed staggered in rows with a scattering of 'S' mines in and about.

An unusual feature of the German field was the fact that they were usually surrounded by barbed wire, and clearly marked 'Achtung Minen', with a skull and crossbones usually present.

The job of the Sapper was to make 'Safe' lanes through these fields wide enough to take the following tanks and infantry. But conditions were never kind and, as said previously there could be a desperate need for speed, shells were usually flying both ways, the Germans nearly always had the field covered by machine gun fire, especially in the dark and it could be in torrential rain with the usual sea of mud to squelch through. One foot wrong was your last!

At first, the only method of detecting the presence of a mine was to probe the ground with a bayonet, or later a modified stiff wire. The body would usually be in a crouching or prone position for this operation, firstly, in order to avoid the missiles flying about and secondly, to bring you closer to earth where both hand and probe could be used. The hand would be feeling for those dreaded prongs of the 'S' mine.

Later the sophisticated mine detector came into operation on which I suppose today's metal detector is based. The first one issued was the Polish detector, a very heavy cumbersome plate on a long pole. Ear phones and heavy back pack were also necessary with this equipment.

Other types slowly followed, each an improvement on the last, the American's seemed to be the favourite, both light to use and efficient in detection.

The 'drill' to clear a lane would be to split into teams of three. A Sub-section (12 men) was the exact number required and a line of twenty plus feet wide could be cleared by two such teams, while the other two teams stood-by to take over, working in relay, or to replace casualties as they arose.

Man No. 1 used the detector, in absolute silence of course, and when detecting a mine would stand still with the detector 'hovering' over the object. No. 2 would place a 'hot cross bun' over it. This was a made up marker of tracing-tape on a circle of wire. No. 3 would lift the mine, by feeling for booby traps first, then gently prising it out. This was the worst job of the three because not only did he lift but also had to carry to the side of the safe lane, marked by tracing tape.

Casualties from the 'S' mines were heavy at first and a 'drill' was worked out to reduce the loss rate. When the mine was stepped on, a loud crack was heard and the words 'S' mine' were shouted causing everyone in the vicinity to fall flat, always backwards or sideways because forward had not as yet been cleared, while the unfortunate chap stepping on the mine took two paces and 'dived', thereby hoping that all ball bearings would pass safely overhead.

It was known, unfortunately, for the base plate to explode downwards, to cause heavy casualties.

Almost unbelievably, it was known for a Sapper to remain standing on the mine when it fired. This saved a lot of casualties but one or both his legs were shattered. Was it ever worth the decoration that followed? One aid to reducing casualties amongst some Units was the wearing of thick clothing such as greatcoat, leather jacket and even blankets. On a hot day in Africa, this could produce heat strokes, but the chance was taken.

Later in the campaign, to counteract this last action, the Germans changed the filling from ball bearings to jagged shrapnel. Bastards!

Mine warfare is a horrible business and one of the worst aspects of war. I visited Tunisia in recent years, and during the tour made a point of calling in the British Cemeteries. It was well known to me the locations where Sapper friends were killed. Each cemetery visited brought back terrible memories and in particular, the one at Medjez-El-Bab as before described when I sought one particular friend, found him surrounded by headstones of sixteen Sappers of all ranks, killed on the same day and obviously in the same minefield.

CHAPTER SIXTEEN

THE BAILEY BRIDGE

This subject will be dealt with briefly in order to avoid boredom, but it is such an important item in the Sapper's life that to avoid describing its capability would indeed be a sin.

Before the advent of the Bailey, the alternative was either very heavy and cumbersome girder bridges or composite wood and metal types which were not only unwieldy but unreliable too, and to transport them for modern warfare requirements would be a headache of enormous proportions. On wider rivers, of course, a system of pontoon or folding boats was used, and later the pontoon or floating Bailey.

Doubtless the war on the British fronts was considerably shortened by its use, and even the 'Yanks' and 'Frogs' were using it later on.

Imagine a Division of 14,000 men and, probably, six or seven of these Divisions waiting to cross, say a deep gorge where 'Jerry' had blown the bridge. This is when the Bailey was the answer to the Sapper's prayer. A bridge long and strong enough to carry that traffic could be erected and ready between dusk and dawn of one night. An alternative type using, say centre piers, would have taken weeks while the convoy was forced to wait.

Its versatility was its outstanding feature. All parts fitted together like Meccano, and no one part exceeded a six man load. The said panels could be increased in width or depth so strengthening its structure. A small gap like a blown culvert, could be bridged by one panel length, six feet, while some of the longest, for example over the Po River, and built on piers, exceeded 600 feet.

The first operational 'Bailey' built on active service was built by the 'Company' and opened to traffic shortly after Christmas 1942.

The railway station. The scene of much bitter fighting. (top)

MEDJEZ-EL-BAB. Photograph taken during re-visit in 1988, of the bridge which replaced the one demolished by the retreating Germans. (bottom)

LONG STOP HILL-MEMORIAL. A French-erected memorial to the British First Army. Long Stop Hill is so called because of its shape and position overlooking the Tunis/Medjerg road. The scene of much bitter fighting late '42 early '43. (top)

Leonard Watkins. (bottom)

EL AROUSSA. An Arab village which became the objective of a German thrust in early 1943. (top)

EL AROUSSA. The road leading to the position taken up by No. 1 Sub. during the offensive by the Germans. (bottom)

EL AROUSSA. The view from No. 1 Sub. Position of the German attack. (top)

THE KASSERINE PASS. Scene of one of the biggest routes of Allied Forces in North Africa. (bottom)

MEMORIAL TO AN ARTILLERY UNIT. It is erected on the main BEJA to MATEUR road in Tunisia, and was the point where the German thrust for BEJA was stopped. (top)

GREEN HILL. Memorial to the Argylls, picture shows a re-visit by an Argyll who participated in the fighting. (bottom)

GREEN HILL. Showing the memorial to the Argylls a key defensive position of the Germans and fought over for a long period by, amongst others, the Argylls and the parachute Regiment. Picture shows a re-visit by Paras who took part in the fighting. (top)

BEJA to MATEUR ROAD. An area for which many lives were sacrificed. (bottom)

British troops advance in Italy. (top)

The 8ᵗʰ Army moves into Calabria, the 'toe' of Italy, September 1943. (bottom)

Sappers repairing and re-launching the Bailey Bridges during the assault on the Gustav Line. The bridges had been previously damaged by dive-bomb attacks and shellfire.

The front cover photograph. (bottom)

Souk-el-Khamis was the site, the Medjerda the river again, which was liable to flooding at this spot. Always dangerous because, having low banks, the bridge would be close to the river surface.

The existing bridge was still in position but because of traffic volume, an 'Up' and 'Down' route had to be established. The approach and exit roads were mammoth tasks because of mud, mud and more mud.

Continuous rain had put the area virtually under water, but a bridge had to be built and quickly.

'Triple Double' was the estimate made to suit the required gap and traffic demand, which was a massive task, being 200 odd feet in length. Work started on the bridge and approaches on Christmas Eve and continued until the 28th when the last decking chess was in position. The work was carried out in relays because of the urgency factor, with all personnel absolutely saturated. The ff-----g stage came and went several times!

Christmas dinner was one never to be forgotten. Eaten in the rain - 'Compo' Rations - straight from the tin and cold.

One outstanding memory of this bridge, beside its being the first, was the name given to it by the Chief Engineer. All bridges were named such as Stirling, Thames, etc. but this one was named because as the traffic started to flow there came a sudden stop, caused by an Arab with a small cart. The air became blue as the traffic piled up. The donkey, or Arab, obviously couldn't read the signs because they said that the bridge would take thirty ton vehicles; he just sat in the middle. If only a camera had been available, it would have made all the newspapers in the country. Imagine a group of very senior Sapper Officers, aided by the 'big guns' of the Military Police practically carrying that donkey over the bridge.

The name, said the Chief Engineer, would be 'The Balaam Bridge', obviously a learned man who knew his Scriptures.

When opportunity knocked, a good many months later, it was very carefully searched for in the Bible, and there under Numbers XXII: 26 –

"Where there was no way to turn either to the right hand, or the left, and when the ass saw this she fell down under Balaam and he smote her with a staff."

Later a 'flap' was on to delaunch the bridge because of the height and speed of the river caused by the torrential rain. But the day was saved when someone had the bright idea to build a boom upstream.

It was almost now that the German airforce started to take an interest in matters and several strafing attacks were made. Casualties were very light thank goodness, just ten killed in the whole attack.

By the time the Italian Campaign had finished, many more 'Baileys' had been built. Each was a different construction from the previous one and each had a story to tell, but only those of interest will be related.

It was just after this situation, which continued for days on end, that people, including myself, started to go down with heavy colds, influenza and even pneumonia. Mine was a good dose of flu but because (a) there was no such thing as a dry bed; or (b) peace and quiet for one to recuperate, the Army panicked a bit because it was thought that an epidemic such as flu could devastate the fighting machine. They would persuade one to attend the 'Casualty Clearing Station', not that you wanted much persuasion when you felt 'rough', a dry stretcher to sleep on and an Orderly to 'present' you with food and pills was heaven indeed. This did not last very long because the 'CCS' was taking in casualties continually, both wounded and 'medical', so 'they evacuated you back'.

This consisted of being loaded 'stretcher bound' into the back of a truck or Army ambulance and bumped down the road to the next hospital.

This turned out to be a huge marquee near Guardimou. The peacefulness was deafening after all that banging, and for the first time in a good many weeks one was not continually looking for a hole into which to dive when 'things' were flying.

In two days, the place was overflowing so it was evacuation again, same procedure again, until a British General Hospital was reached: a collection of marquees with live female nurses, all speaking English. But, of course, by now the flu was on its way out, so heaven could not last any longer and I was on my way back to the 'forward area'.

The system of returning one to his Unit was most inefficient and time wasting. You were transported to the nearest 'Transit' Camp, where you were immediately grabbed for guard duty or any other work to help fill your day and to aid the 'efficiency' of the Camp.

I suppose one could have languished here for a long period, but no thanks; if your Unit, and mates, and personal kit were to be seen again one had to badger the 'Admin.' staff until transport was found 'going your way'. This then would be repeated until the next camp was reached, until out of desperation one felt like walking back to their 'Unit'.

Having reached a point within twenty miles of where the Company should be, and all the time keeping my eyes open for familiar transport, a piece of luck came my way. There was the Company's ration truck loading up from the central Depot, so not only did I scrounge a lift but helped to load up as well!

CHAPTER SEVENTEEN

EL AROUSA

This was the name of a dirty little French/Arab village on the Tunis/Bou Arada road. It had a road junction and a single track railway line and, but for several twists of fate, would have been the place where this Company of Royal Engineers would have been decimated or even written off completely. Here's the story from first hand experience.

It was late February '43 and the Germans were beginning to feel the 'squeeze' between the 1st and 8th Armies. They desperately tried to hold the 8th Army at the southern end of Tunisia and, at the same time, made strong attacks on the 1st Army line, so trying to break the circle around him.

Some of these attacks were successful and punched holes in the Allied lines for a considerable depth. A tremendous amount of damage and hysteria were caused before heavy reinforcements could be brought up to halt these advances. Several Panzer and Motorised Infantry Divisions were used and on one occasion caused wholesale panic and headlong retreat by certain Allied units.

But these are things for Generals and students of War to write about. This story is one little piece of an attempted breakout.

The 1st Para Brigade was holding the line at Bou Arada, the No. 6 British Commando were holding an area near El Arousa, and after some time had elapsed it was found that getting supplies through to these Units was almost impossible. The so called road was a mere mud track, and because of the torrential rain over many days, had been completely washed away with so called bridges disappearing in the mud and muck of modern war.

The usual cry went up 'Send for the Sappers!' The task was an almost impossible one, so this Company was detailed.

The 'road' petered out at a town called Gafsa and so the project was to connect that place with El Arousa where a fairly good road existed.

Distance involved would be about twelve miles over streams, wadis, ravines, various rocky hills and marshy ground.

Immediately it was seen that a quantity of Bailey equipment would be required, together with many thousand tons of hardcore, concrete piping for culverts through the road (and here, as will be seen later, thank God the wise bloke who did the 'commandeering' had the sense to order large diameter) lots of mechanised plant and tipper trucks. The complement of able bodied Sappers would be several hundred, which was not nearly sufficient so, hundreds of Arabs had to be press-ganged but, of course, paid for their labour, albeit on breadline amounts.

As can be imagined the labour force had to be spread over several miles at a time with one Sapper supervising about twelve 'Arabs', and then more guys loading and unloading materials.

Progress was pretty good considering the speed required and the quality of labour involved, and after several days something like a road was taking shape.

Then the Germans took a hand. For sometime a few shells had landed pretty close, but no casualties because, of course, we thought, he had no target to aim at. The weather had been too atrocious for 'recce' aircraft.

The Company was living in a filthy old French farm, just one sea of muck, mud and animal manure. HQ of course, was inside the house (the occupants had long since gone) and cooks, stores etc., in the outhouse. The men were scattered over several fields, sleeping rough. My particular Sub-section had thoughtfully stripped the canvas canopy off our three ton Bedford, draped it from a tree and pegged it down; it provided just enough room for thirteen men. No troop-carrying trucks were allowed in this forward area because, of course, of the intense air activity during dry spells.

This particular morning dawned dry and clear. The road operation was soon in full swing. Myself and two Sappers had come down to the store (fifty yards from the road) to borrow a 'dumpy' level and ranging rods, when out of the blue came six Fokke Wolf fighters and clearly we were their target. How did they know that a new road was being constructed?

Firstly they dropped two small bombs each and then seemed to take great pleasure in raking the length of the road again and again with canon and machine gun fire. Casualties among the Arabs were horrendous, including the 'foreman' killed, several lorries destroyed but, thank God, no Sappers killed, only superficial wounds. The reason for this was the presence of the large diameter pipes they had the sense to dive into. One particular bastard of a pilot had spotted several blokes scuttling into a pipe under the road about fifty yards from the slit trench we had dived into (very wet) and made a point of coming in at ground level, first from the left then the right, in order to get his machine guns firing through the pipe.

Personally I had been issued with a Thompson (Tommy) Machine Gun .45 calibre, just a week before and although I found its effective range was only about thirty yards, could not resist emptying several twenty round magazines at the B, but with little effect, I think. Running to the pipe after he had exhausted all his ammunition, we found several Arab bodies blocking both ends, and inside several Sappers with only minor cuts and bruises!

Early that night while trying to get some sleep under that tarpaulin, the thought kept coming back: why had we been chosen, 'out of the blue' as a target? It was as if it had been a deliberate mission.

The answer wasn't very far away. Soon the usual German heavy bombers were overhead in strength, and, for sure, every man in those fields was lying awake waiting for the 'pop, pop' of those deadly anti-personnel canisters. Would they know, from today's shoot-up, that there were lots of troops in this area? But very strangely nothing happened. They circled several times right overhead, there were several dozen of them, then turned for home.

Fear turned to horror when I realised exactly what was happening; he was unloading a whole lot of paratroops right above our heads. Now paratroopers cannot take prisoners, so there were a whole lot of trained killers floating down. Trained in the use of knife and bullet with no questions asked. I took off from the ground sheet with a shout that shook everyone for a mile around. "PARATROOPS!!" It was as if everyone realised the situation simultaneously and started to blaze away into the pitch black night, rifles, Bren guns, Thompsons (especially mine) until there must have been a wall of steel going skywards, but with no visible target to aim at.

It suddenly occurred to me that there was quite a stiff breeze blowing towards El Arousa. Would this mean that they could miss us altogether? Remember all this took only seconds to happen, and my mind was turning over the fact that a dozen plus giant transports say, Junkers 52 and ME 323; each capable of carrying forty plus men, meant that there were four hundred plus killers on the way down.

It was then that the world went mad again; the Germans had landed on the high ground to our right, smack on top of the British No. 6 Commando. That stiff breeze had, without doubt, saved this Field Company RE from elimination.

As people of a mature age will be aware, the Commandos and Paratroops are the most highly trained killers in any Army, and here was one set landing on top of another who, like us, were sleeping, or nearly so, at the time. The result was the most horrifying carnage I had ever witnessed, hardened as I thought I was to seeing men die in terrible circumstances. It was two days, owing to the fact that the Germans had now broken through our lines in an attempt to capture El Arousa, before we could reach the Commando position.

Saying that the world went mad again was the only expression capable of describing how two bodies of highly trained men fought hand to hand with knife and machine gun. The air was full of tracer fire, in all directions, hand grenades exploding, flares being let off and rifle fire.

From this point on in the episode, there will inevitably be more use made of the personal pronoun, for which I apologise in advance.

The situation now developed into a full scale battle of the 2nd World War, my first experience of such.

The radio waves were going full blast giving details of the fact that the Germans had broken the perimeter line in strength and the main (or first) objective was the important road and rail junction of El Arousa (in other words the dirty Arab village just up the road!). It was 'panic stations!' "A company of Royal Engineers were now taking up position in defence of this important junction," said the local British Forces radio.

"Balls!" said I.

If only the truth were known! Several hundred people running around in circles and doing the disappearing act!

Eventually things were sorted out and the order was:

"Grab everything you can carry from the Stores, such as mines, explosives, picks, shovels, sandbags, barb wire etc., and march to El Arousa!"

There was no transport available of course, so it was the Father Christmas act, in February, with people carrying sacks full of all sorts of things, mostly I suspected full of food and drink but, thankfully all heading in the right direction.

On arrival at the village during the early hours of the morning and, needless to say, in the pouring rain, a parade was called for on the main road. A check of numbers was made and then,

"No. 1 Sub-section (mine) of No. 1 Section will take up position at Map Ref. so and so!" Where the hell was a map? Who could read it in pitch darkness and pouring rain? No lights possible because of 'X' thousand Germans waiting to pounce!

Eventually Bob - the Section Officer was traced and the 'death' sentence given, "Wat, I want you to take your twelve men down this road (Where? Pitch darkness!) for about ½ a mile until you come to a twelve foot high cactus hedge running at 90° to your left (good job I was educated or we might have finished up in Tunis!) This hedge forms the three sides of a square around a French farm. You will take up positions on the far side of the hedge and remember for Christ sake, absolute silence because that is the direction from which Jerry will come. We know that he has got armour but we cannot give you any anti-tank protection until first light. Good luck! Our HQ will be so and so map ref. in the village and remember, he usually attacks with Stukas and Mortars at first light!"

At that moment our thoughts were, 'Will there be a first light for us?'

We crept down this road for what seemed to be about five miles and eventually found, by painful experience, said cactus hedge. It was magnificent in proportion, some twelve feet high and several thick, covered in spikes like bayonets and, of course, impossible to take cover in or strategically withdraw through when *he* came. There was nothing for it but to dig in (thank God we had some picks and shovels) two-man slit trenches on the *German* side of the hedge.

As we dug, it soon became apparent that we were probably draining the whole field, and on account of the high clay contact present, the trenches filled to overflowing with that beautiful soft rain water. As first light wasn't far away we decided to abandon the job and hope for the best!

It was about now that the feeling of terror, first experienced when the Paratroops were dropping, returned. It must have been the sound that every infantry man lives in dread of – Tanks! Yes tanks on the move and obviously German. If any man says that he wasn't afraid, or filled with terror even, during a battle situation, then he is an 100% liar. Your thoughts tell you that at any time now your life could be snuffed out in one of several horrible ways. *Fear* is the first lesson of survival!

In the total darkness those tanks were getting nearer, and eventually stopped in a position which appeared to be just over the other side of the field. Of course, every modern warfare soldier knows that tanks must be protected by infantry in the dark. (How many?)

Now what did we have to stop those tanks? Sweet Fanny Adams!

1 No. Boyes anti-tank rifle, 00.5 inch bore, clip of four which when fired tended to knock your shoulder out of joint and hardly had the power to penetrate a tin of peas let alone the several inches of armour on the front of a tank. 1 No. Bren gun, OK against infantry until the damn thing jams again. 1 No. Thompson (mine) OK at thirty yards range but he had a range of several miles in his tank guns. Ten No. 303 bolt-action Lee Enfield rifles completed the total weaponry.

The next happening of interest was the arrival, just before dawn, of a team of Artillery men, effing and blinding, pulling a 40mm Bofors Anti-aircraft gun (no truck, too noisy); they had to manhandle it across the front of our position to take up a spot against a hay-stack. This was to be our anti-tank defence – an AA gun! As it turned out, George, the Sgt. in charge, turned out to be an excellent fellow who promptly produced a bottle of rum which when shared and, of course, diluted by the persistent rain, was sufficient to get us all coughing. All we could offer in return was French Vin – vinegar like, but under those circumstances delicious!

It was almost dawn, and land marks were beginning to take shape. The first contours to form into any shape were those of a lone hill directly in front and several hundred yards away. It was long and low, almost cigar shaped, with gently sloping sides. This was off to the left of 'our' road which appeared to travel into higher ground behind, probably following a valley.

To the right of the road the ground rose much more steeply and higher. This higher ground appeared to overlook, and run parallel to, the road below. Between our position and these hills were several flat fields with the road running directly across them before disappearing into the distance. Another point which registered was the lack of vegetation, except for a line of low bushes off to the right of the road, and therefore the absence of cover for anyone (or anything) crossing the fields.

It was now full light and I 'felt' a dozen pairs of binoculars watching our every move so I passed the gentle word around,

"For Christ sake keep your head down if you don't want it blown off!"

This was very hard to do, because apart from lying in the mud or sitting in a rain filled trench, there was only 'George's haystack!'

Across the fields everything was quiet, much too quiet for comfort because we knew that those tanks had not moved at all from behind that first small hill. If only we had one small Spitfire to go see! In recent weeks the 8th Army News had been full of the co-operation between Army and 'The Desert Airforce'. Where was it now? A couple of rocket firing planes would have had a field day.

A voice came from the other side of the cactus hedge, "O Group in ten minutes."

This translated, meant that the C.O. wanted all his NCOs around him to hear the latest sit/rep (situation report!).

I squelched my way to the leg of the hedge away from the road, of course running parallel to it, and headed for the village. Some way along the hedge I met the NCOs of the Company coming t'other way, who explained that the C.O. wanted an 'O Group' in the open ground in front of our positions. That, I informed them, was equal to voluntary suicide, or the murder of innocent people on whom it would bring his fire down. The C.O. was adamant that there, and only there was the right place to hold it. Was he trying to show our 'strength' to the Germans? God help such a Dick Head, a leader of men.

He spoke for some few minutes to the effect that the paratroops had now been joined by five battalions of the Hermann Goering infantry, and that elements of the 15th and 21st Panzer Divisions had been identified but, said he, "The news is good because some Churchill Tanks of the North Irish Horse have been located 'in the area' and are even now on their way to defend the village."

He was nowhere near the end of his speech when, flying low from over the German positions, came two Messerschmitts 109, which started to circle us and the village.

My call to the C.O. was,

"We ought to take cover, they are taking our pictures!"

His reply,

"Don't be foolish, they are Spitfires!"

Again another circle and, from me:

"We will be on the front page of the Berlin newspapers tomorrow!"

From Dick Head, looking through his binoculars,

"They are definitely Spitfires!"

At this point, George, who up to now had been desperately trying to camouflage his gun, could stand it no longer and opened up with a clip of five 40 mm shells. Now the noise of a Bofor shell is equivalent to a good many dozen of the loudest fireworks being fired together and caused DH to drop to his knees in the mud. This signalled a general move to take cover from the cameras but, I know, that I lost at least two years promotion when I gently asked DH,

"Should we charge the Artillery Sgt. for firing at Spitfires... Sir?"

On average, as was well known among the men who had experienced this type of warfare, it took about two hours to develop and study the ME's reconnaissance pictures, so that gave us some little time before that piece of field was obliterated by Stukas/Artillery. I enquired of Bob as to whether or not (tongue in cheek) it would be wiser to move to the other side of the road or fifty yards to our left? After weighing it up, he said that the C.O. (DH) had carefully planned out the position of each Sub-section, so that the ones behind would not be firing at the backs of the forward subs, especially yours. (DH2!) So no move.

Shortly after this, all other troops seemed to have disappeared back to the village, except George and his lads, and, of course, thirteen 'brave' lads who were going to stop the German Army.

The water table in the slit trenches had dropped considerably so we spent our 'last few hours on earth' digging deeper and scrounging bits of wood and stone to drop in the bottom.

It was now mid to late morning and the forecasted time of attack had been changed to dusk, when the first of several things happened which I feel again saved this RE Field Company from being decimated. It was also the first in a series of events that led to the village being saved, which probably put an end to German ambition in this area

The rattle of tanks was to be heard somewhere behind us and, after an hour listening to that beautiful sound getting nearer they pulled up on the road alongside. Six Churchills of the North Irish Horse, 6th Armoured Division, had arrived.

A young Captain was in charge whom I was able to study as he walked to meet me. He was what the troops call a typical 'University Boy' – suede desert boots, brightly coloured scarf and, unbelievably, carrying a fly-swat. My first thought was, 'I hope he's got something better than that to hit those Germans with!'

"Take five, boys!" he yelled over his shoulder.

They all piled out and promptly finished off our vino, which we gladly gave, in fact we were so pleased to see them that a pint each of blood would have been forthcoming, if it had been asked for! But fair enough, it had been a long, hot ride in those 'steel ovens'.

More of the Captain. With hand held out he said, "Mine's Harry, what's yours? Len Watkins eh? Well listen Len, I don't want to frighten you blokes but back there in the village there is a Dick of an RE Major and a Dick Major of the Pioneer Corps who both seem to want to take charge of the village defence, so I left them to it, but they've got blokes swarming all over the place and when the Hun shows his 'Dick' above that hill, your blokes are going to get their heads blown off from behind. If I were you I would move at least a hundred yards to left or right and let them fire their ten thousand rounds."

I explained just what had happened previously, all of which he understood perfectly, and said,

"Don't worry we'll give you a decent burial when we come back!"

He was most concerned when he learned about the ME's 'recce' and said,

"Without doubt the Stukas will be here and we will have no defence against them." His next enquiry was,

"What do you know of the Hun situation?" On being told of the tank movements in the night and just where they were now, and also about the infantry and paratroops he said,

"Right, this is my plan. You say that there are at least a dozen tanks hiding behind that hill? We will go straight up this road towards him, because he thinks we don't know he's there, and when we've got them all crapping themselves, we'll turn left at the foot of the hill on this side. Open up in line and slowly climb up the slope until we are in 'hull down' position. This should test his strength and draw whatever fire he's got, but he will have very little target to fire at so most of his 'stuff' will come flying over in your direction so keep your heads down!"

I remember wishing him 'Good Luck' and reminding him to stick to the road on his return journey, because we would be mining in front of our positions.

"OK, understood, and you remember that, God willing, we will disengage at dusk and come up behind that beautiful cactus hedge of yours for the night, for *your* protection. Don't get firing up the road in the dark before you know who it is. Tell George over there."

He explained the plan to 'his chaps', climbed on to his Churchill and called out one word - "Tally-ho!" and they were on their way. What a man!

Just after our 'O Group' I had asked Bob to send up as many mines and as much barbed wire as we could muster and now they started to arrive, Hawkins Grenades only, which really were an anti-personnel weapon and very delicate to handle because of their glass of acid detonator. Three hundred plus of them. It was decision time, so we made up blocks of four, but only armed one of the four, then buried them as a perimeter to our position about fifty yards out. Outside this was piled the Dannet wire.

The mines would at least blow the track off a tank although it (the tank) would still be capable of firing. They would also explode under the weight of an infantryman, so we were now in God's hands, having done all possible.

We were about to witness, at very close range, a tank battle with all the odds, both in numbers and positions (probably fire power too because the Churchills had six pounder guns and the Germans 75 and 88mm) stacked against the British.

He appeared to follow his plan to the letter. On reaching the foot of the small hill, they turned at 90° to the left, spread evenly into line abreast, with Harry remaining nearest the road. They now slowly crawled up the slope, in perfect formation, until just their turret tops and guns showed to the Germans. The reaction was as Harry predicted. The Hun opened up with everything he had and sent a cloud of shells, mostly armour piercing at his tanks. I saw no direct hits because, as forecast, there was little target to aim at and most of the shells landed nearer El Arousa than the Churchills.

All Harry's tanks were soon firing but it was doubtful, in my mind, whether *he* could see much of a target, unless, of course they were using some form of periscope system.

After an hour or so of this, during which time we had an eye on the sky waiting for the horror to materialise, things seemed to have reached a stalemate situation. Harry must have thought the same because he started a move which must have come from 'The Tank Warfare Training Manual'! He reversed his Churchill some forty to fifty yards in a straight line, still of course concealed from The Hun by the small hill, turned 90° to his right, crossed the road, turned left and started to climb the higher ground which, if he made it, would give him a commanding view of the whole German position.

Thirteen men, plus George and his boys, watched, hardly daring to breathe, and then it happened. Harry got himself into a 'hull-down' position at one of the highest points of the feature, where the ground fell away very steeply to the road below, and which would prevent any of the Hun tanks from doing the same.

As he told me afterwards, "I thought that I was looking at the whole German army. Directly opposed to my tanks were a whole heap of enemy tanks, and behind them were armoured cars, half-tracks full of infantry, and even lorries loaded with men who, I bet my shirt, were ready to pounce on your chaps just as soon as they had got my blokes out of the scrap and, of course, you had been Stuka'd. I drooled at seeing this duck shoot but where was I to start? Eventually I decided that it would have to be the tank furthest away from me, and then work along the line, because the black smoke of the 'brew-up' would obscure my target. I hit him with my second shot which went straight through because the armour is pretty thin on the sides and he immediately 'brewed-up', black smoke and his ammunition flying everywhere,. Then I worked back along the line and had six definite hits within as many minutes. In the meantime, Fred my machine gunner, was playing hell amongst the infantry. None of the Dicks knew where it was coming from and all started to panic. This was my chance to radio to my blokes to move forward and select their targets. Can you imagine the hell that valley turned into? Six big guns and six heavy machine guns firing flat out in all directions while they (the Hun) were stampeding back up the road!"

It was now late afternoon and Harry and his boys turned for home. They came down the road as if on a picnic, all of them, except drivers riding outside the tanks. Faces black smoke and sweat but all were 'on a high', and after we had slapped their backs, etc., it was their turn to produce a few bottles from the depth of the tanks and a damn good half hour was had including George's boys of course, by all. It was like a boy scouts day out!

Then it happened! A deafening roar in the sky getting all the time louder; the Stukas had arrived! A whole cloud of them circled overhead.

What a scramble to dive into wet trenches and to batten down the tanks!

Then, by another twist of fate, they turned from us and one by one dived and bombed the very line where Harry's tanks had been an hour before. The sight of that bombing was one of the most frightening experiences of my life. The hill had virtually disappeared under the weight of bombs; had they fallen on their original target – us – there would have been no survivors! George and his boys enjoyed themselves with the Bofors but no hits were registered.

Harry and I agreed afterwards that the German Commander had obviously changed the Stukas target in an endeavour to obliterate Harry's opposition.

The line of tanks now took up position behind, and through, the cactus hedge. There was something very reassuring about having Harry's six pounder above my head!

The thoughts uppermost in our minds now were, had the Hun really been beaten? was he still strong enough to have another go from that valley position?

Harry was convinced:

"No! we had them all crapping and running this afternoon."

The answer was soon to come. After a long, cold and wet night there appeared, at first light, from behind us on the road, a line of British infantry, no less than the Grenadier Guards, and all marching in a dispersed long line (anti-strafing formation) almost like coming down the Mall but in Battle Order and carrying enough kit to make a strong man wince. Apart from the usual arms such as rifles, Brens, mortars etc., they carried bivouacs, boxes of 'Compo' rations, boxes of ammunition and anything else they required (including picks and shovels) in order to sustain themselves 'up front' for days on end.

To say that they were a welcome sight was putting it far too mildly, these were the boys relieving us from that hell hole of water filled trenches and all the other frightful things taking place.

The major in charge (stiff upper lip, what?) still looked every inch a soldier even in the middle of all that muck and mud. He broke his 'chaps' off and came to speak to Harry and I. No Christian names here but right to the point.

"Sit/rep please?"

He told us his fellows had been pulled off another section of the front and had marched all night to get to El Arousa! Hats off and a pint of blood to each man, gladly given! But what soldiers! After Harry and I had filled him in on the day's happenings and, after a bit of thought, he said,

"Right we'll go up and take over the position from where you did your killings and, if there's no reaction from the Germans, we will work our way up through the valley. Sgt. Major get the chaps on their feet!"

That matter of fact statement was exactly what he did, and the last we saw of them they were disappearing up the road and climbing 'Harry's Hill' as if they were on manoeuvres back home.

The thought came back of Harry's action with his tanks, now there were this lot. It is little wonder that an Empire was won with fellows like these, but how the hell did we lose it?

This was almost the end of El Arousa for us, but there are two incidents worth recording before the chapter is closed.

We had packed up ready to move off when a message came through from the Guards Major. They had hit lots of mines and booby traps (and even unexploded bombs) left behind by the Germans and were suffering casualties. Could we help?

Naturally as a Sapper Company we could not refuse, and Section One was detailed for the job.

On arrival in the area it could plainly be seen just where the Commando unit had been sleeping when the paratroops came down out of the black sky. The word carnage is often spoken of in a matter of fact sort of way but, in all my twenty years of living I never ever thought that I would see such a sight. The details of it and how men died will not be described because in these 'civilised' days it is all too horrible to contemplate. Suffice it to say, they fought for their lives and most of them died.

As regards Harry's battle, the evidence was there for all to see. Burnt out tanks and armoured cars everywhere and even half tracks still burning. The smell of human flesh burning is not a pleasant one.

The Major was quite right, there were quite a few booby traps about but, most of them appeared to be ready made jobs i.e.: ration boxes, ammunition boxes etc., which exploded on being opened. It is very hard to imagine an Army, going into battle like the Germans did here, carrying with them a lot of boxes which, if left behind, would kill the people who opened them.

We suffered two casualties this way, one of whom was an expert in mine and booby trap warfare, so from these, we learned our lesson. But there was still a large number to make safe, and eventually it was decided to blow them up in position.

The other incident shows again just what DHs there are in the British army, in charge of men's lives. Towards the end of the day, another Sapper and I were checking the road verges for mines. In this area there was quite an amount of low scrub which made things quite difficult when checking for 'S' mines. We were working a strip about twenty feet or so wide, just the kind of area where a future vehicle could pull off the road and hit a mine.

Up the road from El Arousa came an armoured car, a British Humber with a two pounder gun on the turret which, as it came level, was swung in our direction, and looked, in fact, quite ominous. The turret opened and out climbed a Cpl. (Armoured Corps.) carrying a .38 revolver. He held it at arm's length pointing in our direction and said, unbelievably,

"Put your arms up you are my prisoners. Don't move because the car's gun is also aimed at you!"

Can you believe it? Here were two engineers working their goolies off and crapping themselves (Harry's term) in case they stepped on an 'S' mine.

My reply,

"Piss off! And watch how you go because you have just walked through a minefield!"

This called for two minutes' silence on his part, then,

"Are you British?" pause, then, "The Brigadier says that I am to take you over to his car as prisoners."

That was the situation. This Brigadier, from his H.Q. several miles behind the line, had heard all about the battle for El Arousa and had borrowed an armoured car and driven to go see for himself. After leaving El Arousa we, apparently were the first blokes he saw and was determined to win glory by taking two prisoners.

There was nothing for it but to approach the Humber and explain to a 'soldier' who we could not see because he was still behind his gun. The explanation and realisation of the true position he was in took at least ten minutes. No apology of course from No. 1 plus DH.

Before leaving El Arousa for, we hoped, the last time I spent some minutes plotting the position of our minefield. This was an absolute essential among the Sappers because of the people following on. Some poor devils had to pick them up. It was to be hoped that there were better conditions availing than when they were laid.

Some time later when handing the 'plot' in to Bob I asked him,

"Do you think that a name will be given to this particular battle?"

"It already has," he said. "Steam Roller Farm." To my query he answered, "See that other farm off to the left? Well it was first flattened by German artillery and then, when they took it over, our artillery took a turn."

Our Sub-section had been aware of this shelling in the midst of everything going on but, to my mind, it had very little to do with the battle, and I told him so.

"Well our C.O. has sent in his Dispatch with his version of what happened and that is what *he* has named it."

Excuse me, reader, for repeating myself, but DH1 again!

Many years after the war finished, my job, for my sins, was the supervision of building contracts. Additional to this there were quite a few building tradesmen who also came under my wing for the maintenance of various buildings.

One day an extra fitter was called for to help out during an emergency, a complete stranger. Stripping off for the job I noticed that he had a belt full of brass badges of various regiments and battles etc. On examination, there was to my amazement and in pride of place, one that said Steam Roller Farm!

In answer to my surprised query he said,

"That is one that hardly anyone has ever heard of, but it is the most important of the No. 6 Commando battle honours. You see we were almost wiped out there, and afterwards so few were left that we were almost disbanded, but eventually, after a recruiting drive, reformed again."

My reply,

"What about The North Irish Horse and the Sappers who dug in around El Arousa?"

His face was a picture. Needless to say we took over the bar of the local RAF Club that night and Steam Roller Farm was fought all over again!

But I did learn something from him which had not been common knowledge before.

"In the middle of the night, when those paratroopers dropped on us out of the black, the only thing that I was aware of was men screaming and dying all around me. Knives, bayonets, bullets were being used until the few of us left (about forty I think) were forced to surrender. The Germans took us to a ruin of a farm house but when our tanks started to shoot, the lot of them just handed themselves (and there weren't many of them left) over to us as prisoners, knowing now their lives would be saved."

One more incident that happened many years after this, in 1988 in fact, I was lucky enough to book in on one of those Battlefield Tours of North Africa. It was run as a conducted tour by an ex-para major who as a military expert described the book version of every battle.

When describing the battle for El Arousa, his version wasn't very accurate, but he did say that the village was defended by Sappers and that The North Irish Horse had been involved.

"The Captain in charge of the tanks was one of the most decorated men of the North African Campaign, having received British, French and American decorations for his actions in the battle."

My comment, which he heard and asked for an explanation was: "He had a pint of my blood too!"

So the battle was fought again, but this time pointing out the actual landmarks. Once again, thank you Harry for, surely, giving me fifty odd years of life!

CHAPTER EIGHTEEN

TONY ELLIOT

Tony was a young man, just a year older than myself when he died.

It seems fit that his story should be included in the book because it shows just how futile and unnecessary it is to give one's life for the cause. A young life sacrificed in the fight for his country.

He was a West Country chap, jovial, well built and a very keen sportsman. He excelled at soccer, cricket and sport in general and so, as a member of my Sub-section we soon became firm friends.

It was found that as a youngster enjoying life as much as it was possible to under the circumstances, and without a thought of promotion, the choice very often had to be made between keeping one's friends or taking the offered promotion. I always chose the former.

Our friendship developed long before we left the UK and the first instance worth relating happened in Scotland.

As described before, the Company's move from Monkton to Kirkintilloch was very welcome indeed, and it wasn't very long before Tony and myself were visiting Glasgow just as often as possible. We found it a very good city as regards the servicemen, free rides on all public transport, free entry to all clubs, dances, etc. and the friendliness of the natives had to be seen to be believed.

A friendship with two ATS girls soon developed which called for even more trips into the city. The usual happenings followed, such as cinemas, dancing, walking and talking. Personally I had no ties at home but Tony had a 'serious' girlfriend with whom the bans of marriage were already looming large.

His Glasgow girl (Mimi) was attractive and appeared to like Tony very much, and it was soon became clear that he was undecided between the two. He clinched it by saying that if we went overseas soon he'd leave the decision until the home coming and meanwhile would see if they wrote and remained 'faithful'. His 'faithfulness' did not matter of course.

It is of no importance but the friend of Mimi, and therefore of mine, has been long forgotten by name and almost appearance, but I do remember an awkward and unnecessary line of buttons on the tunic!

When overseas, sometime later, it was plain to see that Tony was receiving mail from, and writing to three people. His mother, fiancée and Mimi. So the problem still remained.

When on board the Otranto and bound for God only knew where, knowing that we were to lead the assault on some foreign beach, Tony asked for these three people to be written to in the event of his death, his actual words were,

"Please Len, explain it gently to Mum instead of her just getting that cold telegram." He turned out to be a superstitious sort of chap and although I didn't understand him at the time requested,

"The skin I was born in, please send to Mum, it is in my wallet."

Some West Country superstition I supposed. It became obvious sometime later after a short time 'up front', that Tony had led a very sheltered life and although having trained in Sapper warfare he had no idea of how to take cover when things were flying, and tended to take a rise out of the 'veterans' who did.

The day came for him to learn his first lesson, and here it is necessary to explain the method used by forward troops of attending to the call of nature. One simply took a walk with a shovel, that is, unless you were under observation or near buried mines.

On this particular day the Sub-section had been dropped off at a small concrete bridge on the Beja/Matuer Road, during the early dark hours because, if travelling by road during daylight hours, it was almost 100% certain that your truck would be destroyed by 'Mutt & Jeff', the ever present Messerschmitt 109s.

The bridge, important in supplying our forward troops, had been damaged the previous night by a German Pioneer Patrol, which was a common enough occurrence if the target was of any importance, but they had failed to completely destroy it.

The blokes were nervous and on several occasions said words to the effect:

"What if Jerry is covering the bridge, knowing that it will have to be repaired?"

As it got to first light, it was clear that we were in the wide open spaces with no cover at all so, and as usual, a discussion was held on where to dive if and when any sort of attack took place. There was only one place, and unanimously agreed upon; under the bridge. The usual artillery were firing their stuff overhead, ours from several miles back, and the Germans replying from much closer but, if you were not in the target area there wasn't much to worry about. Work started well, using the Bailey parts brought with us, when Tony decided to take a walk with a shovel. No sooner had he disappeared into a nearby gully than Mutt & Jeff took a keen interest in what we were doing. At zero feet they came screaming over but, very fortunately for us, they split on to two separate targets. We had the undivided attention of Mutt!

On his first pass he climbed, turned, and dived straight at the bridge, releasing his bomb at the right moment. As this sequence turned out it was very fortunate for all concerned because we were still diving for the safety of the concrete. If he had fired his (eight?) forward firing machine guns first - curtains and Amen! As it was, the bomb missed the bridge by at least twenty yards; thank God for a one-eyed German pilot, and so he climbed to bring his guns to bear. This was the chance that twelve brave men were waiting for and they promptly blazed away at his backside with one Bren, one useless Thompson and ten rifles that is, of course, until he had reached the top of his climb.

It was at that moment Tony arrived! He had done a fifty yard sprint in record time and, having kicked off his trousers and pants on the way (they had been around his ankles) and because some of the distance had been through the mud of the river, he landed, naked to the waist, plastered with mud and gasping for breath! In the meantime the bastard called Mutt was doing his best to kill everybody present. He must have dived from quite a height because it seemed that the bullets would never stop coming. They ricocheted off the concrete with a deafening clatter and mixed with them a whole lot of shells exploding, he must have been firing a cannon or two. Thank goodness for the thickness of concrete and depth of mud in the river bed. This, I'm sure, prevented a lot of the shells exploding.

It was sometime later that we learned the other bastard, Jeff, had caught some British infantry in the open. Fatal casualties were 90%.

The Tony had learned his lesson, and after washing the mud off up to the plimsoll line and retrieving his pants he vowed, "I'll never take the urine out of anybody diving for cover again!"

The job completed and collected at dark by truck we made the journey 'home' quite successfully, but here a shock waited. There was a flap on El Arousa again! Jerry had again broken through and we were to hold it temporarily until relieved by infantry.

There was nothing for it but a quick handful of biscuits and spam, then on the truck and away. The rest of the Company had already left so it was quite a nightmare trying to map read by night with absolutely no light, shells passing both ways overhead and the occasional flare to let you know that his aircraft were waiting their chance overhead.

We didn't finish up five miles behind the German lines as predicted by Tony, and by some magic arrived at El Arousa in one piece, still in the dark.

"Same position, Wat," was the order, and after groping in the black of night, with the usual rain belting down, we found our 'home' in front of the cactus hedge. The mud and water content of the trenches was too awful to face, so it was under the haystack and shut up!

This time there was no George, that wonderful man, but only abject misery and despondency until at last, God smiled, and 'mad' Mac, one of the lads, produced a water bottle full of French Vermouth.

This was enough for a couple of mouthfuls each and raised the morale quite a lot. A pity it tasted "Like licking a Frog's arse," said Tony, "but under the circumstances even a Frenchman tastes sweet!"

What about taking turns to kip? was the next question, which was agreed upon, so the stack was hollowed out and a pile of (semi) dry straw to lie on provided our sweet dreams, which were had in turn.

As Tony remarked in his West Country burr:

"No respectable German would be out on a night like this."

The flap was off within two days, with nothing at all happening out of the ordinary to break the misery of saturated clothes and the discomfort of body lice.

These last devils are mentioned here because not only had we reached the stage, because of not bathing, of total lousiness, we also felt some plague, such as typhus in other wars, would spread to everyone.

Lice were rampant (if that's possible) in every shirt and vest seam. The whole Company was affected. The solution was the issue of AL63 which when showered on to the infected garment not only killed the lice but took the adjacent skin with it.

"German secret weapon," said Tony. "I heard them coming over during the night!"

Things had reached an almost impossible stage with the lice, so a house in Beja was commandeered and a communal shower fixed up. What luxury to pretend to be decent again!

It was while staying the couple of days at this house that the recce of the surrounding houses discovered a small Renault car (bright yellow) in one of the basement garages. Our expert mechanic (Tony) soon had the important bits stripped down and, after a bit of swearing, pronounced it in good working order, with, unbelievably, a full tank of petrol.

It was decided, after some difference of opinion, that four of us would squeeze into the luxury of the car on the next move, so leaving more room for the lucky chaps on the truck. This machine would be ours for the campaign. No self respecting German pilot would shoot up such a beautiful little Renault car!!

The following day Bob - the Section Officer, called us all together for a discussion on the state of play, and during the talk he appeared to stress just how serious it was to loot anything from these French houses and, words to the effect that the punishment for so doing would be almost as severe as that of desertion in face of the enemy!

As to the car, we smelt a rat: did he know something? But of course nothing was said.

A flap was on next day, a serious one too, to the effect that Jerry had broken through in strength from Matuer, with Beja as his objective. Our role was to lay as many mines as possible directly in front of his advance, until reinforcements arrived.

The point where he had broken through was several miles up the valley at a small village called Sidi Nisi, a group of houses and a railway station, with low hills to either side.

Just before first light (it was absolutely necessary to travel in the dark, and disperse the truck on arrival, because of the ever ready Mutt & Jeff) the convoy formed up, fully equipped for laying a very rapid anti-tank minefield. It seemed like ages until we were ready to move off and the boys were getting very edgy. It was then that the reason for the delay became apparent. From the direction of the houses, and to a rousing cheer from the nearby trucks came Bob, and his batman, sitting in the luxury of the little yellow Renault looking like Montgomery himself, and taking his place at the head of the convoy. To the words 'Tally ho! Let's go!' we were away.

My first thoughts were, 'The dirty swine, here was this noble officer giving us a very serious talking to about the dire consequences of looting from the Frogs, and yet doing it himself from his own blokes too!' After a cooling off period on the move, I forgave him because, after all, he wasn't such a bad bloke and the boys were ready to follow him anywhere. No. 1 Sub did not forget it so easily though, and Tony and I took a ribbing for the rest of the journey.

Here I must jump a good many years (at least forty) and come to the time that, through several coincidences of blokes meeting up with one another, we were holding an annual reunion near our old stamping grounds in Hampshire.

This one particular year, who should be leaning on the bar and looking his old self (plus forty) but Bob. After a chat (a lifetime had gone by) the question was asked –

"I wonder what happened to that yellow Renault?"

His face was a study and eventually, pointing to a group of men and wives, he said:

"See the bloke in the middle, he was my batman, ask him."

I did of course and after a long pause he said, "Old Bob had me drive that thing all the way to Algiers and flog it to the highest bidder. Cars were like gold-dust to get then, and we raised a good many thousand francs for it."

On my return to the bar, Bob made the classic remark of the year,

"Never mind Len, have a half of beer on me!"

This chapter is concluded by saying, that a damn good evening was had by all; let us hope that there are many more to come.

Back to the convoy. The Matuer/Beja road area seemed to have gone mad. There were heavy and medium guns firing over our heads from some distance back, and all sounding like trains as they passed over. Their shells were landing in an area not very far in front and getting closer every minute. Then we were alongside the twenty five pounders, a wonderful gun which could hold a rapid fire for some time and on a par with the German 88mm, except the former could not be used for anti-aircraft fire. They appeared to be firing on open sights which meant they could see their target at pretty close range. Not good news for us, having to lay our minefield but, I thought, and being nosy, when the chance came later I'd nip over and have a word with the gunners.

It was some time later that I saw him (the gunnery officer) and he turned out to be a decent sort. He said that two OP (Observation Posts) on the hill, who were protected by a platoon of infantry each, appeared to have been overrun but one of their last messages was to the effect that the German force was very strong indeed and had at least fourteen Tigers, twelve Panzer IVs, and over fifty Panther III tanks.

This was frightening news because we had very little anti-tank defence in the area, except that held by the Royal Hampshires, the infantry in front. A few six pounders, one seventeen pounder and their PIAT weapons.

"The main trouble is," said Eric (the gunnery officer) "we cannot reach them yet with our anti-tank shells (solid shot) and so we're using HE on their infantry. The most effective way of stopping him of course, is your minefield!"

Perhaps a little explanation is needed here to show the position in its true projection.

It is pitch dark except for the gun flashes: our heavy and medium guns were keeping up a terrific barrage, the twenty five pounders were firing 'Intense Fire' which meant a minimum of six rounds each per minute, and I could see eight guns.

The larger tanks were monsters. It was the first time they had been seen in North Africa. A veritable house on tracks with a telegraph pole sticking out from the front. Their main armament was a very superior type of 88mm, various projectiles and two heavy machine guns. The1/8 armour plate was four inches thick on front and three and inches on the sides. Unbelievable, but verified later.

"There are twenty Churchills of the North Irish Horse on the way," said Eric. "So they should help a bit!"

Would we be seeing Harry again? It had started to rain 'heavily'.

Before explaining what happened in the mine laying action, I would like to add here that years later I again met Eric (gunnery officer). He was now a retired bank manager living in the beautiful vale of Evesham. We fought the battle of Matuer again but the big snag was he was stone-deaf from the guns and I only had one good ear!

We exchange Christmas cards and no doubt will meet again for another shouting match!

After dumping (sorry, placing gently,) the mines off, the trucks were got rid of in double quick time, an obvious target. We found that the valley chosen had gentle sloping sides, with a track through the middle and all at 90° to the line of battle. A perfect place for a minefield provided it was sealed completely by mines and very good for us too because all the fire was high overhead.

It was raining hard, so gas capes on, which, with steel helmet in place made a fairly waterproof covering until it started to leak down one's neck! Dawn arrived and the rain continued.

Usual drill, teams of three, each sub having four teams working in lines up both sides of the valley and away from the track. Everything was going fine and we soon had half the valley sealed to his tanks and were feeling fairly good. I was halfway up the hill on one side when 'Bang'! from over the other side and I saw a scatter among my blokes and, of all things, a gas cape floating some way up in the air. After a while Bob called from the track,

"Carry on, we must finish the job!"

Naturally I assumed that Jerry had seen us and was now going to paste us. On walking down the line of laid mines and meeting Bob on the track, my query was,

"What happened?"

His answer turned my stomach over.

"I'm afraid that one of your blokes has gone!"

How I got up the other side of the valley I really don't know.

"Who was it and why?"

Coming up to the crater at last I could see Ernie Bradshaw lying flat and bleeding badly through his gas cape. My thoughts were 'Thank God he is still alive', because he was moving and he still had his arms and legs.

Then he said two words that will never be forgotten,

"Tony's gone! Tony's gone!"

It was then that realisation took over. The gas cape in the air was Tony's with, I thought, his body inside it. One of the mines had exploded so wounding Ernie and killing Tony.

There followed the worst few minutes that I had ever experienced, groping in the mud and muck of that awful place for what was left of Tony and finding very little.

Eventually I found several small pieces, the largest of which was a boot with the foot still inside it, and several other pieces of flesh. These were carefully wrapped in his gas cape and buried near the track. I clearly marked the grave and identity of Tony, ensuring later that the Graves Commission people knew his map reference for collection and central burial.

No uniform, no jacket and no wallet, without which, it was not possible to carry out Tony's request, but just as soon as possible, I wrote to his mother, fiancée and Mimi breaking the news in the best possible manner. The only reply I received was from Mimi in which she said words to the effect: 'Sorry to hear about Tony, but I preferred you in any case, so if you come back to Glasgow..." She, of course, received no reply.

Tony was, in my little gang, the first to die a terrible death, but I'm sorry to say there were more to follow, each one bringing home the futility and stupidity of war.

Meanwhile the German push continued. We had completed our minefield but had to go back the next day and night to lay further mines. Now it was the chance to (1) see if Harry was amongst the tank commanders and (2) find out what was happening.

Apparently the German tanks had been hit by our medium guns dropping shells on the top of them, but not before they had destroyed several of the Churchills.

The gunners were overrun and from nine officers and one hundred and twenty one other ranks, only nine survived (official figures after the battle). There has since been a memorial erected to the 155th Field Battery on the spot.

We also learned that the first Tiger had found itself on the edge of our minefield and had reversed into it and was immobilised. This caused some panic and several more followed.

There appeared to be immobilised and empty tanks everywhere, so during the night our Sappers were requested to go out and blow them up in order to prevent the Germans recovering them. One Tiger had its huge gun, destroyed by a mine, the barrel of which was turned up as if a melted candle.

The chapter will be concluded by asking again, was that minefield worth Tony Elliot's life?

By the way, Harry was not amongst the tank crews. His squadron was commanded by a very stiff upper-lipped 'half' Colonel.

CHAPTER NINETEEN

HAPPY 21ST

It is now early April '43 and life appeared to be settling into a routine of saturated clothes, fighting body lice, diving into ditches (usually very wet ones) and generally being scared out of one's wits by the stuff flying through the air.

Was life that sweet that you tried to keep it at all costs? Or was it that one was afraid of losing parts of one's body in a very nasty way so that it affects one's life for evermore from the age of twenty years?

We had now been going through this lot for five months and could see no end to it. The Germans were still attacking in strength at various places along the line, which always seemed to need to be plugged by some hotch potch means or other, and usually by people who had to give their lives in so doing.

I could tell by the moans coming from the blokes that a change of some sort would soon have to come about.

It was about now that one of the chaps had a letter from home saying that 'Dad' W was a prisoner of war in Germany and not killed as we had feared. Remember that German/Yankee convoy all that time ago? The Germans must have got back to their own lines after all.

One day, when lying in the saturated confine of my bivvy, I heard a plot to celebrate my birthday the next day by 'throwing him in the river!'

Now my memory of the river was that it was pretty deep and fast flowing so in no way was I going in there! But how to escape a ducking?

Luck was in for once because a volunteer had been called for to escort the ration truck back to the central depot for the day's supply, and for once in my service I broke a golden rule and volunteered. It appeared, at the time, to be the lesser of two evils. Either a ducking to celebrate my 21st, or a ride of several miles each way in a nice comfortable army truck. Naturally the latter was chosen. Regret! Regret! never, never, volunteer for anything!

First shock was, driver to me,

"Please would you stand on the seat (passenger side) and keep your eyes peeled for aircraft. Never mind what type because there are no allied planes, so if you see two spots in the sky you know they will be Messerschmitts, and we have to cover 100 yards in record time or its curtains. They regularly shoot-up this road."

Shock two. The journey had to be made standing on the seat, with one's head sticking through a purposely made hole cut through the cab roof and, because he was so convincing, have your eyes looking in all directions at once. Shock three. The road was practically deserted.

"It's only idiots like us who do this journey in daylight," was his very sensible conclusion.

After several hundreds yards down that road the wrecks of shot up trucks began to appear and, very ominously, a small group of graves beside some of them. On some of these wrecks was a painted notice. 'This truck didn't have a spotter, have you?' Alarming to say the least!

Anyway it was foot down to the floor boards and away. It soon became very apparent that what with a drizzling rain, strong wind, streaming eyes, low clouds and holding on for dear life to a weaving truck cab, there was very little chance of seeing a barrage balloon never mind a fast flying Mutt or Jeff!

We gave it our best and amazingly nothing happened. Stores were loaded safely, after gaining a few boxes of 'Compo' rations by bargaining, pleading or fiddling invoices generally (the old Army game) and the return journey started.

We had gone a mile or so when several things happened. Coming down the road at zero feet and at about 300mph plus, were Mutt & Jeff. I had time to yell and bang once above the driver's head and they were over us and gone down the road. If we had been their target it would have been curtains for sure.

Imagine the situation. Travelling at 50mph, you first stop, open the cab door, jump down quite a height and run, all in one second maximum. Impossible! No wonder there were little groups of graves alongside some of those burnt out wrecks!

We allowed them time for the return trip, which did not materialise thank goodness, and set off again. The rest of the journey was uneventful and 'home' was in sight at last.

The next shock came from Section Sgt. Doug:

"We thought you had had it! It's just come over our radio that two ME's have bombed and shot up the ration stores. Six blokes killed and four trucks wrecked. They are appealing for medics."

There but by the grace of God go I! If I had had the choice again I think that it would have been,

"Please lads, throw me in the river!"

CHAPTER TWENTY

DOUG - AN ORGANISED SOLDIER

A word about Doug – a key man to the Section and later, on promotion, a key man for the Company.

To be a good Section Sgt. a chap had to possess tact and diplomacy, physical fitness, common sense and the ability to organise, and discipline a motley crowd of men, who sometimes were at the end of their tether from the bloody war in which they were forced to take part.

Doug had all of these qualities and more, and I, most unusually for a young soldier, admired him a great deal. His was the task of deciphering what the C.O. or Section Officer required to be done and then putting it in motion without upsetting too many people. This he did very well, and if he had made the Army his career he would have gone to the top, no bother.

He was a conscripted soldier and in his early days in the army he saw the opportunities and took them. One of the first qualifications that came his way was that of Physical Training Instructor. The course was one in which he passed because of being physically fit and possessing common sense.

When this soldier (LW) joined the Company at the tender age of eighteen, Doug was the PT instructor and had everyone on their toes, particularly after Monty's request for physical fitness. This included the young officers who thought they were above that sort of thing – but not in Doug's book! Many were the times when the diplomacy was flowing, such as –

"Would you mind raising your arms a little higher (pause) Sir?"

On joining the Company, being pretty fit, he would haul me out to the front of the class saying,

"Wat, you set the standard and the timing, and I'll make sure the blighters follow you!"

This would happen at Section strength - about fifty or seventy men. Company strength 250 odd and even Corps strength with three full Companies plus Field Park a strength of about 1,000 men.

On several occasions he made the remark,

"I wish you were a bit older to help me lick some of these blighters into shape, but they are mostly chaps in their mid thirties and it's just not on."

True!

Doug was promoted Company Sgt./Maj and later (after I had left) to Corps RSM, which was, of course, the limit for a non-commissioned officer.

Today he is the Secretary of the Company's Annual Reunion dinners and get togethers. Naturally they are very well organised, and although thin on the ground now, still appear to make money and be very successful.

CHAPTER TWENTY ONE

THE END IN NORTH AFRICA

It was about now that, at last, the news began to get a little brighter. The two fairly large towns on the Tunisian coast of Sfax and Gabes had fallen to the Highland Division and 2nd New Zealanders. The Highlanders had suffered very heavy losses in both men and materials, but were now rolling along the coastline and therefore squeezing the German and Italian Armies into a very confined space.

Many times the suggestion was made, why not let him (Jerry) break out with lots of tanks and guns – there is nowhere for him to go – and then cut his line of supply. This would save hundreds of Allied lives.

But, of course, ours was not to reason why, that was for higher command.

For the rest of April we appeared to be getting the brunt of all that could be thrown in the way of artillery from his ever decreasing firing circle.

Mutt & Jeff, who were now joined by the rest of the killing family, were ever present, so much so that all tasks (such as clearing minefields) had to be done by night. Even then if caught in the open you were running the risk of the 'butterflies'.

On several occasions we received warnings that because of the great squeeze being executed on him, he would try all manner of desperate measures to break out.

It was about now that a new sound came into the everyday order of normal killings, and a horrible sound it was too! That of the Nebelwerfer, as it was soon called by the British soldier 'The Sobbing Sisters'.

This was, suddenly, one of the most formidable weapons ever designed for attacking the opposing Infantry.

'Intelligence' said that the original had been captured on the Rumanian front and was now in mass production by the Germans. God forbid.

It was a short barrelled mortar 120mm in calibre which threw a bomb weighing 35lb for a distance of 6,000 yards. Rate of fire was about ten per minute. Its recoil was uncontrollable and had therefore to be fired from a trench by an electrical system.

They were in groups of six with the complete battery having six groups, therefore making thirty six barrels.

When fired, the noise they created was exactly that of a woman sobbing uncontrollably. This would then be joined by the other barrels, hence Sobbing Sisters.

The volume of noise was deafening and such that any good soldier would, if receiving them regularly, be driven out of his mind.

My first experience of them was that of a terrible grating sound coming from the German lines, then a trail of thick white smoke looping into the sky, then the sound. It had so much volume that you *knew* those bombs were going to fall on you. They had, apparently, only a thin steel casing and so on landing would do their killing by sheer blast. At maximum firing rate they would have thirty six barrels at ten per barrel each, hence 360 bombs a minute. A terror weapon indeed and, I would say, the biggest cause of battle fatigue (shell-shock, bomb-happy) call it what you will, within the forward area troops.

It was now early May, and at last the rains appeared to have finished their continuous saturation. It was even getting quite hot and the talk was of Khaki Drill to be issued soon, that is shorts and lightweight shirts. Imagine dumping those lice ridden winter clothes!

Shortly afterwards the issue was made and the great bonfire in the cause of peace of mind was carried out amongst great crackling of flames and the smell of burning flesh.

Now the news was definitely getting better. The air seemed to be full of Allied planes. Where the hell had they been all this time when Mutt & Jeff, and the rest of their family were doing all their killings?

We saw planes attacking the German lines in groups of six and even twelve at a time. Planes which had me searching back in my mind to the old aircraft recognition days. Marylands, Mitchells, Bostons, Spits, B17's, P81's, Mustangs to name a few. Where had they all suddenly come from? It was sickening to think of all those boys who had died from German aircraft when these devils could have been blasting their airfield. Thinking back on those Stuka raids, absolute sitting ducks with their slow speed and slow dive, for a good fighter. For sure strong words were said in high places!

The artillery were moving too, there appeared to be guns everywhere and we were kept very busy clearing mines from areas where guns were to be sited. Some Artillery officers were too keen to wait and consequently many guns and gunners were lost unnecessarily.

6th and 7th May were great days. The barrage of 400 plus guns started and had to be seen and heard to be believed. The airforce was attacking continually and, at last, the German Bastard began to give ground. Slowly at first and then much quicker.

My Company went forward with the 4th British Div., North of Medjez, with the 4th Indian alongside. It was absolute delight to ride those trucks in daylight with no fear of Mutt & Jeff!

8th May British troops entered Tunis and the Yanks Bizerta. All that remained now was to clear the German army off Cape Bon.

My diary scribblings read:

Moved through Tebourba to clear 'S' and Teller mines blocking roads. No casualties thank God!

Monday 10th moved further through wooded country. Tanks and trucks burnt out all around, allied and German. Medjerda to be bridged again – Bailey.

Tuesday 11th. German Quartermaster store discovered in wood. Many tons of abandoned equipment.

Wednesday 12th. Moved up to Cap Bon. German and Italian prisoners coming in, in droves. Whole convoys of them, with all their kit, waiting to surrender. What a marvellous sight!

Thursday 13th. German truck broke down here last night. Woke up surrounded by 'friendly' Germans.

THE CAMPAIGN FINISHED AT 11:45 THIS MORNING. THANK GOD!

Now what?

The official figures read:-

Prisoners taken in Tunisia (German and Italian) 238,000, British casualties 38,000.

This latter figure was credible but shocking. All that suffering and misery because some bastard of a German/Austrian house painter had mad ambitions.

Now what indeed!

A week's leave in Tunis; what a dump, followed by training and lectures in all types of mines and mine warfare. It was about now that new methods were appearing of clearing minefields without the risk of loss of life. They were demonstrated and looked really first class in the peace and quiet of a training area. The first method was by flail tank. A drum rotated on the front of a Sherman tank which carried a number of chains, that when rotated exploded any mines in its path. Excellent, but of course exploding mines would soon attract enemy attention.

Another method was by a net of cordtex (explosive cable) fired by rocket over the mined area so causing all mines to explode. Excellent! But we knew that they would never be seen again.

Another task which was to come our way was the containment, by wire, of all those prisoners. A mammoth task, but by using three or four tons of dannet wire coils, reinforced occasionally with metal pickets, several miles were completed in a day. The one blessing of this job was that the prisoners were persuaded to do all the humping and, not surprisingly, they were quite content to do so because there was nowhere to go and they were being well fed. Once a day they were escorted by one Bren-gun carrier to the beach for a swim. We were lucky if one a week came our way.

Imagine the scene, about a thousand blonde-haired sun-tanned Aryans in their birthday suits charging into the water together. The spinster's dream?

By night they would sit around and sing their German songs, and when on the march would render, with great gusto,

"We are marching against England." This *always* called for a burst from a Bren-gun over their heads!

An urgent call was received from the Yanks.

"We are an American Base hospital and, as such, have many hundreds of wounded and sick men all living under canvas. Higher Command has decreed that this must not be allowed to carry on any longer. Could your Engineers help with a supply of your 1/2 round hutting."

Of course they meant Nissens and we took great delight in obliging.

The site chosen was on the edge of a great salt lake near Tunis. God forsaken and, by now, stinking hot.

Nissen hut stores were conjured up from somewhere and work started. All straightforward enough until nature took a hand. A hot wind from the Sahara, called the Sirocco, started to blow. This apparently would last a fortnight and was a yearly event.

The inner skin sheets of a Nissen are placed on the ribs parallel to the ground and held together by sleeves, next a straining wire (a pair) to each bay, which holds these sheets in their curved position. In order to tighten these wires, a ratchet had to be used which rested on the apex sheet, this was finished off straining tight with a hand operated spanner.

With the Sirocco blowing, which resembled a large oven door being opened into an already heated room, the ratchet man had his hands and knees (shorts) severely burnt, and had to receive hospital attention. (They said the Yankee nurses were wonderful) which was, of course, something that had to be investigated before agreeing.

Common sense to the rescue. At 3am or so a special squad were turfed out of their blankets, and were able to crawl over cool sheets, the early parts of the huts having been erected in sequence, and waiting.

A luxury that the Yanks provided was the erection of tripods, some four feet high or so and dotted at vantage points around the site. From these were hung a kit bag type contraption containing, believe it or not, iced tea! Was it a dream? Iced tea, and as much as one could drink in a flaming hot desert!

About this time rumours became very strong about a move back to Blighty - dear old Blighty - somewhere we thought that, at times, we would never see again! My thoughts went back to El Arousa, when the Stukas were coming over in a cloud and one of the chaps said,

"This looks like our burial place!" I can distinctly remember saying to myself,

"That's impossible, I've got a plot in Abergavenny new cemetery," and I prayed with the rest of them.

Rumour appeared to have substance when the order came,

"All kits to be packed ready to move off at first light."

At the risk of repeating myself, it needs to be pointed out that the only relief of stress and tension for a soldier in a battle area was the alcohol bottle, and that evening was a special one calling for more than one bottle. Beer and the occasional bottle of Scotch were now getting through to us, and together with the readily available 'Vin Rouge' a marvellous evening was had by all.

At first light (I wonder why nobody wanted Spam and biscuits?) we were on the move, and sure enough took the Bizerta road. This was the main port of Tunisia and the one from which all sailings took place. Apart from bad stomachs, thick heads, and very sore throats, (from singing) everyone was on top of the world.

As we neared Bizerta it became more and more alarming to see rows and rows of tanks and vehicles strung out for miles alongside the roadway. Every field and any spare space was occupied by troops, Yanks and British, not to mention Poles, Indians, New Zealand, South African etc., etc.

The alarming feeling soon turned to one of awful confirmation. This was one huge assembly area for a mass invasion (of Europe?). One look into the huge harbour area was enough: it was absolutely full of naval capital ships, British and American, with every spare foot of water space taken up with invasion barges of all sizes but all with flat bottoms to get up the beaches. So it was to be an assault landing again, instead of a gentle landing into some friendly port or another.

A space was found eventually for the Company right down by the dockside, and where we remained for some time while other troops were embarking on to the larger ships. The 'drill' now became obvious to one and all in the Company. We were to be the last on to the small barges and therefore the first troops off on the landing.

Rumours, of course, were again rife: Southern France, Italy, Greece, Yugoslavia. Everyone had their own pet theory and appeared to relish explaining the reasons why. In the meantime, sit and wait.

Now this was not a pleasant thing to do by any means because, of course, the Germans knew we were gathering and were determined to do as much damage to that concentration of tens of thousands of troops as possible, and with some success too. How could they miss?

A group of heavy bombers would come over every night with HE or anti-personnel bombs. The barrage that greeted their appearance was one that had to be seen to be believed. I would say that it was the greatest concentration of fire ever. The harbour was full of ships, the ground for miles around was crammed with guns and all doing their best to hit those 'poor'

Germans. Hits there were too, and many a little Fritz regretted leaving the Fatherland that particular night!

The other memory of that time was the sound, and in some cases the feel of the amount of shrapnel returning to earth after such a barrage. The pieces of shrapnel could be heard whizzing all around, and if near the water's edge, heard dropping into the water.

For a week or so this situation continued, until one day it became apparent that the harbour was rapidly emptying of boats full of troops, but we were still on shore with several other Units. What was happening?

The news came through quite quickly. Sicily had been invaded by British and American troops and appeared to be a major operation. Damn good luck to them but what of us?

The answer came quickly enough. Thousands of mines had been laid, and by special request from the 'Frogs', would the British engineers supervise their lifting and removal by prisoners of war. That suited us – anything better than storming those beaches again!

It seemed that, according to the Geneva Convention, using prisoners to lift mines was strictly verboten, and this message was conveyed to us in no uncertain terms by the higher ranking German prisoners. We, in turn, somehow failed to understand this and carried on for several weeks while 'an investigation was carried out at high level'. By the time the confirmation came through, confirming what was already known, of course, most minefields had been cleared. How convenient – the slowness of bureaucracy.

Now it was back to training again.

Lectures on new types of mines, methods of bridging, gas warfare and of course, for the thousandth time, how to strip and reassemble a Bren gun!

The Campaign in Sicily appeared to be going quite well but, judging by the amount of casualties coming into the base hospitals, was extremely hard going.

The big question now being asked was, could Montgomery do without us much longer? The answer was not long in coming!

Before leaving the shores of that beautiful(?) continent Africa, it is worth recording an often repeated statement made by many German prisoners, in English of course!

"When Tommy Spitfire came over - Fritz got his head down. When Fritz Messerschmitts came over - Tommy got his head. When Joe American came over - *everyone* got his head down!"

Slightly embarrassing, but very true!

CHAPTER TWENTY TWO

ITALY

The country noted for - sun, opera, vino, pasta, olive oil and beautiful women.

Few of these luxuries were to be sampled until much later, two bloody long and awful years in fact. Years in which the question was asked repeatedly: "Was all this carnage worthwhile? Was the cost of all those British and American lives justified?" The answer must always be never, never in a million years! Feelings amongst the troops taking part in those bloody battles were, at times, to run very high, almost to mutiny and rebellion. Here were two huge and well trained armies (Eighth British and Fifth American) with the whole coastline of Italy to choose from to make landings which would cut off the German armies which were massed in defence of Southern Italy. We heard daily of pincer moments taking place in Russia, in difficult conditions, which cut off many thousands of men, but it was not for our leaders, we had to land at virtually the tip of Italy and slog through numerous river and defence lines.

Each of these so called defence lines was given a name by the Germans, such as Gustav Line, Gothic Line and even Adolf Hitler Line. Each of these lines was carefully chosen for its suitability for defence, usually on a river where high ground could be occupied by defending troops, so having a field of fire over any crossings by Allied troops.

Each river was a major obstacle in itself, without the attention of a highly trained Army desperately trying to kill, by any means, troops making the crossing.

Some of these rivers had to be seen to be believed. For almost the full length of the country they rose at intervals, in the central spine of the Appenines, and flowed both east and west to the coast. A good many were very fast flowing and, as you will see, at times almost defeated the Sappers trying to bridge them.

During very rainy periods (what rain!) they were known to rise fifteen feet or more, so carrying away any obstacles before them - including low bridges. Floating and pontoon bridges were non-starters, or non-finishers at least because of this rise and fall.

It was not until the Plain of Lombardy, in the North, was reached that the rivers became more normal, and behaved as rivers should.

The size of some of these was really astonishing, far wider than anything in this country. The Po, for instance, made our Thames (God give me those beautiful, cold, freezing, wet nights with a C.O. making believe he was offended by the numerous effing words coming his way) seem like a gentle stream. But of course it still had to be bridged!

Imagine that situation. A river about four times as wide as the Severn at the bridge area, having to have a Bailey thrown across it while an Army queued very impatiently (ff's everywhere) to cross. An Army of some eleven divisions, each of 14,000 men, with all their tanks, guns and trucks. That gives you the idea and, of course, only one bridge possible because of the tremendous amount of equipment required. But enough of bridges.

CHAPTER TWENTY THREE

THE LANDINGS

As described in previous chapters, the Company was transported from Bizerta by an American Landing Ship (Tanks), a flat bottomed all steel monster designed to carry troops and tanks from ship to the assault beach, not for five days crossing a very rough Med in winter time.

Here thoughts return to that wonderful American food: flapjacks, honey, beetroot and cornflakes, not forgetting sweet creamy coffee. All that after a year of very hard biscuits and 'Compo' rations.

The stomachs of all personnel took one look and promptly rejected it, aided and abetted by a rough sea and a flat bottomed boat. Hosepipes on steel decks were on demand for two (or more) days.

The destination of this large assault force was still unknown, even after being at sea for two days. The direction appeared almost due north, but word was circulating that even the Yankee skipper was lost, something that could be true, if he was anything like the pilots who appeared not to know the difference between Allied or enemy troops when off-loading their bombs.

After four days at sea it was possible to see smudges all around the horizon, and one then realised just how large a landing force had been formed up. The wise men knew, of course, just where we were going. Southern France, Greece, Northern Italy, Yugoslavia, they all took a turn at receiving us. On the fifth day the official announcement came. It was to be the mainland of Italy, but news was very much morale boosting too. The Italian Army had surrendered and, in fact, Italy had declared war on Germany.

How now could the Germans resist in Italy with every one against them? Instead of risking one's neck charging up the beaches, was it to be opera tickets and spaghetti in Naples? Official figures after the war show that this total landing force far out numbered the D-Day landings in France, so from this one can judge the size of the operation.

The convoy had now split into three. Our section gently steamed into a very large port in broad daylight with not a German in sight but instead, was I dreaming? hundreds of Italian troops who promptly started to unload our boat. Was this the end of the war?

How wrong could one be?

We soon learned that the port was named Taranto, situated right in the instep of the boot of Italy. This caused genuine disappointment all around because it was felt that we should be landing in the Po valley area, or more north even, in order to cut out that long slog up through the country, and avoid those defence lines, the cause, as it proved, of very heavy casualties on the Allied side.

Word was rife that Churchill would not stick his neck out and risk another Gallipoli, but instead had gone for the 'soft underbelly' of the Axis, mostly to appease Joe Stalin who was pressing very hard for the 'Second Front'!

One other prong of the force had joined the Army from Sicily and landed at Reggio, right on the toe, and one could not get further south than that!

The third British force joined the Yanks and landed at Salerno. This was mostly a beach area, just south of Naples, and, as it proved, a very long and costly distance from Rome.

This landing received very stiff opposition which, as it turned out, was very bad luck indeed because, as shown by official figures later, there were whole divisions of German troops resting in the area, some of these from the Russian front.

Figures published were: 30,000 Panzer troops, 45,000 Infantry and 17,000 Paratroops. Surely enough to repel any invading force!

Many years later, by sheer chance, I had confirmation of this when talking to an Italian farmer from the Salerno area, now living in the UK. 'In 1943 the whole of the area became alive with German troops, they swarmed everywhere, streets, fields, mountains were alive with them. They knew that you were coming!'

Food for thought?

The brightest part of the Taranto landing, for me at least, was to see the masts and superstructure of large battleships. The main ships of the Italian navy, had been sunk by the raid sometime previously by Naval Swordfish (The Stringbags!) a torpedo carrying force from carriers in the Med.

Making a point of querying the local people about the raid, the general opinion was 'they had never seen such bravery before, those very slow moving planes coming through a barrage from hundreds of guns but still dropping their torpedoes on target.'

In particular one old ex-naval veteran said, "After the raid we all asked ourselves how can we be following the madman Mussolini and fighting against the brave Inglesi (English) who are bound to win in the end?"

Be that as it may.

With all the vehicles safely landed, the push north began. The Sappers were soon brought into action. Every bridge, every small culvert had been totally destroyed by the retreating Germans. Even the railways received special attention. Each and every length of metal rail had been cut in order to prevent the Allies making use of the track for transport, but of course these had to be repaired so – forward the Sappers!

Thinking back on all that expenditure, one would ask, "Who pays the hundreds of thousands of pounds spent making things workable again?"

Not the Italians for sure, they were already bled dry, so forward the British taxpayer!

No minefields encountered in those early days thank goodness. He was too busy retreating, or was he?

The story of the very tough resistance being met over on the west coast at Salerno was reaching us and being updated daily.

Where would he make his stand on the Adriatic coast? The answer appeared to be somewhere on a line with Salerno and, for sure, would be on a river line where the Sappers and Infantry would get slaughtered again.

Here an explanation is necessary on the British troops' use of a new word. It was a word which spread like wildfire through all ranks: 'Ted'!

An easy word to say and use in every day conversation, but a word that could bring a variety of reactions, depending upon the context in which it was used.

You can trust the British soldier to abbreviate any word he possibly can, and in this instance it was Tedeschi! The Italian word for German. Here was a word which was entirely foreign to him and rather difficult to pronounce, so how much better to change it to 'Ted', not only easier to say but one that hinted at the slightly ridiculous too.

The occupants (if any were left) of each and every town and village reached on this initial drive were queried as to, "Are there any Germans here?" and, "How long since the Germans passed through?" etc., etc. The reply was nearly always the same.

"I Tedeschi e molto cativo" and, "I Tedeschi potare via tutto" and, "I Tedeschi partire ieri", that is – "The Germans are very bad", naturally, they were talking to the Inglesi. "The Germans have taken everything." There never seemed much to take. "The Germans left yesterday."

Every time the word Tedeschi (Germans) was mentioned, the hand was nearly always drawn across the throat in a cutting action, in exactly the same way as would the 'Frogs' when Boche or Allemande was spoken.

So the word 'Ted' came into existence and being much easier than German to say or write, was soon caught on by everyone. Towards the middle of the campaign it was even being used in official signals, such as 'Ted has been observed on high ground on so and so', etc., etc.

The major towns encountered were Brindisi and Bari. Here again only nominal resistance, but the damage created by 'Ted' when he left was terrific, particularly in the docks area of Bari, a large and very good port for our use, on the Adriatic. So forward the Sappers again, this time the Docks Operating Engineers. These were specialist troops trained in this sort of activity, and they soon had the docks back to virtually full operating capacity. The journey north continued and was almost like training days in UK, bridging and road repairs without the attention of 'Ted'.

Word came through that a breakout had been achieved at Salerno and Naples had fallen. Good news indeed, Rome was not so far away up that coast. Opera tickets in Naples and guided tours of Rome were still on the cards!

What a hope! There was just the little matter of crossing a few rivers and a little place called Monte Cassino to come!

It was about now that the rains started, October to November 1943, and like North Africa, had to be experienced to be believed. Continuous torrential rain for days on end until everywhere was turned into a quagmire and a sea of mud. Not a pleasant experience! The next big step along the way, and an excellent one it was too, was the capture of the Foggia area on the Adriatic. This consisted of several square miles of virtually flat area, and within days was being occupied by the RAF with Spits. from the old Desert Airforce, still in their yellow war paint. At least support was to come when 'Ted' started his stuff.

There wasn't long to wait. The next town reached was Termoli and, sure enough, there was the river, the Biferno, and there too was 'Ted' dug in, in strength on the north bank

The 78 Division of 5 Corps was in the line and calling loudly for two bridges. Apparently two assault crossings had already been attempted but casualties were extremely high without the use of tanks, hence the call for bridges.

Bailey stores were rushed up under cover of darkness and unloaded with the usual total chaos. You could bet your boots on several things taking place at this time in the overall picture of an attack.

1)   The gap had to be estimated in the dark, usually an educated guess, which nearly always resulted in either far too much equipment being dumped at the spot, so causing hold-ups of all kinds (ff's prevalent) or too little, which you could not possibly realise until the bridge was virtually across the gap, and then find a dozen or so panels short (ff's on an increased scale.)

2)   It would be raining with all and sundry taking a soaking (too wet for ff's!) (totally untrue!).

3)   Our heavy guns would be pounding 'Ted' on the far bank while the bridge was being launched. This would mean that from guns being fired from a distance of one or two miles back, the shells would drop anywhere within a 100 yard radius.

'Ted' by now would know that a bridge was being built, and so would do his best to stop it. This would usually mean by shellfire, mortars or fixed line machine guns. The result was usually total chaos!

There was very little difference between his shellfire and ours, except you could usually see his guns firing against the night sky, but our shells were more numerous and sometimes were on target!

Out of this chaos a bridge started to take shape and ff's change to bb's, but casualties in the area were not light, particularly when it was realised that the swine had planted a few mines about, knowing that this was the spot for a bridge, and that people and trucks would be churning the area into a sea of mud. The first knowledge that one had of mines being present was when people started to die or suffer shrapnel wounds from the explosions.

Around this time, an incident happened which is worth recording and which will give you further insight into the life (or should that read existence) of the Sapper at war.

During a particular spell of heavy shelling when everyone was forced to take cover, the word was passed around, "Do not go back on to the bridge, await further orders."

OK by us, that ditch of mud was heaven compared with the open river. Then came, "Make your way back along the track for 200 yards".

What the hell? What could be wrong?

When we were what could be judged as out of the hearing range of 'Ted', the instructions given were, "Proceed a further 500 yards and board the waiting transport". This of course only added to the uncertainty of it all. A half finished bridge with at least 14,000 troops waiting to cross, a few score Sappers risking life and limb for their country being mucked around by the chosen few and no explanation. The intensity of the swearing increased!

Sub-section One groped our dripping way to the White Armoured Car – a new innovation to the Company – several had been issued to us courtesy of the Yanks (bless 'em) together with their mine detectors, which were (almost) a luxury to use. More of that White and detector later.

Now followed an impossible task. Each vehicle had to follow the one in front over a maze of tracks most of which were either half washed away or cratered by shellfire, with no lights possible (much more swearing). When one truck got lost, those behind followed it - naturally! The only consolation was that you could not drive into 'Ted's' lines in the dark – somewhere in between there was a river.

About half the trucks arrived at the right destination after what seemed like hours of stops and starts, and the hell of a battle going on all around. It was of all places what appeared in the dark to be a flat sandy beach, very wet and unfriendly but a beach nevertheless. Rotting seaweed was everywhere and the sea could be heard in the background.

The comparison to a Southend beach must end there because chaos reigned supreme and we were about to do our best to add to it.

The Commandos had carried out an assault landing behind, what they thought, were German lines but had missed their target by several hundred yards. With them they had brought a variety of vehicles which, by this time, were axle deep in wet soft sand and mud. So of course, out went the cry by radio, "Sappers please help!".

What a cock up! – Here was a half finished bridge with most of the Eighth Army marking time and swearing. A Commando landing in the wrong place and all bogged down and bawling for the Sappers', who, when they arrived, had only half their personnel, the rest by now were driving down the Via Roma in Naples. Not to mention, of course, that dawn was only a few hours away when anything moving on that beach would be blown away.

Fortunately three winch trucks had survived the journey, (the good old Morris six-wheeler, the workhorse of the Sappers) and these were soon anchored at the top of the beach, frantically hauling up truck after truck until, that is, a bright 'Dick head' had the idea of laying Somerfield Track so that some of the vehicles could get up under their own steam.

Somerfield Track has been mentioned before. Briefly, a description would be: 'A flexible metal track which assists wheeled vehicles to travel over soft ground, when laid correctly.'

Those last three words are the key to the whole system – hence (if possible) the further chaos!

Imagine a roll of wire netting, wider than a vehicle's wheels, which at intervals of a foot or so has metal reinforcement bars threaded across it at right angles to its length. These are looped at each end, through which is threaded a flat metal bar. These are then held down by metal headed pickets. But – and a very big but as it proved, when used on very soft ground, metal re-inforced duckboards will be used.

In that situation no duckboards were available, and so as vehicles started their journey up the track they sank deeper and deeper into the soft sand until their sumps and lower parts became entangled in the wire, so trapping the truck and ripping up several yards of track at a time. There now follows an interval for swearing (fff_____!!!)

The rescue of these unfortunates had to be completed by winch truck and the tracking abandoned.

Much sweating took place on that cold wet beach in the early hours of that particular morning, in order to finish the job before first light. But someone was looking after us on that occasion and success was ours. So was it now back to the bridge?

Arrival on site brought the surprising sight of the missing 'lambs' (those who had gone astray) having a smoking concert and keeping dry in the nearby barn. One wonders, who were the smart boys and who were the mugs on this occasion? Surely no-one gets lost deliberately when fighting for King and country?

During the journey back – it was nearly dawn now – Bob (Section Officer) had stopped our White with the words, "Wat, I'm afraid your lads will have to lose their sleep, the bridge must be finished as soon as possible, so it means working on in daylight."

Right at that moment we could not have heard a worse statement.

Imagine the situation: by night 'Ted' could only guess our position, but by day it would be goodbyes all around, either VC's or RIP's.

On top of this every man had had a guts full. Completely saturated without a chance of drying out, a terror filled night of bridging, two shocking journeys over very rough terrain, the chaos at the beach, and now this. I knew that I had a mutiny on my hands!

Reasoning and explanation of the situation would not console anyone, and pleading was not in my makeup. So the journey continued with most of the blame being directed at the 'Dick heads' (that's a mild interpretation) responsible for calling off the bridge construction when it could have been finished by first light, instead of going to the help of those (f) commandos who had lost their (f) bearings. It was pointed out that there could be no fault with the Commandos, they were in the hands of the Navy, and as for cancelling the bridge op, orders were from above our 'Dick heads', and no-one argues with that! In any case were you not the people (wise move this) responsible for saving the lives of those British Commandos? That one caused some thought.

It was about now, nearing the bridge site, that something dawned on me which, without any doubt whatsoever saved the day and doubtless saved a Sub-section of Sappers from whatever punishment would be 'awarded' for 'mutiny in the face of the enemy'.

It was the quietness of the place. The truck was stopped to verify, and sure enough, not a bang not a shell, only very high stuff passing overhead. What had happened?

On arrival at the site, now in broad daylight, Bob confirmed my hopeful query.

"Yes! Word of the Commando landing has reached 'Ted' and he has vacated the far bank and is now digging in on the ridge some two miles away."

Never were there sweeter words, at least, under conditions such as those.

It was a simple matter now to organise the bridging party to complete the job while, one at a time, a bloke slipped away for an hour – unofficially – to the barn to wring out his saturated clothes etc., etc.

Job done, now what?

It was well into the next night before traffic started moving over the bridge. This was because of the pounding the far bank had taken from our guns, so making the approach roads a mammoth task in themselves. But success at last and then fulfilment! What a sight to see guns, tanks, lorried Infantry by their thousand, and all going to knock the sh-- sorry, stuffing out of that nasty bloke waiting for us on the next ridge.

But for us it was the luxury of that beautiful barn. It had no sides, the floor was a sea of mud, and the wind and rain whistled through but to that bunch of saturated Sappers it was a luxury villa on the French Riviera!

The next day was an afternoon start, and for this all credit must go to Bob, he had persuaded the 'powers that be' that his blokes needed at least a half a day to clean up and dry out. So the order was 'on the trucks at 1400 hrs'.

During that half day one hundred things had to be achieved. The first of these was a 'bath'. This consisted of a biscuit tin some 15"x15"x18" deep, 9/10 full of heated water. This was achieved by filling another tin with sandy soil soaking it with petrol and within minutes hot water was produced.

Despite all the rain being experienced, good clean water was hard to come by, so was rationed to one or at the most two tins per Sub-section of 12 men plus one (me). This bathing was, by sheer necessity, a highly organised affair, and if one bloke forgot the 'drill' it would lead to heated arguments and even fisticuffs! Plenty of soap and improvised flannels to go around, but most important was the sequence.

The golden rule was, no bollocks - sorry - first time round. In other words everyone in turn kept above the plimsoll line and washed down to the waist. By this time the second tin of water was ready for the important bits downwards. The last couple were lucky and could even stand in the tin, the contents of which now resembled the Company cook's thick soup!

The next operation was de-licing!

This consisted of as before described, applying into all seams of every garment, AL63, the famous delousing powder, a dried mixture of gunpowder, strong carbolic, disinfecting powder, ammonia, etc., etc., etc. This always did the trick for a few days but, of course, removed your skin during the process. Next was the treatment of desert sores. These were something that every one suffered with because of a continual diet of tinned stuff and biscuits, with no fresh fruit or vegetables. They consisted of open sores anywhere on the body, and usually running with pus. These after bathing and drying, were treated by the First Aid bloke with some concoction or other and bandaged but were always sore and uncomfortable, especially under battle dress and equipment.

A discussion followed this beauty salon treatment as to the cause of the sores, and after hearing the agreement that the culprit was the lack of green vegetables, one of the brighter 'sparks' of the sub, one of the lost lambs of before actually, said that he had seen an orchard full of apples not far away. This, of course, caused great excitement and he and two others were promptly despatched with the order 'bring as many as you can load into the White'.

A little explanation is required here.

In North Africa, when the call of nature was heard, one took a walk with a shovel and buried the result but, here in Italy, being a little more civilised, 'thunderboxes' were constructed, usually one per Sub, and made from a strong wooden box, bottomless, but with a tight fitting lid (toilet flap). This fit being essential because of the ever present plague of flies, a particularly vicious strong type, always ready to spread all manner of disease.

But back to the 'thunderbox'. After construction, a quiet spot was found, a hole dug and the box planted over the hole - absolute luxury, particularly if a screen of hessian was erected to stop the viewing public.

Before the return of the fruit gatherers it was announced by Bob that only 'recce' parties would be required at 1400 hrs, the others to stay put.

As it turned out, this was a very fortunate state of affairs because, when the scrumpers arrived they brought with them a whole truck full of shining green apples, so many in fact, that

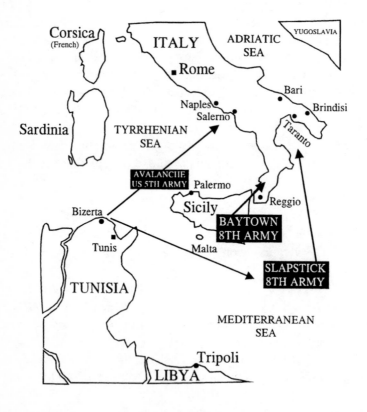

THREE-PRONGED THRUST
AT THE ITALIAN HOMELAND

there was enough to share with the whole Company and every man to eat his fill.

Then it happened!! And I'll pause here in order for you to get your imagination working! ....

At first it was only a slight stomach pain, then, as the day wore on, it became a severe gripe, and what followed had to be seen to be believed. Trouserless people dashing in all directions. The 'thunderboxes' very quickly became obsolete and Mark2 was urgently required! Trenches were rapidly dug by those able, a forked vertical post erected each end and a stout pole rested across where one could perch one's backside but still retain one's feet on the ground. These 'meeting places' soon became crowded and, of course, popular with all ranks. I wonder if this was (many years previously) the origin of Officers', Sgts' and OR's Messes? Conversations there must have been very enjoyable because, it was said, some people did not leave there for hours on end!

Green shining apples, probably very expensive today, but on that particular day they were the means of moving an Army!

Some time later when this item was under discussion, the majority of voices were convinced that it had been a ploy by the evil minded 'Ted' to leave all those beautiful apples behind, after all they were just as effective as a booby trap, and they did effect the whole Company!

Anyway, No. 1 Sub. kept a low profile for some time for reasons other than 'Ted' throwing stuff at them!

Nuff said!

After a couple more of those 'restful' days it was on the move again. Over the bridge and forward about two mile to 'Ted's' new position. On these moves, and there were many of them in the years to come, the stench of death was everywhere. Bodies of horses, bloated in a pantomime of positions were lying everywhere, together with the dead of both Armies, waiting to be collected for central burial by those who followed.

It was now getting well into the wintry days of '43, and rain, mud, muck and frozen appendages became prevalent, so much so that it was becoming obvious that soon we would be bogged down for the winter.

Rumours were strong at this time that 'Ted' had formed a very strong and formidable defence line north of the Sangro (a very big river), running from Ortona on the Adriatic coast, across to Cassino on the west coast, calling it the Gustav Line.

The Sangro was two rivers away yet, so there was one other first, the Trigno, a river similar to the last, to be crossed. This one entered the Adriatic at a small port called San Severo and was overlooked by a high ridge running inland and parallel to the river. The larger town of Vasto lay astride the ridge and was almost a mile inland. This geographical layout has been described in some detail in order to help you to understand the following events.

A quick recce was made of the river and Bailey stores were soon arriving on site. It should be pointed out here that air activity by 'Ted' had been restricted to one or two glimpses of Mutt & Jeff (or other members of their family) and certainly no attacks as yet on us personally. Perhaps these would come later, but what he lacked in air strikes he most certainly made up for in shellfire.

The bridge was started the following night and went very smoothly with only the occasional thump of his shells to worry us, but no direct hits in the bridge area. It really was a well designed piece of equipment, with all praise going to Mr Bailey. With every man knowing his job (except the new replacements of course) everything went without a hitch. A river of considerable width (say the Wye at its mouth) could be bridged in one night by trained personnel, and the crowning glory of this equipment was the fact that (stores available) it could be strengthened by adding panels to suit the load required in proportion to the width of the gap.

Building and Rocking rollers were soon in position, the single nose rolled out with its usual lift to counteract the sag of the bridge before touchdown on the far bank, and as panels and transoms were added, counterweights were placed on the deck on the building side of the Rocking rollers in order to prevent the whole thing running away and plunging into the drink.

A typical example of this mistake was at the Empire Exhibition 1951, where insufficient weight was used and the whole lot dropped into the Thames for all the world to see. I wonder whose head rolled for that?

On the Trigno bridge all that could be heard was the occasional shell burst, numerous but quiet (Ff's) and the thump of the mallet persuading the awkward panel pin to behave.

Dawn arrived and very anxious moments with it. Would 'Ted' now blow the bridge away?

But no, and the explanation was soon to come. Our big stuff was keeping his head down up on the ridge, ably assisted by close mortar fire, and then we were to witness the most determined and devastating attack imaginable. Remember that he was holding high ground, so it was plain for all to see.

Firstly it was Al Bostons in groups of six attacking his position, quickly followed in very well organised groups of six and twelve Marylands, Mitchells and even B24 Liberators. We nearly felt a twinge of sympathy for 'Ted', getting all this attention, but thinking back on all those horrors he had committed in recent times – 'the lust awoke to kill, to kill', so please keep 'em coming!

Next on the list were fighter bombers – each carried two small bombs, and after dropping those on target would return again and again to empty their guns into his positions. They were a continuous stream of all types and received loud applause for their action.

The idea was, firstly, to make him keep his head down, then finally to shift him off the ridge.

Now came the master stroke. From out of the mists of the Adriatic came a 'group' of large British warships, at least to our ignorant minds they were large warships. I'd never seen bigger anyway (agreement). They formed up in line – what a

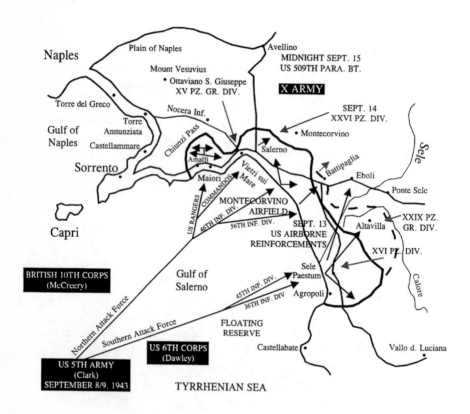

THE SALERNO LANDINGS SEPT. 1943

magnificent sight – and each in turn fired all its guns as a broadside into 'Ted's' position. The wise men said they were 16" but again, ignorance reigned. What we were witnessing was something never to be forgotten. A large group of shells leaving each ship in turn and erupting into the German positions. Each group contained a quantity of tracer shells so that the trajectory was easy to follow by eye. I shuddered to think of the destruction caused, both physical and mental, to the recipients of those salvoes. The overall result of these operations was a complete success. An Infantry attack followed which gained several miles and, thank goodness a bridge completed with no casualties.

Before moving on to the next chapter of our miserable lives, the opportunity is taken of printing the words, for what it's worth, of a song which circulated amongst the troops from Italy, after the war. This song gave an answer to Lady Astor who is supposed to have accused the Eighth Army in Italy of dodging D-Day. Whether or not there was any truth in this will, I suppose, never be known, but someone took the opportunity to answer in song so, for what it's worth, a verse has been included at the end of some chapters.

Another statement credited to that lady was:

'Beware of the men
With brown arms and knees
They are the carriers of disease!'
Where *do* these rumours start?

The tune by the way, is Lily Marlene, what else?

We're the D-Day dodgers, out in Italy,
Always on the vino, always on the spree
Eighth Army scroungers and the Tanks
We live in Rome, amongst the Yanks
We are the D-Day dodgers in sunny Italy.

THE SITUATION
AUTUMN 1943

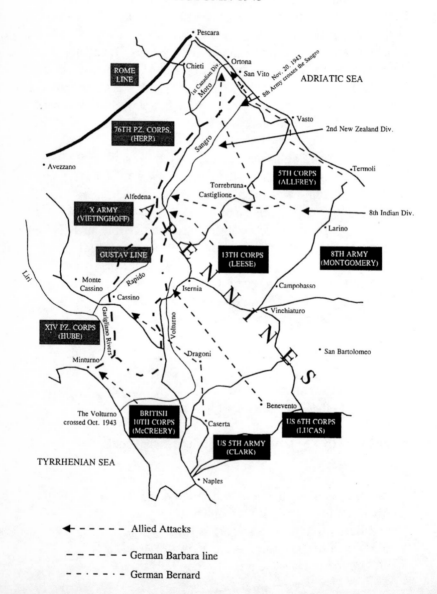

Pescara

Chieti
Ortona
San Vito
1st Canadian Div.
Moro
ROME LINE
Nov. 20, 1943
8th Army crosses the Sangro
ADRIATIC SEA

Vasto
76TH PZ. CORPS. (HERR)
2nd New Zealand Div.
Sangro

Avezzano
Termoli

Torrebruna
Castiglione
5TH CORPS (ALLFREY)

Alfedena
X ARMY (VIETINGHOFF)
8th Indian Div.

Larino
GUSTAV LINE
13TH CORPS (LEESE)
8TH ARMY (MONTGOMERY)

Liri
Monte Cassino
Rapido
Campobasso
Cassino
Isernia
Vinchiaturo

XIV PZ. CORPS (HUBE)
Garigliano Rivers
Volturno
San Bartolomeo

Minturno
Dragoni

Benevento

The Volturno crossed Oct. 1943
BRITISH 10TH CORPS (McCREERY)
Caserta
US 6TH CORPS (LUCAS)

US 5TH ARMY (CLARK)
TYRRHENIAN SEA

Naples

Allied Attacks

German Barbara line

German Bernard

CHAPTER TWENTY FOUR

THE SANGRO

Italian rivers have the strange habit of ending with the letter 'O' e.g.: Po, Trigno, Volturno, Senio etc., etc. So the Sangro was no exception.

The letter 'O' made it of masculine gender as opposed to 'A' for feminine.

It was never understood by 'us rough British soldiers' why a river should be masculine and (say) a table, feminine, but perhaps those Latins have something which might be an advantage over the English way (or should that be weigh, or even whey?) of spelling and pronunciation.

The point in this case was the fact that when an enquiry was made by yours truly of an ancient peasant, before leaving the Trigno, 'What is the name of the next river?' Received the reply which I can still hear today.

It was delivered with the genuine earnestness that only an ancient Latin could muster and, of course, with gesticulations!

"Filio mio! Quel fiume - il Sangro - e il fiume de sangue-sangue d'uomini! Stare qui! Stare qui!"

Some time later when checking with an Italian speaking colleague, the reply received was both surprising and, perhaps, frightening. He said, "That old Italian was quoting an old local proverb to you. What he actually said was, 'My son! That river - the Sangro - is the river of blood - blood of men! Stay here! Stay here!' In other words don't go near it!"

As things turned out, if only that old man had been the General in charge, and given such an order, many lives would have been saved and, for sure, would hardly have affected the course of the war at all. But, the river was there, the Germans were holding it from very heavily fortified positions on the high ground of the far bank, and we had to cross.

Here is the story of that crossing, at least, the small part played in it by No. 1 Sub-section of No. 1 Section!

There are no pleasant memories whatsoever of the river Sangro, particularly when one's thoughts go back to the mud, rain, cold and, above all, the needless casualties suffered on both sides. Among the casualties in our small area, was a close friend who died an awful and totally unnecessary death, caused by the fiendish mind of modern science.

Around this time, conditions were really becoming atrocious. Continuous rain had turned all roads and tracks into a sea of mud, and there appeared to be no respite from it all. Men were continually being saturated with no means of drying out, and this, combined with the incessant shelling of the forward area, began to take its toll.

Cases of 'battle fatigue' were gradually appearing. This was what was known as shell-shock in 'The Last Lot' but was something fairly new to us at that time.

Every man has his breaking point of course, some sooner than others, but this must have been in the back of every thinking man's mind.

You will remember that this small group of people had been through the North African campaign, and after a short, but not peaceful break, entered the scrap for Italy, and always in the 'forward area'.

Just how much shelling and other forms of killing could the mind take?

This form of illness, for that is what it is now acknowledged to be, would take various forms, and if the chap was not known very well to you these symptoms were very hard to spot.

It was never like the typical Hollywood scene where a chap grabbed a machine gun and ran screaming at the enemy, but rather something which transpired over a long period and, if the chap in charge failed to notice the first signs, could rapidly get worse.

There were two common symptoms. One of these was when a chap withdrew into his shell, had no sensible conversation and never answered back even when provoked by his mates. This form of 'fatigue' was seldom understood and the ridiculing would grow to an unnecessary level until at last the bloke would be 'guided' to the M.O. and was seldom heard of again.

The other form of 'fatigue' was when the bloke, and this was much more common, would grow more and more nervous. He would ask to be excused dangerous jobs, such as mine laying or clearing, and would find any number of reasons for not going on them, such as going sick on the slightest pretext, boils, coughs, colds etc., etc. Another symptom was, at the slightest bang, immaterial of what it was, he would be in the nearest hole or ditch trying to dig deeper with his fingers.

This was a state of affairs which, of course, could not continue, and the end of him was in sight. Again it was the path to the M.O. and no return.

The enquiry was made, some forty odd years later, after one of these cases, a personal friend, and one of the stalwarts of No.1 Sub. Still in a mental home and no hope of recovery, was the reply! What a tragedy! And to how many?

On the lighter side of an unpleasant period - it was about now that we acquired the Pig. A medium sized porker from a litter in a deserted farm and, with the aid of a converted trailer attached and adapted to suit the White, we were able to transport around. There was still some time to go before Christmas and so every man in the Sub. was committed to scrounging and saving scraps (including green apples) for the fattening up process.

The butchering should prove no problem because Cyril, one of the lads in the sub. was, so he said, a professional butcher in 'Civvy street'. Well his trade test would be coming up shortly!

Meanwhile the order of the day was 'the pig is to stay in the trailer, no walking or exercise of any kind, just feeding, with refusals of food not accepted. To be cleaned daily'.

Over the next month or so, many were the envious eyes cast on that pig with a fortune offered in bribery 'for just a couple of slices, a bit of stuffing and, just a taste of crackling'. The answer was always the same. There are 12 men plus one to have their fill first and the remainder will be divided amongst the most deserving cases. This, of course, meant to those who could offer the best bribes. It was well known that there was at least one bottle of 'Scotch' among the deserving cases. But more of the pig later, meanwhile he was beginning to fill the trailer.

The attack across the Sangro was about to begin and we knew from the amount of retaliation from 'Ted', that he was well and truly dug in, in strength.

The Official Record, after the battle read, 'General Alexander ordered the main attack by British forces, to go across the Sangro River, the main turning point of the Gustav Line. It was found that they were opposed by six German Divisions (of 14,000 men each) who fought with great tenacity and skill'. You can say that again! 'A combination of deteriorating weather plus the skill of the opposition made progress very slow and extremely costly. Any further attacks were halted until the weather improved.'

Balls! Here's what really happened!

Reconnaissance of the river first from high ground some 500 yards back in order to pinpoint possible crossing places, and the general lie of the land. It could plainly be seen that 'Ted' had complete observation of anything that would take place on or near the river. The high ground on the far bank started at almost river boundary and then climbed in a series of rolling hills into the distance. Astride two of the ridges were villages of fair size, which from the map, appeared to be named Mozzagroggna and Santa Maria (one of a hundred such named in Italy!). While further back, and out of sight from us was the larger town of Lanciano. Both villages were already receiving a pounding from our heavy guns, and for certain would be mere ruins by the time we arrived looking for dry shelter.

Two crossing points were discussed, but this was soon changed to one because of the access situation from this side, i.e.: no road or fairly good track approaching the river, bearing in mind that an Army of heavy (very heavy) vehicles would be using it. Perhaps the alternative could be used as a 'Down' route at a later date, for returning vehicles.

It appeared that on the site selected there had already been an existing bridge which 'Ted' had completely destroyed. There wasn't much sign of it now apart from two clues:

1) A fairly good track from the lateral road leading right down to the edge of the river, and

2) Quite a lot of debris just downstream from this point.

It was to be hoped (very sincerely) that any pier bases were still existing because otherwise we were really in the muck – to put it mildly!

The river itself was fairly fast flowing and so a floating bridge was ruled a non-starter. As things turned out this was a very wise decision because, as you will see, 'someone up there' (or was it 'down there' in this case?) took a hand in matters. In width it was about as wide as the Thames in its lower reaches, so a single span was impossible.

Viewing the overall situation it was obvious that this was going to be one hell of a job, particularly for the Infantry who would – somehow – have to do an assault crossing to establish a bridgehead ready for bridge construction to start. The bridge itself would be the main target in the area for the German gunners, so every movement, never mind how small, would have to be done by night. Not that this would deceive 'Ted' of course, he knew exactly where that track ran down to the river, and so where the bridge would have to be built.

They told us that a man called Churchill (cigars and brandy) said that the river had to be crossed, never mind how many 'Teds' were over the other side, so who were we to argue with that.

The first opposing factor was something that had not even been considered at the planning stage, all thoughts were on

'Ted' and just what opposition he would put up. This factor was the rise and fall of the river. Imagine a river rising in the spine of the country, the Appenines, some 6000 to 9000 feet high and with a relatively short run to the sea, and with numerous tributaries feeding into it. All that was needed was one good day's rain to increase the volume of water with a sudden rush. Torrential rain would produce a rise of 15 feet plus, in a very short time, and turn a fairly placid river into a raging torrent. But of course there were no locals about to warn us of this fact, everyone had fled the area. They valued their skins more highly than wordly goods or chattels, and in any case 'Tedeschi potare via tutte' - remember? - except, of course, one lucky(?) pig.

Establishing the width of the river was very important and, because it was essential to know the amount of bridging stores required, educated guesses were not good enough, it had to be measured physically!

The only method possible was to cross it. In total darkness and absolute silence, no boats because of the current, so get wading! And look out for the mines which he must have scattered pretty thickly around here.

The small group that crossed were roped together and as their leader progressed, he established the depth of water and (thank goodness) the position of the existing pier bases. The length of rope, with due allowance, gave the river width and, again thankfully, it was found that the water at this point was only armpit depth on the average man. God help the short arses if wading for all became necessary!

Based on these figures, the Bailey stores necessary for the job could be whistled up. The supply of these stores should by this stage of the campaign have been a highly organised affair and, to a degree it was but, with roads washed out by heavy rain, and choked by a thousand and one vehicles, long delays were nearly always on the cards, and of course, it was always the poor old Sapper who took the blame for the bridge being late. Sorry to natter on so much, but I was only trying to give you a complete picture of the situation.

One or two small incidents here are worth relating. The events started with the request being made for a volunteer to pick up stores from our last 'resting place', an old brickworks on the Vasto road. The message asked for an intelligent bloke, so I volunteered.

By the time the return journey was made it was well into the darkness of the following night and, with no lights available, it became one hell of a job to find the Unit who, in my absence had moved down nearer the river. Eventually HQ was found (kisses all round) and polite enquiries made such as "Where the hell have you been, Rome?" etc., etc. But also from the Sgt./Major, "How's that pig of yours?"

It was coming up to Christmas, and naturally he was enquiring after the pig's health. A passing remark said something to the effect that No. 1 Sub. really did appreciate a drop of Scotch!

Back to the serious side of things. In reply to "Where are the Sub?" came the answer, "Your blokes have taken over a farmhouse on the left of the track leading down to the river. They are out on a job where you won't find them tonight, so keep your head down and (ominously) good luck!"

In complete darkness the farm was duly located, completely deserted of course, with only the blokes kit scattered about the concrete floor. This was luxury indeed, our normal floor would be ankle deep in mud. My stretcher bed could not be found – the blokes had it out with them – so it was two blankets on the floor and sweet dreams of home.

But not for long! Within minutes of 'kissing that blond on the corner', the whole farmhouse experienced something unknown in it's previous history – it lifted at least 4" off its foundations as a barrage of 1000 plus guns of all calibre opened up. All were on intensive fire: this was obviously the start of the assault across the river. Dante's *Inferno* was a quiet church service compared with this.

How can the noise be described to one who hasn't experienced it? Imagine standing on the platform of a station and the old steam express roaring through! – that's about the noise of one heavy shell passing close overhead. Now multiply that by a thousand and also realise that they are all landing just a short distance ahead. The world had gone completely mad!

After several minutes of this unbearable noise one became completely deaf, and with the deafness came an agonising pain in the ears. Stuffing the ears did not help and the awareness that permanent damage was being caused was ever present.

Then out of this first nightmare another one started, rats! Yes rats! A whole horde of them came charging into the room from, I suppose, the barns and outbuildings, obviously terrified from the sound of the guns, and who could blame them?

In the darkness there appeared to be hundreds of them – were they looking to me for protection? – I never stopped to really find out, but just took off through the door and straight into the cab of the White Scout Car, there to shiver out the rest of the night!

The barrage went on for some time and it became more and more obvious that this really was a big attack across the river. Soon it changed to the continuous rattle of machine gun fire interspersed with the crump of mortars. Were my twelve mixed up in this? And if so what were they doing?

The noise of battle said that the slaughter of men on a great scale on both sides was taking place, and for what reason? Not, surely, because a group of people wanted to cross a lousy river? Or was it because a freedom loving people had to stop a mad house decorator leading a power-worshipping people into the conquest of Europe and beyond? Whichever way it was, I prayed to God (How did he get into this? The slaughter outside said that he did not exist!) that my twelve were alright. Father and Mother at age 21? Of blokes twice that age!

The unmistakable crumps of the 'Sobbing Sisters' were now landing quite regularly, together with the whack of his shells, so a stiff fight seemed to be on the cards.

I had long since given up hope of the farmhouse surviving this madness, because by now the shells were falling thick and fast all around, so obviously the armour of the White was the best protection.

Daylight at last, cold but dry, with a fairly clear sky. This was good news indeed because now the RAF would soon sort 'Ted' out on the far bank.

How right that line of thought was! Mitchells first in groups of twelve, plastering the bank and ridge opposite, quickly followed by many and varied types of aircraft with the dear old Spit buzzing around everywhere, probably looking for Mutt or Jeff and family. What a difference to North Africa! If 'Ted' had dominance here he could have 'taken out' a thousand targets a day.

Something new in battle now occurred, new to us anyway, and awesome it was to witness. The news came later as to the cause of it.

Apparently a small force of Infantry had fought their way across that river of blood in the hours of darkness, but were being confronted by a strong force of German tanks, so they called for air strikes and here came the answer. Rocket firing Typhoons!

This was a weapon never before seen on our front, but as you witnessed it in action you had the feeling that the war was won! As the first aircraft dived to its target the thinking amongst the troops was 'here we go for a burst of machine gun fire', but when those rockets were released with that terrible roar, and that trail of fire shot down to destroy its target, it became apparent that the Germans had lost any chance of resisting the Allied advance in Italy. How could they win against such a weapon?

As each plane used up its rockets, so it returned to the 'queue' to dive again using its machine guns. Was there still sanity in the world?

Now the blokes were coming back. Filthy and covered in stinking mud, but twelve faces which was pleasing to see. The usual friendly greetings followed, "You lucky bastard getting out of that lot!" etc., etc. Then in answer to the question, "What happened last night?" The story came out.

Three British Divisions attacked after the barrage, lst, 5th and 78th, the latter being our old friends from Medjez-El-Bab, nicknamed 'Monty's Butchers' taken from their Div. sign the battleaxe.

The slaughter that followed was totally unnecessary, and predictable by all who took part in the battle. Where were our brilliant leaders? Why was all this carnage ordered to take place when all that was necessary was for us to hold down a German Army in Italy, so relieving the Eastern and eventually the Western Fronts?

The orders were for a frontal attack across the river. This meant wading in cold fast flowing water, armpit deep on an average man (again God help the short-arse!) against heavy and concentrated fire. 'Ted' was dug in, in strongly prepared positions of months ago and, of course, by nature of the river, knew exactly where the crossing would be attempted. In order to protect these positions, he had thickly sown the whole area with mines, mostly anti-personnel, our old enemy the 'S' mine. Casualties from these amongst the Infantry were very high, particularly on the home river bank.

Two main criticisms will be made here:

1) Why when the Infantry ran into so many mines, wasn't the attack called off until the Sappers could do their job? To be fair here, one local commander did this, and that's how my twelve were involved, resulting in much lighter casualty figures.

2) Why not wait to give the RAF a chance to 'take him out'? Several days of what we had just been seeing would surely have achieved this? Our Bailey would have been constructed under cover of darkness, over which tanks and Infantry could pass with dry feet.

Amen to criticism for a while. There will be more for sure. There are military cemeteries in Italy today which should have been fields for growing corn and orchards of apples.

The other news was that another small force of Infantry had managed to cross at a shallower place, and had actually been able to get several six-pounder anti-tank guns across with them. They were now isolated but still trying to enlarge their bridgehead. The planners 'up top' apparently now turned to the Sappers again.

"Can you get a bridge across in a hurry?"

"Yes," said our 'top brass', "in two nights."

The 'bottom brass', those who had to do or die said definitely not because, although appreciating the situation in full and realising its urgency, firstly the bank had to be cleared of mines, a mammoth job in itself, and secondly, the pier bases for the bridge had to be found before any construction work at all could begin. When and if the bases were found, how could piers be built to support the bridge, bearing in mind that only Christchurch Cribs were available, a metal rectangular grid of three cubes, so called after the bridging training area at Christchurch near Bournemouth – was there such a place still in this mad world? The only other material available was the Bailey panels themselves. These could be placed on end off the bases, pinned and braced together. Brilliant but highly doubtful because of the height required.

Eventually a combination of the two was decided upon and, tongue in cheek, the necessary stores ordered. This was by far the longest bridge we had tackled to date and was certainly more than double in length to our previous achievements.

The day was given to scraping and cleaning mud off bodies and equipment, then sleeping until dusk when the mine clearing job would start in earnest.

For my sins the day was spent in preparing all the gear necessary to carry out the work. First on the list were the mine detectors, the most important piece of equipment of the lot.

Gone, thank God, were the old days of prodding with bayonets or the old Polish detectors, we now had, as before mentioned, brand new Yankie detectors, and excellent they were too! Light to handle and very efficient at detecting buried metal. Then came the other thousand and one bits and pieces, tracing tapes, hot cross buns (remember those mine markers?) a supply of safety wires, to neutralise as and when found, the stretcher, thick with mud but please, unnecessary for use this coming night.

Dusk arrived and with it a drizzling rain, fine stuff at first then a good old dose of torrential Italian rain, the sort of stuff you get with no end in sight. The journey down to the river, through thick squelching mud, was made on the existing track. Goodness only knows what the fields either side were like now, but it was pitch dark and they were quite invisible. Nothing to disturb the journey from 'Ted', most of his stuff was passing overhead.

The awful and I mean awful, smell of war was everywhere, sickly, sweet, once experienced never forgotten. There were torn bodies about.

All stores had to be humped by hand over that long wet journey and the 'moans and groans' of Churchill's and Montgomery's ancestry were to be heard on all sides. About fifty yards from the river bank was the collecting point for all and sundry, and here all the Subs. were divided up so that their full sweep would clear at least 250 yards of the bank.

The usual drill would follow with tracing tape laid to show the cleared paths for the tanks and Infantry to follow. Fine up to now but here was a difference. Some miles back a large number of searchlights were combing the sky, obviously looking for enemy aircraft, and these threw a moonlight glow over the area which proved a blessing in disguise, one could actually see a hand in front of face.

Shortly after this Sangro episode, the system of using searchlights in this manner was adopted nightly, and proved very effective, it was nicknamed, naturally, Monty's Moonlight.

Sweeping began in almost knee deep mud which almost prevented one leg being dragged out to replace the other. Progress was proving painfully slow and the question was asked, 'why sweep 250 yards of the bank when all personnel would be using the track only to get on to the bridge?' The answer to this was, of course, that the whole of this area would be required as assembly points and dumps for the bridging stores.

The next few hours were ones that would stay with me for the rest of my days. Several mines were discovered within the first few minutes, but being buried in a sea of mud did not need digging out, instead No's. 2 & 3 would reach down to elbow depth to bring up a large lump of mud with a mine inside it to be cleaned off and (if free of booby traps) insert the safety pin.

So far so good, but then the shock and horror of last night's battle suddenly erupted. Instead of mines, No's. 2 & 3 were beginning to bring up bits of torso of which arms and legs, or parts of, were most prevalent. These poor devils had been lost in that dreadful sea of mud. Retching could be heard on all sides as these objects were passed back to be stacked on the trackside.

Who could have blamed any of those blokes for refusing to carry on? Surely only those people with red tabs sitting in their dry billets some miles back!

Religion next took a bashing. It is a well known fact under conditions similar to these, particularly if one's life is in danger, it is the recognised thing to pray. It doesn't matter to whom the prayer is being addressed as long as the person making it believes that it's helping him or even protecting him. To my knowledge 100% of people followed this natural action but some were loath to admit it. This saying of prayers is normally in thought, or done quietly to oneself, but in this particular instance when the horror of it all was gripping everybody, there came a loud and clear voice quoting the words of the 23rd Palm 'The Lord is my shepherd, He leadeth me in green pastures, etc., etc.,' to my left, probably being said by one of the recent replacements. The sound of this had a grating effect on nerves already at breaking point so, easing my way in his direction, I was about to gently tell him to say his prayers to himself, when a voice from the darkness behind did the job for me: "If you don't shut up I'll ram my bayonet up your arse!"

That voice was never traced and that prayer never heard again.

Then it happened, something we all knew was bound to come, our first casualty of the night. A terrific bang from our neighbouring Sub. and several voices, one shouting, one crying! Soon the words became clear, "Wilf's gone, Wilf's gone!" This could mean only one thing, Wilf, who was a particularly good friend of mine, and did the same job, had been killed on a mine.

It turned out to be rather more serious than first thought. Wilf was killed and his two nearest chaps badly wounded. Did that thick mud help to save others near by? My prayer regarding the stretcher had not been answered.

Now 'Ted' took a hand. Up to now it had been his big stuff only which was passing safely overhead but, after the explosion on the bank, he gave us his undivided attention. 88s, mortars and, the worst of the lot, his Nebelwerfers (Sobbing sisters) remember those bastards?

This lot caused further nightmares. To save one's skin there was no alternative but to dive into that stinking mess, deep enough to swallow a man, and not knowing if mines were below you, or even bits of torso!

All this, and work to the bridge was yet to be started. It was nearly dawn before the job was completed, and a sorry looking bunch of blokes it was who finally dragged themselves back to what was now a ruin of a farmhouse, but heaven after that lot.

Living conditions were vile. Clothes and bodies covered in that stinking mud. Skins could be scraped but clothes had to be dumped in wet piles until time could be found to sort them out.

Dry, or rather, semi-dry clothes would have to be found for the following night's work.

Sleep did not come easy to anyone, although totally exhausted, because mostly of the thoughts of what was to come on that night. Would 'Ted' realise what was happening and give us hell? Would casualties be heavy etc., etc.?

Some time during that day panic reigned when a terrific barrage of Bofor and 37AA guns opened up on a whole group of German fighter planes, they came sweeping up the river at zero feet, obviously looking for any bridge under construction. Thank goodness they were one day too early! These were the first enemy aircraft we had seen in 'our' sky for some time. Shades of Africa!

Before moving on - there are a body (or two rather) of people who should here be mentioned. They are the Salvation Army and Women's' Voluntary Service. These two groups of people (always women) would turn up when most needed, usually when the 'shit was flying', with a van of heavenly tea and cakes. Can that be credited? Not of course, right in the forward area but, as in this case, at the junction of 'our' track with the main lateral road, which would be some 500 or 600 yards back from the river bank, and so well within shelling range. Remembering the days of youth, the 'Sally Army' was almost a figure of fun – with jokes about whose turn was it to carry the banner etc. But just see how a set of circumstances can alter a well established opinion. Today, my generation, particularly the blokes who participated consider them to be one of the finest voluntary bodies of any people doing that kind of work. It was well worth losing an hour or so's sleep in order to drown in tea and cakes, and to listen to the voice of a sane and calm English woman telling us just how bad the weather was at home when she left last month! Was it all a dream? Or was this the sort of thing that helped to prevent many more cases of 'battle fatigue'.

Some very true words were written by DE Curtis during the 2nd World War.

These come from 'Death's Harvest'.

Around these green fields torn, death lies in every form
Broken mangled bodies that once were men.
A shapeless crumpled heap, some as though in sleep
Groups of four or five or sometimes ten.

We push on through the din, though our line is wearing thin
Then halt to hold more firm our hard won gains.

Quick, every red rimmed eye, is turned towards the sky
To catch the tell tale glint of planes.

They come in one by one, with cannon bomb and gun
We dive beneath the tanks to dodge their fire
The men on Ack Ack guns, fling off empty drums
They work like hell, too scared to seem to tire.
The planes come screaming down, and sometimes even
drown, the remainder of the battle's din and roar.
When their devil's work is done, they climb up to the sun
And we feel a ghostly silence reign once more.

Where the battle rolled its tread, we gather up the dead
And lay them in the ground near where they fell.
Hat or helmet give the name, an officer his cane
We lay across the grave as well
Whatever be its name, these forever will remain
Just Britain and the price men had to pay.

We learned, after the Sangro crossing, that the artillery barrage was made by 9 Regiments of Field Artillery and 3 Medium Regiments. This of course was additional to the AA Regiments and mortars.

CHAPTER TWENTY FIVE

THE BRIDGE

All stores, and there were masses of them for a bridge of over (from memory) 400 feet in length, and of double panel construction, had been off-loaded during darkness, along one side of the track leading to the river.   This of course was essential because of the depth of mud once off the track.

The overall battle situation was that the small group of Infantry who had bravely forded the river were still holding out, although 'Ted' was giving them a whole lot of attention. On the home bank tens of thousands of Infantry and hundreds of tanks were waiting to cross once the bridge was completed. Meanwhile the grapevine said that there was to be another attempt to get more Infantry across by night, using a ford some way downstream from the bridge. PBI – Poor Bloody Infantry – expressed the feelings and sympathy of every thinking man.

Because of the size of the job, the whole Company was to be employed on the construction of the bridge.   The sequence would be firstly to find, establish and build the piers, construct the bridge and then connect up the approach and exit roads to existing hard surfaces. All this of course, in spite of 'Ted' sitting on the high ground opposite, doing his best to stop what was going on.

The river was behaving itself but was quite fast flowing, and despite this current, several ropes were strung across in order to help the people getting stores into place for pier construction.

It was amazing how many sleepers appeared from nowhere – the Italian railway people must be very generous! Another source of amazement was just how quietly several hundred men could work in the dark. Silence of course, was essential, one bad slip and it was curtains for everyone.

Several times during the night 'Ted' sent a flurry of shells and mortars screaming over, obviously suspecting that something was going on but not really knowing what, and inevitably some of the chaps were hit by shrapnel. Among these was one of my 'leading lights', Geordie, surely a man amongst men whose wit and humour kept us sane when all were at their wits end. His was a language of its own, most certainly not English, and his songs when drinking time was here just had to be learned by all and sundry: 'The Bladon Races' 'Keep your feet still Geordie boy' and, I think, 'Her name is Kitty Butterworth (she liked her beer)' were all part of his repertoire. Was this goodbye to Geordie after coming all this way together? We never saw him again. So old chap if you are alive and able, there's always a welcome in the hills of Wales for you!

A replacement would come within days. Still the job went on.

Pier construction was just about finished at first light so it was then back to the holiday villa for a soya link and porridge breakfast, biscuits (very hard) - (I wonder why they were sometimes called Breezy Blackpool?) and, of course, tea beautiful tea. Then it was heads down, 'Ted' permitting, for a few hours.

Most unusual during that day, there were several 'sweeps' by German fighters, low and fast, but no actual strafing took place, not in our little area at least. Was this just a show of strength, perhaps for the morale of his troops? or maybe he was telling us to keep our heads down, we are not finished yet!

After dusk that evening the bridge construction work seemed to go with a swing. Everything seemed to be falling into place (some bits into the river) and apart from a few (sorry many) Ff's and B's, the launching nose and first few bays were soon completed.

The complicated business of spanning from bankseat to first pier was achieved via counterweights on the Rocking rollers, and the 'kick' of the launching nose. The words from 'up top' were well done lads, a few more nights like this and the bridge will soon be over. Then it started to rain. The next day it rained, and for the whole of the following night, rain, torrential rain! Not the rain of this country, but one continual outburst, until everyone and everything was completely saturated.

Then the river started to rise, slowly at first, barely visible until it was realised that our newly constructed piers were now under water with the river still rising. It would be a miracle if those piers held out against such a volume of water, which was now rapidly approaching flood proportions.

Daylight arrived and still the bridge survived. Another 24 hours was the estimated completion time. Now it was back to the farm, but with an around the clock watch on the bridge. All sorts of ideas were suggested to strengthen the piers – anchors upstream, extra weight on the structure etc., etc., but nothing, yes nothing, could change the inevitable end, and the bridge went!

Panic and chaos reigned! From the sag in the structure it was obvious that two centre piers had gone completely but, by good fortune they were not adjacent, or the whole structure would have been swept down the river there and then.

At this stage 'Ted' appeared to appreciate the situation and decided to put a 'stonk' on the bridge area. By good luck again, there was nobody working on the deck at the time because it was hit by several shells with some of the panels suffering severe damage. The situation was now critical. Word was coming back across the river that there were quite a few wounded troops to be got across for life saving operations, ammunition and stores of all types were short, and unless action was taken immediately there was danger of 'Ted' overrunning the bridgehead.

News was coming through that a Company of Sappers had managed to build a single/single Bailey somewhere on the river and this was being used for foot traffic.

Later that day came the news that this bridge had suffered from river damage too, and later still had been totally swept away, but most of the wounded had been evacuated, supplies taken over and several battalions of Infantry had managed to cross.

DUCKs were now brought into our patch, particularly to evacuate the wounded, but they had one hell of a job battling against that force of water, and were soon called off, so there was once again no means of crossing the Sangro.

It was now conference time for the 'Top Brass'.

This consisted of three senior Sapper Officers walking gingerly across the bridge, gingerly because at any moment the whole structure might be carried away by that mighty torrent and, because it was now broad daylight, 'Ted' might take another hand in matters.

Having successfully crossed and partly recrossed, it was decided to try a Jeep. Journey across OK but on the return, when almost home, came a terrific bang from the pier area on the enemy bank, and the whole bridge in that area dropped at least six feet and the pier lurched over as if to compete with the leaning tower of Pisa. There was now no support for about 170ft length of the bridge which was sagging dangerously near to the water level.

This indeed was a serious situation. We were back to square one with no means of crossing that river. Could 'Ted' possibly know what had happened and take advantage of it? It was heartbreaking to think of all those lives already lost in vain and, obviously, many more to come in making the crossing.

Morale was at a very low point at this time, what with continual soakings, no real respite from the shelling and mortaring and now the defeat of all efforts. Perhaps this danger was not appreciated by the 'Top Brass', but, most certainly, down at ground level feelings were at zero.

Just about now, to cap it all, 'Ted' started to bomb, in broad daylight, the Infantry positions across the river. Was this the start of an all-out attack because he had read the situation? The RAF were caught off guard and several heavy raids were carried out before the 'Spits' arrived. There followed the only two bright spots in an otherwise very grim sort of day. One was the glorious sight of two German bombers coming down in flames (they never showed up again for days) and the second was that of three very senior Sapper Officers running for their lives off a sagging Bailey.

Decision time had arrived: do we abandon the bridge and dismantle, or do we attempt to salvage and strengthen by some as yet unknown means?

Fate appeared to take a hand here because it suddenly became obvious that the river level was falling, just as quickly as it had risen. A typically Italian phenomena.

This really was help from above. Amends were being made, at high level, for His absenteeism during the past few days.

The decision was taken to construct new and stronger piers, at a slightly lower height, support the bridge meanwhile, and then jack down the structure to the new pier level. Really this was a brilliant idea, if it would only work. A lot depended on 'Ted' because it was decided to work, provided the water level had fallen sufficiently, from dawn around the clock, until the bridge was opened to the (estimated) 100,000 troops now waiting to cross, with their relevant tanks, trucks, guns, etc., etc.

The sequence and efficiency of the attempt to rescue that bridge from near disaster was proof indeed that, when the need arose, the British engineer was among the best in the world. Speaking from the point of view of 'the man on the ground' where all the expletives, and the effort, originated, it somehow seemed inevitable that success would come in the end.

Somewhere in the middle of the operation, which, by the way, took several days, there suddenly appeared a group of Russian Engineer officers who obviously had heard of the engineering work being carried out on the Italian front and had travelled a long way to learn first hand. Somehow I found myself as a representative of the lower ranks – selected? – well detailed anyway, to explain to Boris, Ivan and Co. exactly what was going on. Fortunately some spoke broken English so, together with my broken English, they appeared to understand most of what was going on, and were full of praise for the operation. What a cheerful bunch they were and, after the Vodka bottle was passed around a few times and toasts duly drunk to Father Stalin and Winston Churchill, it was unanimously decided that the Nazi hordes would all be wrapped up within twelve months.

New pier bases were found among the debris of the river bed and the unbelievably successful operation of filling sandbags with a dry concrete mix of strong proportions began. These then, by the hundred, were lowered into position on the pier bases, keeping to the perimeter. Where the bases were above water level, the same operation was carried out by teams of bricklayers (and a mason) building a one brick thick skin with all speed and possible efficiency. I felt sure that old 'Bill' was watching my mortar joints from somewhere down in the depths of the river, and every time the 'Cooee drill' took place, he received a mouthful of Sangro. (Please!)

Where all the cement etc. came from really was a miracle because the supply was endless. A master stroke now followed the initial operation. Liquid concrete was poured into the huge perimeters created by the bricks and sandbags. This was an operation new to us, but a Company of Canadian Sappers had been located in the vicinity with the necessary pumping equipment to do the job, and were very happy to oblige.

Hundreds of gallons, (or should that be cubic yards?) of concrete were used until the piers were high and solid enough to withstand the Sangro's next onslaught. It was to be hoped that we were a good many miles further on by then.

Next operation was the crib piers on which the bridge would eventually rest. The stores for these, while the concrete was setting, had to be ferried from the lateral road where they had been off loaded. During one of these trips in the White armoured car, on the narrow track leading back from the bridge, we came face to face with an open-topped Humber staff car. As we had already travelled 400 of the 500 yards journey, it was the driver of the staff car who should back up (it being impossible to pass) and he was told to do so in no uncertain terms. In any case we were much more solid and heavier than he was and therefore ready to stand up to any nonsense a 'jumped up' Staff-captain may care to dish out. Two figures were seated in the back and when one of the figures stood up, I heard the words from my gang, "Blimey its Monty!!"

This little chap with a big beret then said, "Corporal we will reverse and I want you to follow closely to us to the cross-roads."

Well having done nothing wrong, except to swear at his driver, we duly followed. On arrival at the lateral junction we were amazed to see the large numbers and variety of troops about the place, British, Canadians, Poles to name but a few, were everywhere.

Someone yelled for all within earshot to gather around and He stood up in the car and started to explain that He was sorry that they had all been kept waiting to cross the river, and how these Sappers were doing a magnificent job and they would be all across soon etc., etc. Then came, "I will be leaving you all soon for duty elsewhere with very sad feelings etc., etc., but feel sure that you will give my successor Gen. Sir Oliver Leese (I think from memory) your full support."

The other chap in the car stood up and acknowledged.

Monty then handed me several cartons of Player cigarettes saying "Please distribute amongst your chaps," and then he was gone.

The first and last sighting of the great man. He to Blighty, to prepare for the 'second front', and me to the mud and muck of the Sangro.

Because there were only four of 'our chaps' in that White, those Players would last a very long time. Actually they were shared between the seven smokers of the twelve in No. 1 Sub.

'Victory V's'! What a stupid name to give to an awful weed masquerading as a cigarette. These were the only ones available to the troops for a very long time and had to be smoked to be appreciated. Manufactured somewhere in the back streets (of Cairo?) by a native firm who lacked complete respect for the recipient's lungs, their approximate specification was 90% camel dung, 9% desert sand and the remainder tobacco. Whoever arranged the supply of millions of those weeds must have received a back hander large enough to live in comfort for the remainder of his days. You will now appreciate the value of Monty's handout, they really were like gold-dust.

Back to the bridge. The concrete received its full setting time, thanks to 'Ted' behaving, although there were two further strafing raids by his fighters, but not actually on the bridge. The piers completed, it was now time to jack-up, complete the resting points and jack down again on to the permanent bases.

Everything worked perfectly with very few Ff's apparent. It could have been the training ground back home, and soon many thousands of vehicles a day were passing over the bridge.

'Ted' was on the run again but not too far this time. He had crossed the Moro river and dug-in around and in the town of Ortona, right on the Adriatic, the extreme eastern point of the 'Gustav Line'.

The task of taking the town was given to the 1st Canadian Division, a very fine body of troops indeed, but 'Ted'was determined to hold and soon the casualties were mounting.

The signal came through that urgent Sapper help was required, so up sticks and away again.

It was now December 17th, 1943 and all thoughts (of No. 1 Sub. at least) were turning to the 'Day of the Pig'. Would we be in a position to cook and eat him in the luxury of some farmhouse?

Or would it be that rain, mud, muck and whatsoever else would come to sabotage the feast?

When we left the Sangro, it was about a month from when we had arrived. Tired, sadder, more experienced in modern methods of a Sapper's war, and really down-hearted to see new faces replacing the familiar ones 'that had left'.

We landed at Salerno, holidays with pay
Jerry brought his band out,
To cheer us on our way,
Showed us the sights and gave us tea
We all sang songs, the beer was free
To welcome the 'D-Day' Dodgers. To sunny Italy.

CHAPTER TWENTY SIX

THE FIRST 'WINTER LINE' – 1943-44

The River Moro was a totally different barrier to cross than the Sangro: less than half its width and, in most places, having much steeper sides almost resembling a ravine type formation. The amount of water flowing through the gorge was no problem, and provided 'Ted' would allow us a clear run, the bridge, which he had totally destroyed two days ago, would soon be replaced.

But a peaceful period was just not on the cards. He, 'Ted', had sunk a lot of his tanks into the basements of various buildings of the town and these were proving virtually impossible to shift by normal means i.e.: anti-tank guns or shell-fire. The Canadian Infantry were fighting almost house by house and using hand held flame throwers against the Panzers.

Some areas of this ancient port were built in a fortress type construction with walls several feet thick. The Germans again took advantage of this fact and manned them with their best troops. Again, normal artillery could not penetrate these defences and so other methods were called for. A little further inland was a battery of British 7.2 howitzers, a very heavy gun indeed, and they were quick to respond to the Canadians' call for help.

It was quite a sight to see those four monsters taking up position just slightly downstream from our bridge site. Thank God they were on our side and thanks also that, for a change, they would not be firing over our heads when the noise would mean the destruction of any normal hearing.

The sighting of these guns had, by necessity, to be either below ground level i.e.: dug-in, or protected by the nature of the surrounding ground formation because, just as soon as they opened fire they became the target for retaliation from all that

206

'Ted' could throw at them. It was not a prospect to be enthusiastic about, seeing as we were in the close proximity.

The Battery Commander decided to place the guns within the protection of the rather steep sides of the river banks. This was a good idea because it avoided the necessity of digging in, or filling numerous sandbags, but still allowed the guns to fire howitzer style as designed.

At dusk a strong force of Canadian Infantry began an attack on the town which was supported by a very heavy artillery barrage. Most of these guns were firing from behind and were creating an unbearable noise as the shells passed overhead, a noise which one could never get used to because of the horror of it all. The 7.2s joined in the killing and nearly blew the beginnings of the bridge off its bankseat! The German artillery were quick to respond and very soon a full scale war was taking place. The only blessing, if that is what it can be called, was that there were so many guns firing it was impossible for him to trace the position of the 7.2s.

Then it started to rain. Saturating rain which just kept on and on, drenching everyone and everything unlucky enough to be in its target area. While the attack went on so did the rain. All night and through the next day.

By dusk it was realised that the attack had been a failure and casualties were very high.

What a totally unnecessary waste of lives. Brave men, good men who were sacrificed for a minor town of no importance, when surely it was only essential to hold down the opposing German divisions, so preventing their use on the Russian front or elsewhere. This madness was becoming very hard for the man on the ground to understand.

Then came catastrophe! Just like big brother Sangro, the Moro suddenly started to rise and soon became a raging torrent. Nobody, of course, had thought of warning the Battery Commander of the danger of heavy rain, even after the very hard lesson just learned, and away went the guns. All four of them just like children's toys, rolling and pitching away downstream. Very fortunately there was no loss of life because the night sentries had been able to give sufficient warning for all personnel to scramble clear.

This time the bridge was high enough, and without piers, to escape the flood, and, 'Pig-day' was only two days away! Surely that was some consolation from it all. Christmas comfort, for that one day at least, was high in the mind of everyone and a desperate search was taking place for a reasonable billet. No. 1 Sub. was lucky in this and a small cottage type building was commandeered several hundred yards back from the banks of the Moro.

Here a surprise was waiting. It transpired that the civilian owner of the house was living in the basement. Imagine that, a civilian living in the front line area with all that shot and shell flying about! Firstly when the Germans occupied the area, the British and Canadian artillery put down several barrages, and now that 'Ted' had retreated some distance it was his turn with guns and mortars.

The surprise of his presence was soon diminished when his character was revealed. It turned out that he had spent a good many years in the USA. A thick set heavy type of bloke in late middle age. When he spoke it was the vernacular of the Bronx that emerged in a strong Italian accent. We were face to face with Al Capone! The British were all bootiful boys! and the Germans were 'Goddam sons of bitches'. This attitude to the British persisted throughout our acquaintance with 'Old Nick', and some of his stories about the evil Germans were repeated so many times that one almost believed the accounts of 'Ted' stripping the whole area of anything that could be moved. He must have had enough large trucks to fill most of the roads of Italy.

When 'Nick' was at last made to understand that we were taking over his house and outbuildings he wasn't too happy but, eventually, as long as we kept those 'Goddam krauts' away he was pacified.

208

'Nick' turned out to be a useful ally and in addition to assisting Cyril(the butcher) in killing and preparing The Pig, he supplied us with as many vegetables as we could eat, potatoes, swede, greens etc., in exchange for a portion of pig and a few unwanted tins of 'Compo' rations.

There was more than enough of that gorgeous animal to go around, and so the other deserving cases had their share as promised long ago. Several bottles of Scotch appeared as if by magic and coupled with 'Nick's' vino bianco, a truly marvellous Christmas Day was had by one and all.

Because the bridge had been completed in good time and was unaffected by the flood, Bob made sure that all personnel had as much time off as possible, and every advantage was taken.

Here it is pointed out that in no way did 'Ted' respect the day. Instead of 'Stille Nacht Heilige Nacht' as in 1914, he kept up a heavy barrage of shells and mortars. So much so that 'Old Nick' at times had a cellar full of bootiful drunken Sappers, who were in 'fine voice' and rendering such arias as 'O Solo Mio' and 'Mamma Se Tanto Felice' in (almost) perfect Italian. Let 'Ted' send 'em over, this was the one night of the year when they just sounded like Nov. 5th in the garden back home.

The Christmas 'holiday' period brought no respite whatsoever from the continual bombardment by either side, and during periods of good weather, strafing and bombing raids were carried out too. It was during one of these German raids that another of the lads was hit by shrapnel. This meant another one lost out of the original 13 of No. 1 Sub, making 7 altogether, so leaving 5 of the originals. With so many things designed to wound or kill flying about, it was little wonder that one's thoughts turned to the question. Who would be next? And by what method? When lying in a mud hole of a night time these thoughts just had to be obliterated. Making mad passionate love to that beautiful blonde around the corner back home helped a lot!

The Canadian Infantry were having a hell of a time of it during these last few days of December. It appeared (so rumour had it) that Hitler had ordered his troops to 'bleed the Allies white' before giving up any ground. This they were doing very effectively.

How strange it was to hear those big Canadian soldiers being referred to as Princess Patricia's Own and Van Doos Regiment etc. What fine troops they were and always showed great affection for the British. One recollection will always remain in the mind. In the middle of all the rubble they had set up a canteen selling coffee and buns. In or near the entrance a purposely made sign said 'All British Troops Welcome'. What a gesture of friendship amongst all this killing, and how marvellous it was, after coffee and buns to smoke their Sweet Caporal cigarettes. Nobody offered a 'Victory V' in exchange! The presence of camel dung was too embarrassing!

News came through around this time that the New Zealanders who had been on our left during the battle for the Sangro had lost 1,600 men during that crossing. That was one Division only, what of the three British Divisions on our front? The 8th Indian also and the Canadians? Never! And I say again, never was the sacrifice worth it!

We were to co-operate with the New Zealand Division later, in fact, from memory it was a whole year later. Could that be possible? Another year of this type of sacrifice?

Numerous booby traps were now being found by the Canadians in Ortona, and these were causing many casualties to the Infantry as they fought street by street.

At that time the Section was engaged on another bridge and so were not called upon to clear those pretty nasty bits of work.

That fell to the Canadian Engineers whose casualty figures for doing the job were pretty high.

The particular bridge for our operation was one the Canadians had built earlier and was now in danger of collapsing because:-

1) the flooding Moro had washed away one bankseat and

2) it was in constant use by heavy vehicles and tanks which were in excess of the weight for which it was intended. A wonderful feature of the Bailey is the fact that, provided the bankseat supports are strong enough, it can be fitted with extra panels which greatly increase its strength.

Two things of importance now happened which were to affect the course of the war in Italy over the next few months.

The first was that the Canadians had taken Ortona and 'Ted' was retreating into his Gustav Line. This now appeared to be a ridge of high ground overlooking the Moro and running between the towns of Ortona and Orsogna, and from there across the central mountain spine to Cassino and the west coast.

The second was bad news indeed. It had started to snow! Sitting now in the comfort of home, many years later, that statement appears very insignificant, particularly to a layman with no idea of warfare conditions.

The snow, combined alternatively with sleet and heavy rain, soon turned the whole area into a quagmire. The scene was one of utter chaos. Literally thousands of vehicles were being bogged down to their axles in thick stinking mud. Most Italian roads run laterally across the country, and those that there were running north/south appeared to be little better than minor roads, that is with a few exceptions of course.

These roads soon disappeared under mud, and the drainage ditches on either side were soon claiming numerous victims. The Germans, sitting up on high ground in positions prepared months previously, knew that the danger of an allied attack was now fading fast.

It was time to call a halt to proceedings. The messages coming down the line from 'up top' were to consolidate on our present positions. This, thank goodness, meant that there were to be no more suicidal frontal attacks, at least, for the time being, and this was exactly as it turned out for a period, believe it or not, of several months.

What a strange war this was turning out to be! The overall picture was one of complete stalemate on the whole of the 8th Army front on the Adriatic coast, but savage and very costly attacks – casualty wise – going on the other end of the Gustav Line at Cassino.

What the man on the ground had great difficulty understanding was that here was a very narrow country with a very high mountainous spine, which therefore was far better for defence in prepared positions, than for the type of warfare being pursued by the Allies, that is, suicidal frontal attacks. On both coasts were stretches of flat and sandy beaches which were ideal for beach landings and, of course, no prepared positions from which to defend them. Why not a series of leap frogging assaults instead of trying to dig 'him' out of a strong defence. Surely a very strong landing would cut off the German forces to the south of it.

For the 8th Army it was rest and consolidation, that is rest from attack, but in the meantime continuing training for any future operations which could be foreseen.

One of these must have been for a wide river crossing, because it was back to the Sangro for the Company for training in watermanship and floating bridging. The only river wide enough for this type of crossing was the Po and that, at this rate of advance, was more than a year away. Could anyone stand another year of this without cracking?

It was now getting to mid January and, if anything, the weather was deteriorating even further. Reports were coming in of roads totally collapsing under the weight of traffic using them, so obviously it would soon be the same old story 'Send for the Sappers'. Sure enough, training was knocked on the head and it was back to the forward area reconstructing roads which had virtually become non-existent as such.

In a way this type of work was a change from previous months and really was quite welcome, because you were not a specific target for shell or mortar fire as on bridge construction or minefield clearance, which could be covered by fixed and previously set-up gun positions

The rain was torrential and incessant. Saturation of all clothing became a daily occurrence and this, together with the bitterly cold weather, soon brought its crop of coughs, colds and flu. Practically everyone was suffering in one form or another. The only life saving fact was that, because of the lull in the fighting, we had been able to commandeer a billet, as had all the Company in the various towns and villages around. Here with two lots of clothing it was possible to change every 24 hours, so at least the clothing you were now putting on wasn't so wet as when it was being removed. All types of fires and stoves were soon roaring away in an attempt to dry the soaking clothes, and the billet more often resembled the drying room of a laundry than somewhere to eat and sleep.

All sorts of troops were now beginning to appear in the front line areas and, obviously, their job was to hold while the well trained fighting troops were being rested and re-equipped.

Among these were Italian Paratroops (Paracaduti) who resembled something from Hollywood - bristling with all types of weapons and with bandoliers of ammunition draped all around them, until they could hardly walk. They strutted around the deserted village streets ready to take on the whole German Army single handed. Strangely, when the shells were pitching close they were nowhere to be seen. Am I being too hard on them? They were probably as brave as the next man. Was it then a lie that their armoured cars had more reverse than forward gears? It became impossible not to think of the time when Gen. Wavell's Army, the original 8th in North Africa of 30,000 men captured 300,000 Italians in a short campaign.

As January dragged on with artillery duels, occasional bombing raids, continual soakings, colds and flu, desert sores, lice etc., etc., came a very bright item of news. My diary for that day reads, 'Allied landing north of Cassino. 50,000

American and British troops have landed at Anzio in order to cut off the German Army at Cassino'.

It was January 22nd, 1944 and, at least, a new strategy was being tried. An American General named Lucas was running the show and from all reports he was an excellent soldier, chosen especially for the job.

The point of landing, although north of Cassino, was still some way south of Rome but with such a force, and with the Germans now facing the Allies on both sides, that they were bound to crack. A link up between the two forces and Rome within days!

It wasn't long before that dream disappeared in smoke, the smoke of the German guns.

The landing was unopposed and soon consolidated. The build-up of troops and stores took place with little interference from 'Ted', but meanwhile he was being given time to build a defence line around the perimeter of the bridgehead.

What a waste of what could have been a first class move. There was a quote in the Army newspaper by Winston Churchill to the effect that 'We thought that we were landing a raging tiger, but instead it turned out to be a stranded whale!' That is how the situation remained for five long weary months, with 'Ted' easily able to control any attempt at breakout. Perhaps this was the point of it all, just to contain as many of his troops as was possible.

It was to be the following June before any movement of significance took place, and by then the whole of the 5th and 8th Armies were on the move. The strategy behind this was obviously to draw attention away from the so-called 'D-Day', which was to take place within a few days.

On our 8th Army front, the daily slog was continuing but with a difference. Could it be true? Was it just a rumour some awful swine had started? But the stories persisted. We were on the move, and by the appearance of all readable signs for a very long journey.

Naples and Casino were taken in our stride
We did not come to fight there
We just came for the ride
Anzio and Sangro were just names
We only came to look for dames
The randy 'D-Day-Dodgers' in sunny Italy.

CHAPTER TWENTY SEVEN

TRÉCASÉ

The destinations were given a sequence of priority:

1) England
2) A landing in the South of France
3) Transfer over to the Casino front
4) A long rest in the sunshine of Southern Italy.

Monday 31st January 1944. Advance party left for unknown destination. Rumours still persisting on all four destinations.

Thursday 3rd Feb. Same job on roads. Winch trucks very busy hauling ditched trucks back on to a 'solid' surface. 'Ted' lobbing big stuff today. Too close for comfort!

Friday 4th. Preparing for long move. Big stuff coming over again.

Sat 5th. Moved off 6.30am. Travelled all day via Lanciano, Vasto and the South. Slept night in truck, no room for stretcher.

The diary reads: 'No bangs, no screams, ears ringing from the silence!'

Sun 6th. Journey continued south down the coast, and then turned inland on to the Naples road. The final destination was a small village called Trécasé (Three Houses) near Torre Annunziata on the outskirts of Naples.

The message was, this is to be your home until further notice. You are being rested from front line duties.

What welcome news that was. No shot nor shell until further notice. No diving for your life into mud filled ditches, and here I say without fear of contradiction, there is not a person who did not dive when nasty things were flying, to save his life, and in this I include VCs, MCs, DCMs, MMs, etc., etc. Let no man say otherwise!

The village was small and right on the lower slopes of Vesuvius. What a magnificent sight it was, towering above the village with a cloud of smoke as a capping. I vowed there and then that she would be climbed before leaving.

The people of the village, whose school we had occupied, turned out to be very friendly indeed. Friendly, that is, after they had decided whether we were Tedeschi or Inglesi.

No English had been seen before, so the Company was quite a novelty and everyone soon set about 'getting their feet under the table'.

The majority of the men folk appeared to be either called up to the forces or were already prisoners of war in England. In either event there appeared to be a serious shortage of Italian men.

Welcome Inglese! Soldiers who had not seen a female for many long months! And that was the basis for the story of the time spent in Trécasé.

The following day was a little light training but mostly the day was spent in cleaning up clothing, washing underclothes, bathing, delousing, etc.

Next day came a further surprise. All kits to be packed, we were moving to the 8th Army Rest-camp at Bari. At 4pm we moved off, back across the snow of the mountains (no sunshine here) to the city of Bari on the Adriatic coast. It was to be five days of cinema and Ensa shows with some visits to Bari in between, just to wander around the city, rubbernecking, and listening to the small boys calling, "Cigaretta Joe?" or "You wanna know my seesta, Joe?" etc., etc. It was amazing to see just how many areas displayed the 'hot cross bun' sign, which meant to British troops 'Out of Bounds' and to the Yanks, 'Off Limits.'

The sixth day saw the journey back to Trécasé. It was good to be back, not only for the peaceful atmosphere, but to start the routine of the restful life again. Mail from home was waiting. Good old Mum, she never failed. Dad wasn't very well and from her letters it was plain that he was more than just not well, but she was not going to cause unnecessary worry for me. Dear old Dad. How I remember those days we spent in the garden together. He in his shirtsleeves digging for his life, while I tried to shoot sparrows with an airgun which fired around corners. All that was another world away. Would it ever be the same again?

The mail I should have been getting, but just wasn't arriving was from girlfriend Peg. We met during the Southampton blitz and spent quite a few weekends at her home, and one of my leaves at home with my Mum and Dad. During the North African campaign, some of her letters were getting through but she was not receiving mine, so she thought that I was not writing.

It was then that I suspected (and this could have been the only explanation) her Mother was intercepting the letters. I wonder just how many times that happened to people during the war? Mother not wishing to lose her darling daughter to that rough soldier!

The way around this particular problem was to either write to her local priest or to her place of employment. The second was chosen because the local curate was, by coincidence a lodger in dear Mum's house.

Contact was made, explanations given, upheavals at home resulted, and regular correspondence resumed until somehow, later in the war, it gradually trailed off. Good luck Peg!

Light training was resumed, which included a visit further north to the Volturno river for a floating Bailey. The weather was bitterly cold, and living under canvas after getting saturated all day produced bitter resentment against the people whose idea it was to 'give us a rest'.

Back to Trécasé again, and resumption of the pleasant life which, for me at least, was spending the evenings with an excellent Italian family who had 'adopted' me. Mother, Father, small son, and four daughters. The second eldest daughter was a dark haired Italian beauty – Carlotta – and it was plain from the start that we were going to 'hit if off'.

As a family who had suffered as a result of the war, from having very little food or the necessities of life, they were more than generous to their English soldier visitor, and I responded to this generosity by sharing all I had, and in this way very soon got into their way of life. She (Carla) was studying English and with me being keen to learn Italian, no opportunity was lost in getting together under the watchful eye of Mum, who was a keen chaperone, except of course when, after a hard day's work in the kitchen she would fall asleep so soundly that nothing would wake her!

In order to avoid turning these scribblings into an autobiography of an uninteresting everyday individual where little action of interest of any kind takes place, it is stressed that what was taking place involving myself was, and could have been, happening to any individual in that Sapper Company, and so was part of a Sapper at War.

Various light duties were being undertaken during these wonderful days. It was truly marvellous and, for once, it was felt that the people 'up top' were trying to help the 'lower order' to have a rest. There was, of course, the ever present thought of 'What was there to come when the weather improved?'

Judging by the enquiries made about Vesuvius, and how long it would take to climb and which was the best route etc., etc., the family realised that this 'Soldato Inglese' was determined to see for himself. Luigi, the son, had at one time been most of the way up and was able to help but, he said the best way by far was the 'tourist route', which meant taking the cable car from over the other side of the mountain.

The day came and after wangling a day free of duty and with Mamma's sandwiches and a bottle of vino rosso slung in an Army pack, this soldier set off for, hopefully, the top of the most famous volcano in the world. Here I must explain about the sandwiches provided by Mamma. They consisted of one

Italian long (very long) loaf, cut lengthways and absolutely crammed full of all the herbs, spices and other tasty foods she possessed. They were absolutely delicious to a very hungry young bloke who had lived on biscuits and tinned food for so long. The red wine was out of this world and blended perfectly with the countryside in the early stages of the route. Mile after mile of vineyards with the grape just beginning to form. A return visit would have to be made when maturity had been reached: harvesting would be a pleasure.

I would sacrifice a great deal just to repeat that day again, exactly as it happened, fifty years ago.

The surroundings soon changed to less greenery, with increased rock and shale formation, and all the time the smell of Vesuvius getting stronger.

Towards the summit, after a good many hours of walking (climbing steeply in fact) a young Italian uomo (man) appeared from somewhere and after an exchange of 'buon giorno, come state' etc., we talked, he in the local dialect (Napolitano) and me in the Italiano of an English soldier, that is, more English than Italian, but with the hand gestures which said far more than the tongue ever could.

He was learning to be a guide on Vesuvius and was very keen to learn English, so we walked and talked to the top.

It was the nearest thing to a moonscape that it was possible to imagine, but more rocky than dusty. The most surprising thing of all was the size of the crater itself: could it be a mile across? If not then nearly so, with the centre built up by numerous minor eruptions. Molten lava was being thrown up from somewhere in the middle of all this, and at times reached well above our heads. Above all was the smell, acrid, sulphuric and choking! The nearest thing one could imagine to Dante's *Inferno*.

Hidden in the rocks was a group of beautifully shaped ashtrays, made from the lava when fluid and then allowed to cool. They resembled a shiny open textured tarmacadam. He had made them for sale, obviously to the tourists, and insisted on presenting one, one which I treasured as a reminder of that great day until unfortunately, it was lost with all my kit and valuables during the worst, and, I suppose, the luckiest day of my life. But more of that later.

A good camera would have captured all of that scene but it wasn't to be so, the return journey started.

Carlo the guide (note the terminal masculine 'O', as compared with Carla) made sure that we called at his house (casa) which wasn't much out of my way, on the way down, but still very much on the slopes of Vesuvius.

His Mamma, plump, dark haired and very jovial, produced a soup which was well worth the journey. The flavour was out of this world and of course, while we were waiting for the 'zuppa', the vino was flowing, this time a bianco from their field on the mountain, which really was excellent.

Goodbyes were said with the promise to return one day 'dopo la guerra' (after the war), with the full intention of doing just that. Little did I know the future.

Early March came much too quickly and saw the Company on the move once again. It had been a very enjoyable period of light training, recreation, and above all, resting from that stupid series of killings.

Meeting the people of that small village had been the most enjoyable event in our lives for a long time, and great was the sorrow at the moment of parting. Never had there been scenes, involving ourselves, like it before. On the day of departure the streets were full of knots of people, hugging and kissing their tender farewells. Were these folk really our one time enemy? For sure it was a scene to be repeated many times, by other individuals during that war.

One day I knew that there would be a return visit but now, on with the war. The journey back to the front was long and miserable, the weather in the mountains was atrocious, both snow and rain, with ice covering most of the roads in the high ground areas, making them almost impassable. An overnight stay in an open sided barn with the wind and rain lashing

Sappers repairing and re-launching the Bailey Bridges during the assault on the Gustav Line. The bridges had been previously damaged by dive-bomb attacks and shellfire.

Time to catch a quick sleep during a lull in fighting. G.I.'s in Italy
(top)

A typical two man trench. One man must stay awake at all times.
(bottom)

TYPICAL ITALIAN TERRAIN. Impossible to dig in a shelter from ice, snow or rain. (top)

ITALIAN CAMPAIGN. Bringing in the dead. (bottom)

ITALY 1944, German Paratroopers bring in a British Tommy minus his left foot. (top)

The ruins of an Italian town. (bottom)

Time for a quick smoke. (top)

Walking wounded. Allied troops in a dazed condition awaiting evacuation. (bottom)

CHEPSTOW COLLEGE. A re-union of old friends. Author is on the right. (top)

CHEPSTOW COLLEGE. A re-union of old friends, 1993. Author is 4th from left, seated. (bottom)

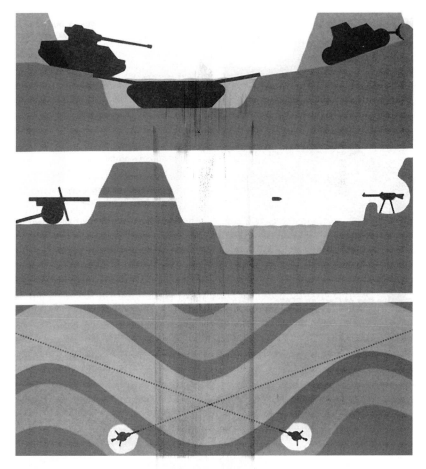

Coping with Italy's Water Barriers.

Method of crossing the Senio. (top)
Attack through a flood bank. (middle)
German machine gun sitings. (bottom)

THE ARK. One of 'The Funnies' used in the Italian Campaign. (top)

THE ARK. A slightly different type to those used during the crossing of the River Senio, Italy, 1945. (bottom)

through, made life appear to be its normal miserable self once again.

Next day saw us in the Lanciano-St Vito area once again.

Here there were thousands of troops all in winter quarters, waiting for the weather to break. Then most of them would be replaced by 'front line' troops ready for the big assault which was bound to come within the next couple of months.

As a consequence of this situation, most of the reasonably habitable buildings had been taken over long ago, so we were left with shell torn buildings little better than heaps of rubble. Conditions were atrocious. What with icy cold winds and snow, saturated clothing and sparse shelter, it was little wonder that influenza hit with a bang. Days were spent shivering and feeling lousy. After the second passing out spell, they decided, via the M.O., that it was time that the patient had a spell in hospital.

Here followed a period of embarrassment which should never have been meted out to a human being. The Casualty Clearing Station at Lanciano was full of wounded. Stretchers everywhere with chaps who had lost limbs or suffered shrapnel wounds and into the middle of this arrived a NCO – RE with flu!

The operating section of the building was always full, with a queue of stretcher cases filling the corridor outside with badly wounded chaps waiting their turn for surgery. Most appeared to be quite cheerful under these terrible circumstances, while others were either unconscious or too far gone to care. The more cheerful ones explained that their particular wound was sufficient to get them back to 'Blighty'. I wondered whether they had given much thought to their future, or was getting the hell out of here good enough for the time being?

Whenever an orderly paused at my stretcher to read the attached card he always said in an incredibly loud voice - flu? - flu? - not FLU? The embarrassment was complete, so much so that when the M.O. made his round the request was, "Please could I return to my Unit? This is no place for me, occupying a valuable place, etc."

The reply, "You're damned right and if you give these blokes your flu in addition to what they've already got, you will answer to me for it!"

What a pleasant situation. He didn't want me there, I did not want to be there and now the Germans didn't either. They started to shell merry hell out of the place. It was a stonk which lasted intermittently for two days, and as a result, the wounded were overflowing into all the corridors and even into the grounds outside.

This of course meant evacuation for all the cases able to be moved, down the line to the next CCS. In my case it was a very bumpy ride, on a stretcher in the back of a truck, along with about a dozen others.

The first destination was a distinct improvement on Lanciano. It wasn't muddy, it didn't smell of death and, above all there were no shells flying about.

There were several British nurses here and a pleasant sight they were in their prim uniforms. It was almost pleasant to be told by them to, "Shut up, and drink your medicine!" But they really were to be admired, giving their 100% to the badly wounded. The sight of strong men crying from the devotion and care they were receiving from those girls was something always to be remembered.

Further down the line was the drill once again (memories of North Africa) until reaching the final destination, 98 British General Hospital at Bari. Why couldn't that have been Naples, with a chance of seeing Carla and family again?

By this time the flu was running out of 'steam', and with the improvement in weather, all the balconies of the building were occupied by such cases as mine.

On the third day of this balcony trip I noticed a distinct layer of red dust on the sheets (yes sheets) of the stretcher and more falling. So much so that when the visiting Padre came my way, he was asked, "Why the red dust?"

His reply absolutely floored me and went in like a knife!

"Obviously my son, you have not heard, but Mount Vesuvius blew off its top yesterday. It is the biggest eruption for several hundred years with seven villages already destroyed and thousands of people evacuated."

What a bombshell! Trécasé was right on the slope of the mountain and would obviously have suffered. What of Carla and family? What about all those other wonderful people in the village? Probably the nearest populated area to the point of eruption.

On the way to Florence we had a lovely time
We ran a bus to Rimini
Right through the Gothic Line
Soon to Bologna we will go
And after that we'll cross the Po
We'll still be 'D-Day' dodging in sunny Italy.

CHAPTER TWENTY EIGHT

VESUVIUS

What to do next, how could I get over there (150 miles) to find out or to help? The Padre was my answer. The next day he was told the tale of the soldier who had fallen in love with the beautiful Italian girl, and wished to take her back to England after the war, and here she was in mortal danger from that terrible dragon Vesuvius. Would he please see the officer in charge of Admin., and arrange for me to take some of my accumulated leave before returning to my Unit? The next day, his answer - "Yes, they will consider it."

That was good enough for me, so down to the store where one would be fully kitted out ready to return to Unit. There followed two days of thumbing lifts from Army trucks over to Salerno, some thirty miles or so from Vesuvius.

Here came the first shock. The air was thick with dust and lumps of solid clinker were continuously falling from the sky without warning, so 'tin-hats' were the order of the day.

Getting a lift north to the Naples area was a more difficult job than the crossing from Bari because there was very little traffic on the roads. The clinker and heavy grey grit was building up on the roads and consequently most drivers were loath to venture very far. For once my luck was in, a lift from a Sapper Plant Troop in a Scammell low-loader with a D-8 (bulldozer) on board.

This lift bore fruit at a later date because during that very slow and often precarious 20-odd mile journey, much useful information was gleaned. The Cpl. and Sapper on board were members of a Plant Troop RE who were being sent to join their Squadron at Torre Annunziata, about three mile from Trécasé. Apparently all British plant and mechanical equipment had been offered to the Italian government to help in the clearing of roads in the Vesuvius area, hence this journey, and what a mammoth job it was going to be.

Precarious journey because the Scammell at times was crawling over clinker piled some two or three feet high. Only a strong and very heavy truck could have survived the journey. To make matters worse we came across the odd car and even ox-cart abandoned in the depths of the clinker. As you will appreciate, this entailed either skirting or pushing the object aside. Meanwhile a steady snowstorm of grit, mixed with heavier clinker continued on all sides.

The useful information gained was the fact that one of their colleagues was an old Chepstow School mate of mine, one 'Spud' Jackson, a very good all around sportsman who had excelled at swimming and, in particular, boxing, having won his 'weight' in the School competitions. This latter training was to prove useful later but, as to that, we'll have to wait a while. My thoughts were already running along the lines of 'Spud', living so close to Trécasé, acting as postman, through the military network for Carla and myself. That is if the FAMILY HAD SURVIVED!

As we reached about ten miles or so from the mountain, breathing became very difficult indeed. The only possible way to survive was to wrap wet towels and rags around our faces. This helped a great deal, but driving now became almost an impossibility, and progress slowed to less than walking pace. A rendezvous had been arranged at a point ten miles from Trécasé, and without that Scout-car as a guide we, for sure, would never have reached our destination. Imagine ending up as one of the 'relics' of Pompeii which, after all wasn't so far away! Within the cab itself conditions were just about tolerable, but this was only achieved by blocking all gaps and holes with rags and anything else to hand.

By now serious doubts were beginning to arise as to whether the journey to Trécasé itself would be possible, especially once the shelter of that cab was lost. But top priority had to be given to that Italian family who had been so wonderful to me. Did they now need my help? Or, worse still, were they in fact still alive?

Either way there was no turning back now! (Was this young love?).

At the next village we found in the 'snowstorm', the news we gleaned from the 'locals' was that two villages had been definitely 'overrun', and members of several families had been killed. But of Trécasé no definite news, only extreme doubts as to its survival because of its high position on the mountain.

HQ of the Squadron at last, a meal with 'Spud', and a long chat about the Chepstow days. Then followed the production of a rough map of how to get to Trécasé, if it still existed, and a discussion of the future system of sending and receiving mail.

The last stage of the trip was a real nightmare. Two of the miles were completed on an ox-cart, where a local farmer was going to see if his 'figlio' (son) and 'moglia' (wife) had survived.

By now, between the dust clouds, the lava could be seen spilling from the crater, and what a terrifying sight it was. Thank God that there appeared to be no lava heading in the direction of Trécasé.   Goodbyes and well wishes were exchanged with the farmer and the last mile or so of the journey started on foot.

It was a long uphill gradient to the village with clinker falling all the time.   The air was acrid and choking, with breathing only possible through the wet towel. Grey dust and clinker were piled so high that some of the smaller houses were virtually buried.   Someone had attempted to clear a path through the main street of the village, and this now was the only means of access.

The family home was on the top floor of a block of houses and, because of this situation, had escaped the material piled high in the streets below, but because of its flat roof construction appeared to be physically groaning under the weight of ash and clinker piled high.

The family were all OK.

All of them had been at home when the eruption started except Papa who worked in Naples, and had quite a hard time getting home because, as he said, of the absolute panic that had gripped everyone when the eruption started. The driver of the electric train which he took to work every day refused to leave Naples because of travelling in the direction of Vesuvius. He was very fortunate in knowing a friend with a car, who brought him most of the way.

When they had got over the shock of seeing this apparition, dressed in a British 'Tin-hat' and wrapped in wet towels coming through their door, my welcome was complete. And here it must be said, that when an Italian wants to express an emotion there is nothing like it in the world. 100% crying, laughing, kisses, handshakes and hugging lasted for the next half hour or so, and then it was questions and answers. It was amazing just how much of the Italian language had been mastered by yours truly in the time available, but then, of course, 90% of it was hand gestures!

When it was learned that their Soldato Inglese would be staying for a few days, the best vino was soon on the table, and Santa Maria was thanked for theirs, and my deliverance, many times over.

Thank goodness that I'd had the sense to pack in as much tinned stuff as could be carried, and this included chocolate, cigarettes and the inevitable soap. There was a total absence of soap in Italy at this time. The family had very little left in the way of foodstuff because, of course, they had already been trapped for four or five days, so my supplies were very welcome.

Papa, wise old Papa, immediately set about rationing out the available food, ably assisted by Leonardo, who of course, had to translate the contents of each tin. It was decided that with Mamma's supply of pasta, herbs, formaggio (cheese), 'potats', beans (fave), tomatoes (pomodori) etc., we could all survive fairly comfortably for about four days but, after that, if conditions outside had not improved considerably, the going was going to get pretty grim.

It must be remembered that it was wartime and food was pretty short in Italy in any case, and here in the poor south it was even more so. Some varieties of food had become totally unavailable. It was only on my return home after the war that I learned that the situation was much the same here.

Water would be no problem because the well, although on the top floor, was immediately outside the rear entrance door and well under cover of the roof. The toilet too was available (more of that later) and although not inside the house, an access path had soon been cleared to it.

Within an hour of arrival the absolute urgency was stressed to Papa of shifting some of the build-up off the flat roof, which was ever increasing, and in my opinion becoming extremely dangerous. Papa agreed, and a couple of shovels were produced, and then began the task of getting on to the roof. This was going to be no mean operation, because not only was the access door extremely small but the weight of ash and clinker built up on top of it was almost unbelievable. There was nothing for it but to 'sweat and strain' until success was ours, and eventually the job was done and we were through to the roof.

Here the situation was even worse than anticipated. The heavy grey grit was lying in a solid bed about chest deep, worse still the stuff was still coming down like a heavy snowstorm. Its choking sulphuric content made it almost unbearable and without the protection of wet wrappings it would have been impossible to stay up there more than a few minutes. But it had to be done or else we were all in serious trouble.

It was organised so that one was working while the other two rested and recovered aided by glasses of glorious vino bianco, supplied by the lovely ladies of the house. Luigi and Papa were good workers and we at last made headway, concentrating our efforts mainly on the centre of the roof, which the Royal Engineers deemed to be the weakest area, and the one which needed that solid mass shifting as soon as possible.

After a few glasses of that refreshing (and life saving) liquid the work appeared to become much lighter, and even a song or two came mumbling through the wraps. Was that 'O Solo Mio' competing with 'There'll Always Be An England'?

The shovelling went on until well after dark, until we decided that the real danger was over, for the immediate future anyway, and Papa declared that the 'snowstorm' was for sure ('per securo') easing up.

In the darkness Vesuvius became an awesome sight. A huge mountain towering above us shooting flames and red-hot rock to a tremendous height, and all the while spewing lava over the lower parts of the crater lip. There and then I made the vow that before leaving, the monster would be climbed again, firstly to see how Carlo and his family had survived the eruption, and secondly to see the terrible damage done by the lava flows.

My thoughts that night turned to the fact that, although not yet twenty two years old, life in all its aspects had been experienced, and death in all its terrible forms had been seen and heard, and now here was the experience of a huge volcano erupting with all its awesome power. What *could* the next 21 years bring?

The evening saw a family gathering. Mamma, Papa, Luigi, Christina (Tina), Carlotta (Carla), Rita and Anna, surnamed Cirillo. Anna and Rita, the youngest were soon packed off to bed and the rest of the evening spent in gentle discussion of the situation, that is locally, and the war in general. The vino supply seemed endless and gradually, gently at first, the singing began. The songs of Italy were performed, and explained, with gusto. In between came England's best (there didn't appear to be many clean ones) and, of course, the songs of dear old Wales (would I ever see it again?). The wine was in and the wit was out!

Some time during the evening there was a classic statement from Papa in beautiful hand waving and gesticulating Italian. Who would have thought, Leonardo, that you, an English soldier, would be here with my family tonight and really enjoying each others' company, when just a while ago Mussolini declared war against you, and our soldiers were bitterly fighting each other in North Africa? Yes who indeed? That evening was, again, something to be stored in the memory for ever.

When at last the throats became too dry for any more singing or talking – or did the vino run out? A bed was made up for me in the corner of the living room. It consisted of a pair of trestles supporting several planks and some beautiful soft bedding which, surely, was robbed from their own beds. After the sleeping conditions in the front line area, never, never was such bliss experienced. Was it the vino? The nearness of the beautiful Carla, or the fact that nothing was going bang?

After several days the storm of grit and clinker slowed down and eventually stopped. People started to emerge from their homes and other places of shelter and there was much wailing (Italian fashion) when the enormous damage was assessed. Several people had died in the village and the stories of injuries were told time and again. A good many houses had totally collapsed from the weight of grit, and with the collapse of the concrete roof, any people below were bound to suffer the consequences.

Gradually over the days life began to return to normal. The Sappers came with their dozers and scrapers to clear the streets and Papa even returned to work in Naples. His workday seemed very long, leaving home very early morning to catch his train and returning well into the evening. He could be seen moving about (my) living room before leaving but never disturbing me.

With Carla, who worked as a stenographer in a Naples bank, it was an hour later before she was up, and I would become aware of her presence when that long black hair would be draped over my face. This, of course, was our only chance of being alone together and occurred every morning. Never a word was spoken because of the presence of Mamma in the next room, so it became a silent romance in every way. For sure Carla would get up a little earlier than necessary in order to achieve those few moments together. Happy days!

The Italian food and the ways of cooking it became more and more enjoyable every day. Mamma and I were alone together all day when work and school saw the others away, and she would teach me just how simple it was to make, for instance, the ordinary potato taste delicious just with the addition of garlic and herbs. Tomatoes dried on the windowsill were gorgeous when added to her dishes. The method of eating spaghetti correctly was demonstrated until perfection was achieved. That night, when the ceremony of eating the evening meal took place, all eyes were on me. A spoon to the left and a fork to the right, Mamma came in with a steaming bowl of spaghetti, and Pappa dished it out, person to person, onto a smaller bowl and each person was named as the bowl was handed over.

"Leonardo mange (eat) and buono appetito!"

I was aware that after everyone had received their bowl of spaghetti, all eyes were on this English soldier who was about to get himself tangled up with several yards of the stuff. Mamma I knew was all on edge and nervous, so after a polite 'grazie, buono appetito' and without hesitation in went the spoon, in went the fork to meet it, a few deft turns of the fork the spaghetti arrived safely in the mouth to the shouts from all around the table of "Bravo, bravo, Leonardo!" I felt as proud as if I had built the Sangro bridge by myself, and I knew that Mamma was delighted.

As the days passed that old brain of mine kept sending out little alarm signals to the effect that a couple of weeks would soon pass, and so get cracking and do the things promised.

The lava was still flowing but more slowly now and the clinker stopped altogether so, taking a chance, the directions to the most badly affected areas were obtained and the journey started.

It was more or less on the same contour around the mountain and, after less than 20 mins walking from the house it was easily possible to pick out just where the lava was flowing. Both smoke and noise acted as guides and, although prepared for a shock, what actually came into sight was almost unbelievable. At this point the lava was flowing quite fast, about normal running speed, was about six feet wide and had cut a channel through existing rock as a normal water stream would have done over many years. The heat generated was unbearable and so, keeping a safe distance from it, I followed its course down the mountain. No vegetation of any kind remained on either side for about 30 yards, and piled everywhere was the grey grit and clinker.

The first village to receive the full fury of that awful stream, from memory named Santa Maria, came into sight and a shocker it was. The lava at this point was slower wider and higher, and had rolled over everything in its path, right through the village. Where houses had been was now a red seething mass tumbling over itself down the mountain, destroying everything as it went.

There were other villages reported destroyed, just as was Santa Maria, but this one was enough to see in one's lifetime, so the homeward journey was started. The sight of that destruction will live in the mind for ever. Surely this was nature in its most destructive mood.

Safely home and a discussion over the evening meal which, by now, was almost normal fare because supplies, although meagre to our standards, were much more plentiful.

None of the family had been to see the lava streams at all, so Leonardo held the centre spot and in fluent (after several glasses of vino to ease the dry throat) Italian/English with a Welsh accent, and much use of the combined dictionary, told the whole story of the day's trek to a wide eyed Italian audience whose gasps of, "Mamma Mia" and "Dio Mio" did wonders to keep me going.

The whole family was against me going up the mountain tomorrow to look for Carlo's house but, with only a few days left I knew it had to be done. The two greatest dangers ('pericolosi') were, they explained, that the mountain was still very active, and had dramatically changed shape so that now there was a good chance of getting lost.

Just how right they were! Nowhere could the original track or any path be seen at all, instead it was one heaving mass of loose clinker, almost impossible to climb. The determination was there, so it was do or die in the attempt. The bearing of the peak with relation to Carlo's house was firmly fixed in mind, so the struggle began.

It must have taken all of six hours to reach the place I knew that house to be, whereas before it had been done in half the time. There was nothing there! Nothing but masses of black/grey clinker!

This just wasn't good enough, so it was climb and search, across and search, climb and search again, until my numbed brain made me believe that there was just nothing there any more. Nothing but moonscape as far as the eye could see. Surely this wasn't the end of a whole family? Had they all died? Who could give me any confirmation of the tragedy?

Total exhaustion and dusk said head for home 'subito'! (at once). The slipping and sliding journey home wasn't as bad as the climb and the lights of the village were a good guide. The family were extremely worried about the absence of their visitor, and were already organising a search party when the grimy black object arrived!

They could tell the sadness I felt at the thought of Carlo, house and family were buried under tons of clinker, and Pappa confirmed that this was indeed so. He had made enquiries in Naples that day and it was officially confirmed, that all houses and buildings above the line of Trécasé had been totally destroyed and the families lost. He said that it was a very 'triste' (sad) time indeed for all concerned. Agreement was unanimous.

The days were passing and the 'addio' (goodbye) time was looming. There was a niggling doubt in mind. Had they granted those two weeks' leave? Could they possibly have been refused? If so was I now a deserter? A deserter on active service? Did that mean the firing squad? Well good luck to them! None of my blokes could shoot straight anyway!

The only way to confirm any doubts of course, was to return to Unit, and this would be done exactly to the day, allowing for travelling time of course.

The day came, Carla sobbed, the other girls cried, Mamma cut and filled her long loaf with marvellous tasty morsels, added a bottle of her best vino rosso, then cried. A cry like my dear old Mum – 'Leonardo returna a la guerra' (Len goes back to the war). Pappa shook my hand until I thought it would fracture. Luigi, who I had talked into a job with 'Spud' in the cookhouse, walked me to the 'AutoStrada' (motorway) and said how 'molto triste' (very sad) he was in saying goodbye but, please you must come back again because Carlotta has set her heart on 'matrimonio' (marriage) to you and living in England.

A Yankee truck soon came along, full of airmen who had just spent two weeks' leave in Naples, all fleeced of money and broken hearted at saying goodbye to their girlfriends. They had never met a 'British guy' before, so it was question and answer time for about 100 miles. One Yank (name forgotten) became very friendly, and eventually, when we said our so-longs, vowed he would look me up in England one day.

At Foggia, the airfield complex, he extended the invitation to stay overnight in his hut. Gratefully accepted and, after vino and sandwiches (mine), we arrived at his hut. It was, surprisingly, the crate of engine parts delivered from the USA and was big enough to sleep two, cook in and still had enough room to swing a large cat! Compared with us 'Limeys', these Yanks were having a 'luxury' war, and who could blame them? Good luck to them and a Government who could create conditions such as these for their armed forces. Of course their front line troops were undergoing conditions similar to ourselves.

Morning came with no dark and beautiful soft hair being dangled on my face. Instead it was the terrific roar of dozens of heavy bombers taking off for an early morning raid. The thought came of the recipients, who were they and where? It only lasted a fleeting moment and then was gone. There could be no sympathy in war. What of the bomber crews themselves, how many of them would not be returning? How mad the world had become!

Chuck - I think that was his name - soon had bacon, eggs and beans going and very welcome they were too. Someday he would make someone a good husband.

An ammunition train going north was my next lift, and took me to within 20 miles of where the Company should be. At the train stop was a transit camp which catered for personnel returning from leave etc. So taking the chance, I booked in and was promptly booked for Guard Commander that night. This at the time seemed a pretty nasty trick to play, but it turned out to be the answer to a maiden's prayer.

A dash for the Unit on my last day of leave, and after many enquiries found them in the St Vito area.

"We received 'discharged from hospital' papers for you about a fortnight ago, but assumed something wrong when you didn't show up. What happened?"

It was then that the bottom dropped out of my world. The two weeks leave had not been granted. A deserter while on active service! What could be more serious?

The answer was simple but life saving.

"As you know Sir, the Bari General is about 200 miles from here, and I have been handed from Transit Camp to Transit Camp along the line in order to get back to the Unit."

"What was your last camp?"

"No. 202 at ---------- Sir."

Sgt./Major to Orderly-room Clerk: "Telephone them and confirm, and tell them that he is now returned to Unit."

No more questions asked and no more answers given. And so back to No. 1 Sub of No. 1 Section. It would be quite wrong to say that it was good to be back because, frankly, it wasn't, in fact quite the reverse. The only bright note was that there had been no incidents of a serious nature during the last few weeks.

The war had not moved on at all, and the everyday routine of trying to live 'as best one could' was being practised by all concerned. Before Trécasé slips from the mind and is replaced by the happenings of war, there are a couple of incidents which you should be told about.

The first one relates really to the everyday routine of life in the family but, being a stranger from another system of so called civilisation, it registered and is worth relating.

During the first few hours of arrival at the Cirillo family home it was noticed that at intervals, one of the family members would take down off the wall a straw or raffia ring of some 18" in diameter. It was thick and solid and on each occasion the same procedure was adopted. Firstly came the word 'scusare' (excuse me), the ring was unhooked, a walk to the door, a varying absence of minutes, then return replacing the ring.

Eventually by nature's demands, I was forced to ask, via the dictionary,

"Dove il cabinetto?" (Where is the toilet?).

There followed a rapid discussion between the family in Napolitano, obviously concerned as to what action their guest was about to take in the cabinetto. Pappa solemnly handed me the straw ring and pointed to the door, through the clinker covered steps, on the mezzanine floor.

The thought came, 'What a curious thing to take to the toilet', but on opening the door all was revealed. The structure inside consisted of a hollow concrete column about the size and height of our toilet pans but straight in design and very uncomfortable to sit on – hence the straw ring.

The rim of the pedestal was extremely thin so the straw ring required quite a balancing act to be successful. Sitting and thinking the thought occurred, 'God help the bloke who's had a feed of green apples and a couple of glasses of Mamma's vino!'

There was no flushing system to be seen anywhere so, curiosity aroused, the question was put to Luigi when the opportunity arose. Where, how and what happens to the contents of that multi-family block of buildings?

In front of the family and with no evident embarrassment he explained that at the bottom of the block of houses was a pair of metal doors. These were the means of access into a concrete chamber, the contents of which, once every year, having been 'fed' for those twelve months by all the families and visitors concerned, were opened by a team of 'special' men and emptied and washed out on to the field of peach trees at the rear of the block as fertiliser for the peach trees. The completed job would cover the field up to knee depth, and this task would be repeated throughout the district.

"Surely," I said, "you don't eat the peaches afterwards?"

"Oh no!" he said, "we can't afford to. We send them all to England."

The second incident concerns 'Spud'. Remember him? The military mail service worked well for Carla and myself via 'Spud', and he usually enclosed a note saying that the family had entertained him with wine etc., when he was collecting or delivering mail. On one occasion the enclosed note was from a mate of his saying that 'Spud' had been involved in a fight, and it was over Carla. Here's how he told it.

"'Spud' and I had caught the electric train from Naples. On board was Carla who was being annoyed by a 'Springbok' Sgt. (South African). When 'Spud' told him to stop his nonsense he became very abusive and threatened all sorts of dire consequences if this so and so Limey didn't shove off! No-one talks to 'Spud', as you well know, like that, the train was duly stopped, a ring was formed by all the hundreds of passengers and 'Spud' took him to pieces, bit by bit, cheered on by the spectators until forcibly stopped!"

Well that's the story as told to me and later confirmed by Carla. I can well believe it, remember he is a tough egg and did win his weight in the School boxing! 'Spud' and I still meet yearly at the School reunions. This is one of the items on the agenda!

Back to the war situation. The front seemed quite static, 'Ted' was dug in his 'Gustav Line', and apart from the intermittent shelling and bombing raids, there appeared little attempt or desire to shift him. In reply he would have a 'stonk' or two in the general area of our positions, but nothing really serious. It was as if both sides knew exactly what the other was thinking and preparing to do.

Everything would depend on the weather now, once that improved the next 'push' would be on.

Early May saw an issue of Khaki Drill clothing in readiness for the coming hot weather so it was stand-by time! How long could it possibly last? Surely not another year and another winter? When would the Second Front start? When would Rome fall? What lay in store for us after the Gustav Line?

We were now 5 of the original 13 of No. 1 Sub, that meant 8 replacements since landing in North Africa - over 50%. How many would be alive at the end of it all, and how many without scars of any kind? It was a blessing that the truth wasn't known to us at that time.

The Italian 'Paras' were still conspicuous by their strutting around the town and this could only mean one thing, there would be no big push while they were in the line. Once they were replaced it would be skates on time!

Now it was the turn of the 5th Army over on the west coast of Italy. It became obvious that the initial attack was going in from there.

On May 13th reports were coming in from the Cassino front, which was the other end of the Gustav Line, that the

French had made a flanking attack in the area, the British 4th and 8th Indian Divs. had attacked across the Rapido and Gari Rivers. Their Sappers had managed to put two bridges over under heavy fire and a Canadian Tank Regiment was attempting to cross. All of this was being fed to us by our radio operators. The big Cassino attack was on at last!

The next big news was that the 78th British Div. had cut the Cassino road, the New Zealand and Canadian Divs. were also involved while the main assault on the Abbey itself was being carried out by troops of the Polish Corps.

The Americans meanwhile were heading for a link-up with the Anzio beach-head, which, if they succeeded would mean that the whole of the German forces (10th Army) in that area would be cut off. This was good news indeed and to us seemed to be the beginning of the end.

The radios were red hot with the news and all commanders were in praise of Gen. Alexander, the overall commander and 'brain' behind the attack.

It was the 25th of May when the news came through of the link-up with Gen. Mark Clark's Americans and the Anzio beach-head, and caused a big cheer through the whole of Lanciano. Now surely with the Germans cut off at Cassino 'Ted' must start withdrawing on our front.

The next report could not have been more disappointing. Instead of Clark linking-up with the British, Polish and other troops, so cutting off the whole of 'Ted's' army, he was 'high-tailing' north in order to have the glory of liberating Rome.

The comments all round were 'Typical Yank! But Alexander will have his arse for it!' But to us of course the news was still marvellous, Rome was about to fall and indeed did so on the 4th of June 1944.

There must have been 'rollickings' at high level because of Mark Clark grabbing the glory of Rome but of course, that did not reach down to our level, and by being declared an open city, it had been a 'piece of cake' for the Yanks to walk into.

Once we heard a rumour we were going home,
back to dear old Blighty never more to roam.
Then someone said in France you'll fight
we said no fear, we'll just sit tight,
We are the D-Day Dodgers
In sunny Italy.

CHAPTER TWENTY NINE

SUMMER OFFENSIVE - 1944

Elements of the 4th Indian Div. (The Shite Hawk) were now beginning to appear in the Lancio area. This definitely meant that things were afoot, especially when the convoys of Italian paras were to be seen departing for safer areas.

Our first move was several miles along the Perano road, so out of billets and into 'bivvys' again. The site was an olive grove, on the hillside, which was such a tangle of roots and rock that it was impossible to adopt the usual sleeping position of digging in the stretcher, for both reasons of safety and headroom. So grin and bear it; well bear it anyway. Fortunately 'Ted' seemed preoccupied elsewhere and was not sending any shells our way.

How wrong can one be? How we regretted choosing that particular site of rock and roots! In some uncanny way 'He' became aware of our presence and put down a barrage of heavy shellfire which had every man bleeding at the finger tips from trying to dig into the hard ground. There was no end to it, so it seemed, and as you lay there you were aware that nearly every shell crash brought fresh casualties. Above all was the helpless feeling that there was absolutely nothing one could do except to take it. The end of the shelling brought a sorry sight. There was no opportunity to count the wounded, but there were 13 Sappers requiring burial. How much longer was this carnage going to carry on? How much more could the human mind stand?

It was much later before we heard of the terrible atrocities and death camp policies being carried by the Germans, and it was then that we thought back to those moments of terror during his attacks and attempts to kill anyone in opposition to him and his Army. Were such incidents as last night worth while? Were the deaths of those Sappers, and sacrifices of

242

many others, worth stopping these mad people from trying to rule Europe and, perhaps more?

By some quirk of fate, one of the fatalities of that night's shelling was the CRE's (Colonel RE) batman – someone who very seldom visited the forward area. What was he doing there to get caught up in that lot? I remember thinking during one particularly nasty period of shelling when the Olive branches were being torn from the trees above us, 'Does the Olive branch really offer peace?'

Here the words of a 2nd World War writer, Martin Southall, make grim reading, but at the same time report a fact of war – in dramatic form. He refers to the burial of the dead after such a night as that night.

> Arms and legs were broken
> Brought closer to the trunk
> Not from respect
> But simply to lessen
> The burden of digging.
>
> God! how I hate the sound
> A dead branch makes
> When stepped upon.

6th June, 1944. D-Day! D-Day for some indeed but of course, we had our D-Day a long time ago with the landings in Africa and Italy so we, to ourselves, became the D-Day Dodgers. It was really amazing just how quickly the 8th Army song went the rounds;

> We landed at Salerno,
> Holidays with pay.
> Jerry brought his band out
> To cheer us on our way etc., etc.

To the tune of, naturally, Lili Marlene.

Apologies for the repetition but there will always be bitterness and resentment felt at the commemorations (celebrations) of D-Day 1944, when it should be remembered that there were British cemeteries created, with thousands dead, long before that date.

This news of the opening of the 2nd Front was indeed marvellous. Just how long could 'Ted' hold out now fighting on three fronts? Christmas at the very outside!

There were several bridging jobs came up while 'living' in that olive grove (should have 'high-tailed' it out of there long ago), but nothing of major importance until the order came to move across to the coast again, through Ortona (devastated) and out on to the Pescara road.

Here 'Ted' had done as much damage and mischief as he possibly could in order to delay any advance. There appeared to be mines everywhere, both anti-tank and personnel. As they were the types we were used to, they caused little bother in lifting (except of course the new comers had to be carefully initiated in, to them, this new form of death) but, to our cost, the cunning swine had suddenly introduced mines made entirely of bakelite and even wood. These, of course, were impossible to pick up by mine detector, so a very hard lesson was learned. One particular type of the latter was the 'Schu' mine, a small mine designed to take one leg off to the knee and, of course, to create panic by being undetectable. These were sewn in their thousands and so virtually every yard of the way had to be cleared.

'Ted's' Sappers had really enjoyed their retreat. Every small road and rail culvert, every bridge, large and small, every length of railway line had been blown up and destroyed. He had (amazingly) employed some sort of towed device which ripped in half every railway sleeper along the track. What a headache in repair work! And what a bill for it all! I felt sure that the British tax payer would come into it somewhere!

Our 'recce' party, in conjunction with the local Artillery OP (Observation Post) reports that there is a large bridge ahead which, as yet, has not been blown - wonder what's cooking there?

By now the reader will have gathered that the whole front was on the move forward again, and the reasoning for this was because of the rapid advances being made over on the west coast. But complacency must not be allowed to creep in because somewhere ahead there is (100% sure) a very awkward river to cross, and it will be overlooked by commanding high ground, and 'Ted' will have been preparing strong positions for many months.

Meanwhile these quiet advances still involved the nastiness of war where people were killing and being killed. Mostly, of course, these deeds were being done indirectly from miles apart, say by long distance shelling, or by a group of Sappers laying a minefield this month for a tank crew to get themselves blown-up on Christmas day!

No-one had to tell us that the bridge had been blown-up. There was a terrific whack from up the road which meant that 'Ted' (by usual method) had stacked a load of bombs below with a delay fuse. God help the bloke who tried to defuse it!

A careful advance followed, mine sweeping all the way (looking out for the bakelite and wooden mines), paying particular attention to the verges. It was here that the most damage was being done. Trucks would pull off the road for a short spell or to set up a gun emplacement and, of course, the usual stop when nature calls with a truck full of troops. Often it would be the last stop for some of them!

By the time things had settled, after the big bang, and the bridging area was reached, it appeared that units of a dozen different armies were arriving and waiting their turn to cross. Never as yet had so many varieties of uniforms, nationalities, forms of transport etc., been seen in the campaign before. Lots of them had their own language, but all had one purpose in mind. The leading thought right then of all thinking men present must have been 'What chance do these criminals and murderers from Germany stand when all these nations are against them?'

This could plainly be seen over the course of the next few days: Poles, Canadians, New Zealanders, British, Indians, South Africans, French, French Colonials and even units of the Jewish Brigade.

One of the problems of an 'Allied' Army was co-ordination, i.e. achieving a purpose together at the same time. This was a mammoth task and needed a very well drilled Organisation. A glaring example of how a language barrier would almost defeat one of the major attacks of the Italian campaign will be seen later.

Meanwhile on with the bridge. As said before, every bridge and every crossing was different and this one most certainly was. The river was the Foro, fairly wide and deep but, again a ravine type of crossing where piers would be impossible to use, so making the bridge, of a necessity, stronger and therefore more work to build.

The difference in this case was the spectator element. The waiting army had, by now, spread over the fields as far as the eye could see. Thousands of trucks, tanks, guns and troops of all kinds waiting to cross and 'get on with the job'! If the river had not been the ravine type, fords would have probably been set up and most of the rabble would be crossing. The term rabble is used, because as you know by now, every bridge built was given a name and some wag had christened this one 'Rabble Bridge'. That name along with all the others, is still recorded in the history of this Field Company RE.

The bridge, because of its length and strength, took some time to construct, but amazingly enough there were dozens of volunteers to off-load and carry stores. One of the lasting memories of that occasion was the number and variety of types of cigarettes proffered and smoked. One moment they were strong enough to blow one's hat off, the next was like smoking a ladies' filter tipped!

The truly wonderful thing about all this was the absolute difference in the situation to (say) two years ago. Then, if one truck had shown itself on the road in daylight, it would have been very few minutes before Mutt & Jeff 'took it out'. Here was a situation which would have sent them both 'high-tailing' for the Fatherland for reinforcements!

On completion of the bridge came a new sight, one that, thank goodness, we had not encountered for some time: Redcaps to organise the huge volume of traffic into some order of priority.

Obviously tanks, fighting vehicles and supply trucks first, with the mobile brothels (sorry, wrong army) mobile canteens bringing up the rear.

It was about now that one of the perks (if it can be called that) of war occurred.

Water, particularly water for drinking, was hard to come by because of the pollution problems, so a recognised 'water point' would be set up in each area and all water trucks from various units would fill there to keep their own unit supplied.

The type of trucks used were a smaller version of today's milk-trucks and from memory held, I think, 300 gallons. The water truck driver would be equipped with radio and a simple call would bring him to any Section of the Company (say) out on detachment.

For several days after the Foro crossing the whole of the Company had been split up into small units. This was a necessity because of the ugent demands for dozens of smaller jobs, i.e. road craters, minor bridges, mine clearance etc., etc.

No. 1 Sub-section was detailed to clear a mined area near a small village (name forgotten) somewhere off the main track. It was completely deserted as usual although there was always the feeling in these places that *someone* was around.

A word of explanation here again. One of the more favourable ways of easing the tension of the forward area was by keeping the ever dry throat well oiled with the wine of the area. Sometimes it would be vino bianco and sometimes rosso.

All of it was fairly easy to come by and could be obtained from the store of most deserted farm houses. If we didn't safeguard it, those that followed would probably pinch it anyway. When a good quality wine was found and if there was plenty of it, the word was passed to all and sundry and, one and all, would fill his water bottle. I have known some of the more honest (like myself) chaps to leave 'Compo' rations and Victory 'V' cigarettes behind in exchange.

Sometimes a real luxury would be found, such as Italian Vermouth. This was a slightly more 'scented' drink than vino but much more potent and therefore achieved its target much more rapidly. Unfortunately one of its after effects was terrific indigestion but, all things considered this was overruled by the pleasure of 'forgetting the war' on the night before!

No. 1 Sub. hit the bull's eye!

On the outskirts of this village was a group of buildings around a centre courtyard. Each building was large, vaulted and contained – wait for it – huge containers, each as big as the average single room in a house with the very best quality Vermouth Italiano inside!

At first it was just a sip, followed by an unbelieving mouthful and then realisation of just what it was. What could we do with thousands of gallons of the stuff?

Someone suggested a pipeline to follow us, and to be extended as we travelled up Italy, but soon all water bottles were full and then the 'Jerry' cans were emptied of contents and refilled.

Now what? Radio to water-cart driver, 'Please come (map ref.) immediately. Do not – repeat not – bother to fill with fresh water. Come soonest, out!' Within the hour Bob had arrived, any water emptied out, and suction hoses into vats. By the time the tanker was full, Bob would never have passed a breath test, but just a couple more wouldn't do any harm!

Then it happened! Radio message, the C.O. requires the water truck immediately.

248

They do say that looting, as a crime, comes next to desertion so, here we go again, there could be no possibility of emptying that valuable cargo on to the ground.

Radio message to all Sections of the Company.

"Water truck making immediate circuit of all personnel with special treat. Please taste and if liked, fill all possible containers. Water for drinking follows! Out!"

It was at least six hours before Bob came back to me on the radio and I quote his exact words.

"The fucking truck is empty! The fucking war is over and the fucking Company have all gone home. Goodnight!"

It was the middle of the afternoon – so, goodnight!

No apologies are forthcoming here. You were warned in the very early stages of the book that all writings would be from the 'other ranks' point of view, and Bob was expressing his.

No particular reaction for some days to this little episode except, of course, thanks from the boys. They said it was marvellous stuff to sleep on but who the hell could fancy fat bacon and soya links for days afterwards?

Just as things were settling nicely with our job completed (casualty free) except for sore heads and stomachs, the recall came for return to HQ. The usual moans about carrying heavy kit seemed to have disappeared because nearly everyone appeared to be carrying extra water bottles!

Rendezvous HQ and a greeting from Bob (Section Officer), "The C.O. would like to see you, 1400 hours."

'That's it!' was the immediate reaction, 'this C.O. is a stickler and has been known to hang people up by the balls for less than this.'

14:00hrs and into 'The Presence'. A long hard look which, I suppose, could have had several meanings and then, "A Subsection is required for a very special mission, and I am awarding your enterprise by selecting No. 1 Sub. During the present advance there has been a new division formed called 'Y' Div. (We had heard of these, they had been formed up by all the odds and sods from other units, sorry Sir, you were saying), 'Y' Div. are cutting across country to join us on this front. Already they have cut-off a large force of The Hun but, have encountered numerous mines and booby traps so I want your chaps to go out to meet them. You will be aware that most of the time you will be working close to or even behind the enemy, so travel light by night only, take any necessary kit and keep radio silence. Good luck!"

Oh! The password is! Long forgotten, so this was the reward for 'bringing a little happiness' into the miserable lives of several hundred men? Next time, if there was a next time, the water truck would deliver water only!

Map references and routes decided, twelve 'brave' men, plus one, left at dusk, equipped with various mine and booby trap clearing equipment and, in the pitch darkness became like walking ghosts.

After some way down the road an infantry unit was passed who 'thought' that 'Ted' was several hundred yards ahead but had been very quiet for a while. Was this good news?

Soon it was time to turn off the main drag and take the track which we had all memorised,. This achieved, we progressed in dead silence with the occasional flare causing us to freeze (how does one sweat and freeze together?) and more disturbing, the bursts of differing types of machine gun fire. It was surprisingly easy to tell the difference between the British heavy, then the Bren, and very ominously, the Spandau. This latter German weapon must have been a marvellous piece of engineering, its fire was so rapid that a whole burst sounded almost like one shot, and it was reputed to be absolutely accurate.

Those were the sounds of that night and were really a good guide as to was were where regarding troop positions, or at least where their machine guns were placed.

After some time down this track there came a junction, one to the right, the other to the left and both of about equal width. No one remembered seeing those marked on the map and, of course, producing a torch at this point would probably have both sides firing at you. The majority decided left so, once again, on into the night. After what seemed miles, and by now of course we must have been behind the Jerry line, a couple of houses were spotted.

Long deliberation and then the suggestion 'Let's leave well alone'. That seemed common sense until suddenly a bloke (a Civvy) appeared from nowhere and got quite excited on seeing us. Obviously the tin hats gave us away and he wanted to run into the house to tell his moglia (wife) that the Inglesi had arrived. These were the first Allied troops he had seen since the Germans took over.

This didn't sound too good, so the interrogation started. 'Where were the Germans?' was the leading question. The word Tedeschi was known to all but 'where' appeared to stump him completely until one of the bright sparks said he had seen it written in his phase book. - DOVE - So the next attempt was 'Dove Tedeschi?' but still it was 'no capito', until we decided to use a small torch in the shelter of the wall, and show him the dictionary. He immediately understood and said 'DOE VAY!' Trust the stupid 'other ranks' not to know that every letter was pronounced in this beautiful language - unlike our own lot of nonsense. So it was 'Do-vay Tedeschi?' The answer was frightening.

"Tedeschi qui, Tedeschi qua, Tedeschi la." 'Ted' *here* was the first word and then 'Ted' there, 'Ted' there pointing in turn to every point on the compass.

"Oggi (today) he was here drinking vino!"

Now what? I decided that if 'Y' Div. could not be contacted within one hour we would retrace our steps, with the few hours darkness left to us.

No 'Y' Div. so it was back the way we came. Obviously the wrong fork had been taken.

The road back appeared to be much longer than the outward journey but, thank goodness, nothing out of the ordinary until that is one of the sharp eyed boys said, "Troops ahead!" so it was all down and a 'recce'!

Unbelievably, several hundred yards in front were hundreds of Indian troops, all in the firing position and all facing us. What a nice welcome that was going to be!

There could only be one way out of that, in a loud voice shouting, "We are British!"

Jabbering followed then an 'Oxford' voice said, "Show yourselves!"

Hell, all's well that ended well!

This is of course until the C.O. unit wanted to know, "How did you get on?"

He, of course wasn't very happy when he heard our version of the story and was only half convinced when assured that if 'Y' Div. was out there, we would have found them!

The following day came a message to report to the C.O.

"I would like you to hear this piece of information first hand," he said. "The news has just come through that 'Y' Div. ran into a strong force of the enemy last night and suffered severe casualties. As a result were forced to withdraw but, unfortunately, during the action they were mistaken for German troops and were fired on by Indian troops."

Nuff said!

The next few weeks of June saw the Company working in a dozen different places at the same time. The demand for urgent work was so great, and from so many people that there was no alternative but to split the Company and Sections (now called Platoons but no-one was familiar with this term so Sections they remained) in to smaller groups. No. 1 Sub was called upon to build a Bailey well forward from the previous position, and found that they were working with Tom, Dick and Harry from other Sections. This was quite a large structure, and the question was just how did it get across that gap without disaster, because it appeared to be a disorganised rabble of odds and sods doing the job. I wonder if that's why it was named 'O's Bridge'.

This area was really good to be in at that time. 'Ted' appeared to be in retreat and obviously would be doing as much damage as he could during that action but, for us, the peace of it all was heaven. This only lasted during daylight hours unfortunately, because by night the Jerry heavy bombers would circle round dropping anti-personnel bombs wherever they thought fit. Most of them were the butterfly type again, our old enemies and usually caused chaos whenever they were scattered. One just had to be under cover when these things were landing.

The project now was to bridge the Chienti river. This again was an unusual job because of, firstly, its appearance (at least before 'Ted' sent it skywards). It had been one of Mussolini's show pieces and had large marble columns at both ends with the Fascist insignia still showing. These were soon covered by our unit signs.

Secondly, its length and height above ground: from memory it was at least 400ft long and a tremendous height above river level. Thirdly, there were numerous craters all around the bridge where the RAF had carried out at least one raid. I wonder if they had any success? No means of knowing because now, of course, there was only rubble left.

The site was situated very close to a beautiful sandy beach, and being the hot June of an Italian summer, who could resist the call of the cool Adriatic, only a fool of an Officer would attempt to prevent the men from wallowing in it, and there were no fools around!

That night was shattered by German bombers who had decided that their target would be the town of Macerata, situated some small distance inland. A fearful raid and delivered with the Hun's uncanny accuracy. He just 'took out' the whole centre of the town, and why? There appeared to be nothing there of military importance, no troops, or very few, but just a few miserable Italians, who somehow had escaped the war as it passed through. These people were virtually starving already and had no possessions to speak of, so why bomb hell out of them? Their former ally. Only 'Ted' knows the answer!

Bridge finished, we were on the move again. This time it was almost twelve miles north and took us through what had been the town of Pescara. The place was a complete shambles and, judging by the state of the buildings which were near converted to rubble, had probably suffered the artillery fire and bombing of both sides.

From now on it seemed to be continuous moves. This was the result of being under the beck and call of several different formations. One minute it would be a Canadian Division then British and even Polish. They all had their priorities and all were different.

Mine sweeping was a daily occurrence and without doubt, saved many a life and limb. 'Ted's main minefields were easily found because under the rules (if any) of modern warfare, he was forced to form a wire perimeter and place warning signs on it. He did this, sometimes, with the sign, 'Achtung Minen' together with a skull and crossbones. It was the scattered mines which caused the trouble and ended the war, by death or disablement, of many British soldiers.

One memory that sticks in this old mind is that, whilst on the move north, we set up a living area in a small village just north of Chieti – name forgotten – where just about every house was flattened. On enquiring as to why, the answer from the locals was that the Americans had bombed them 26 times in three days. And were the Germans here at the time? Never saw any Germans at all! Why the bombing? Only the Yanks know the answer!

The next move was another 25 miles north, and it would appear now that we were reaping the fruits of the '2nd Front' in France, the fall of Rome and the further thrust north. It was absolutely marvellous to crawl along at 30mph without shot or shell, when only weeks before we were bogged down to no forward movement at all for months. The question now was, 'Where would he make his next stand?'

There had been a lot of talk recently among the boys who knew of a 'Gothic Line'. This apparently was a very strong defence line of wire and pillboxes somewhere in the mountains to the north, and was to be his 'last stand' before the Plain of Lombardy and the Po valley.

The next incident in this story comes right out of the blue and was a complete surprise. At the time it was quite enjoyable and made a nice change from the humdrum of daily routine.

"Get your kit brought up to scratch with effect immediate. You have been selected to meet a 'Very Important Person'."

So it was a day bulling up boots and equipment. The following day we boarded a truck with six other blokes and headed south through Perugia and then inland to Lake Trasimeno. Bivvied for the night in an area which could only be called a holiday camp. Flat countryside on the shore of a sky blue lake. Query to driver – 'What's the destination?'

"It's the map ref. of an airfield about 40 miles from here, and we have to be there by 10:00 hrs."

So it was up anchors and away. On arrival we were shepherded into some sort of parade formation by a Guards RSM. He then handed over to a 'brass hat' who called the parade to attention and left us standing and wondering.

He meanwhile wandered off to a large tent pitched to one side of the parade, and disappeared inside. It was minutes before a whole bunch of people came out with King George VI in the middle. Surprise, surprise! He had asked to meet representatives of the units who had successfully driven the Hun out of Africa and Italy, and here were hundreds of idiots standing and sweating, 'bulled' up to the eyes, having travelled all this way just to meet the old boy.

Anyway that's life I suppose, 'Ours is not to reason why!' A friendly chat, a meal afterwards (not a seven course dinner, believe me) and then on the truck for home.

Nothing unusual on the two nights journey except that on the second night the stop over was high in the Appenines at a small village called Seravalle. What a beautiful place it was too, clean and bright and so unlike most of the other places which had been shattered by war. The Germans had not been here and it was virtually untouched. The whole village turned out to see their first British soldier. The vino flowed freely and the songs of Italy were sung with more gusto than ability, and a great time was had by one and all. For some unknown reason the belle of the village, a real dark eyed beauty in her late teens, selected me as her beau at dancing (if you could call it that) and the whole thing went on until the small hours because, after all, we were their liberators from the 'Nazi-yoke' and she, for one, wanted to show her appreciation! Seravalle is one small village never to be forgotten!

The action of the next few days is well worth describing because it suddenly brought us, at least a small group of us, back into the war with a bang, several bangs in fact.

Dear Lady Astor you think you know a lot
standing on your platform and talking tommy rot
You, England's sweetheart, and its pride
we think your mouth is very wide
That's from the D-day dodgers in sunny Italy.

CHAPTER THIRTY

ALBACINO

The last day of July saw kits packed again and a journey south which took us through Macerata, then inland along mountain roads and passes, then northbound. Eventually the destination was reached, a village called Albacino.

Here was a partisan stronghold. Apparently the local partisan group had held out from the Germans for days, and they had been supplied from the air with arms, ammunition, food and uniforms by the British. So it was 'Vive l'Inglesi' on all sides and, once again, the vino flowed.

The word came down that this was to be a big job and the village would be our home for some time. Who could ask for better? Away from the bangs of war, living on a beautiful hillside (actually in a field of grapes not ripe, but very pleasant) and a village of friendly people with a good supply of vino.

The job. The powers that be had decided, apparently, to switch the main attack from the west to the east coast. This entailed the rapid move of five divisions (average 14,000 men in each) with all their heavy tanks and guns across a mountain range and a lateral road which had been designed (probably) for ox-carts. No one told the boys up top that 'Ted' had blown all the bridges and carried out a series of road crater jobs, just to stop such a move happening. So forward the Sappers!

In total there were 17 large bridges and numerous small ones. When was this move to be done? In two weeks or two years?

First full day was recce day and it was spent scouting out the lie of the land and establishing priorities and who would do what and when. So to No. 1 Section fell the job of the bridge, slap bang in the middle of the village. It was a beauty and obviously would cause numerous headaches when (and if) completed.

The largest and (eventually) the strongest of 17 it was again going to be unique in construction. The river, at this time of year, was a mere trickle at the bottom of a deep ravine, whose sides were steep and unassailable. The complications came about really because, on the far bank, the existing road ran parallel to the river and the whole of the area where the new bridge would eventually rest (the bankseat) was non-existent, it had been blown away with the bridge. Headache No. 1, and while Bob was sorting that one out, we took the chance in the evening to have a look at the nearest big town.

Fabriano. A fair sized place but with few civilians about. This was surprising because the war seemed to have passed by without knocking it about.

Once again it was 'Welcome British soldier, you are the first troops we have seen,' and soon, of course, the celebrations were in full swing. What a marvellous grape for wine in the area!

The natives were very friendly, after they had established that we were not Tedeschi, and soon there wasn't a bloke of ours to be seen in the streets. They all had got their feet under the table, or other place, and some had managed no doubt, to get their shoes and socks off too!

Next day was headache time, not only for the job but mostly from the larger amounts of vino safely stored away. There is one little house on the Via Roma, Fabriano with a small family whose men had gone to 'la guerra' (the war), which will be always remembered with affection.

The Company had, apparently, been given plenty of warning on these projects, so Bob decided that the best, and really only way, to construct the far bankseat would be by building it up with brick and concrete. What a job!

Memories of the Sangro! Firstly there was the problem of materials. Bricks, sand, aggregate were available by the ton but what of cement? Secondly were there enough 'brickies' in the Section to build up those enormous skins of brickwork ready for the concrete centre. This second problem was solved by including the stone mason (I wonder who) and cannibalising from the other Sections not engaged on brickwork.

When the local partisans knew of our problem with the cement they assured us that in the next town north, Sassoforata, there was a large cement works which supplied the whole of central Italy. There is one snag they said, the town is still in German hands. Bob said he doubted this because all reports clearly indicated that 'Ted' had withdrawn and the town was now ready for British occupation.

"We must ask for volunteers to fetch the cement, how about you Wat?" asked Bob. "You've got the White scout car, and I feel sure that your blokes would like the trip!"

He couldn't have said a truer word, that is if the trip was due south instead of north but, once again who are we to ask the reasons why? Ours is just to (better not finish that quote).

I agreed and decided to take only three blokes, thinking on the lines that if we did get cement and had to make a rapid exit, the lighter the load the better, particularly with a few bags of cement on board.

Only a few characters of No. 1 Sub. have been written about as yet which, I suppose is wrong of me in a way, because by bringing the individual into the story a much more interesting tale could be told. Really this was not the object of the book but instead it was started with the idea in mind of telling the reader about the 2nd World War from the view point of the 'other rank'. His thoughts on just how stupid it all was, just how wrong our leaders could be and how the ordinary soldier, in this case, the Sapper, had to make the best of his lot and get on with the job in hand. Now, after all that, to continue.

The ideal vehicle for the cement job would have been a formula one racing car but we had to do with the old White. No complaints really but it could be damned slow when loaded. An open back to the truck surrounded by fairly thick armoured plate with the obvious cab (and the NCO of course) hemmed in with thicker armour and in addition, when things got unusually hot there were visors which could be dropped all round, leaving slits to see through. Good old Yanks!

For weapons we had one Bren gun, a Boyes anti tank rifle, a Thompson .45 (mine) a 303 Lee Engield and the driver's .38 revolver, and with these we were prepared to take on the might of the German army to get our cement.

After about a mile along the road north (not south) we started to see British infantry and indeed it was rather good to see them because most were stripped to the waist in the glorious sunshine, some playing cards and generally lying around the place.

My thoughts then were that this wasn't a bad sort of war after all, with these front line chaps obviously making the best of things. But then another 1/2 mile or so the mistake was realised because we started to see blokes with battle kit on. No card playing here, this was the real thing. A little farther and the heavy machine guns began to appear, I counted six close to the road, all dug-in and pointing towards Sassoforata. Not good news at all!

The Officer in charge made a point of waving us down and enquiring in an 'Oxford' voice, "And just where do you think you are going with that vehicle? We bring our truck up by night and if the Hun sees yours we will get a hell of a shelling here!"

What good news indeed!

The story of the cement was told, and greeted with derision.

"Good god man! Don't you know that the Hun is in the town and your appearance will cause all hell to break loose?"

My next remark was one of supreme diplomacy.

"If you tell me that we should not pass your positions and give me a firm order to turn around then I shall do so."

A long pause and a reply to the effect that he could not do that and then something about you bloody Engineers think you run everything etc., etc. Then came a nice bombshell.

"You have just four hours to get your damned cement, it is now 10:00hrs and at 14.05hrs we fire. All guns (machine guns) will fire and the whole of the ground that you see in front of you will be covered from end to end. If you and your cement are still there you will not stand a chance!"

'What a charming bloke', I thought. 'If 'Ted' didn't get us - he would!'

We left without saying thanks, and as we progressed, the thought occurred that buying cement from the builder's merchant back home was dear enough, but this situation was ridiculous. Those many lives for a few bags of cement?

It was time Errol Flynn took over this job and fought against all those odds to get his horde of gold (sorry cement).

With apologies, the story will now be described in detail, just as it happened.

Slowly forward to the ridge in front and, as we breasted it so the whole of the valley below came into sight. I suppose, being the first troops there, we should have stuck our flag in the highest point and shouted 'God save the King', but we didn't have a flag and no one felt like getting out from behind that armour anyway.

Quite a fair size town right at the bottom, with the chimney of the cement works way over to the far left. Our road was very much a zigzag affair snaking down a very steep hillside with, I noticed, a similar one climbing the other side. Everywhere was dead silence but we *knew* for sure that 'Ted' was watching us. My hope was at that moment that he didn't want to give his positions away because he would have no idea how many tanks etc. were following us. Little did he know that it was just the local jobbing builder fetching cement!

Slowly down the road to the town, no hurry at all, that would be saved for the return trip. Outskirts of the town reached and still not a sound. Through the streets following the chimney knowing that there were dozens of eyes following us, but still nothing.

Cement works at last and as far as could be judged, bags of cement in piles everywhere to the tune of several hundred tons. Truck reversed up to platform and commence loading bags.

"Don't hang around boys because I believe that something is about to happen!"

There really was no need to say a word, we - including myself and driver - worked like slaves. It was at this point that Bob the driver made a point.

"If you stick any more on we'll never get up that hill!"

That caused an immediate stop and without a word, the boys, knowing what was to come, took up their positions on the floor of the truck lying prone with the cement in the centre, neatly stacked and looking every bit the part of the local jobber. Would 'Ted' know the difference?

Then things started to happen. Before we could get out of the yard, the first shell went ranging over the top and pitched some one hundred yards away. Within seconds the second followed and taking our cue we dived into the cab, visors down and away. Horror of horrors the load was obviously too heavy because we only managed a 'chug-chug' with a speed of about 10mph. Not nearly good enough, but because *he* now had the range of the building, (who could resist a chimney like that with a battery of guns at one's command?) and was raining them down thick and fast it was unanimously decided to dump cement while in motion, though not a word was said. It is guaranteed that Sassoforata had never before, and never will ever again, see a truck moving through the main street with bags of cement being thrown off the back!

Speed achieved by this means, 20mph, by no means good enough, on the flat, with still a very steep, and long hill to come. His 88's (shells) were by now hitting the main road and, obviously, he was plotting our route. At the end of the houses, we knew, that it was open ground and the start of the climb, what would be waiting?

The German accuracy with mortars is very well known and respected throughout the British Army, and we were about to witness a practical demonstration.

The truck was stopped in the shelter of the last house of the village in order to plan the course of action. I was determined to get at least several bags of cement through. Bob was still very doubtful about his truck being overweight with the steep hill to climb at any speed at all so for me it was lightning calculation time, and with a problem in which the Army 1st Class certificate in maths was no help. How many bags of cement (in metric weight) would be needed to build a 3 to 1 mix brickwork, and 4:2:1 concrete, a bankseat of unknown width depth and thickness to carry a Class 70 Bailey Bridge? There were far too many unknowns to rely on algebra, so it would have to be physical trial and error.

The 'White' was still loaded to virtual capacity, so there would be scope, if necessary, to dump a few more bags. This was the 'drill' worked out in detail. Bob was to drive the first two hundred yards, which would include the first one hundred yards of incline, in order to see what speed could be obtained with near capacity load. The decision would then be taken whether it would be necessary to start dumping more cement or not.

'Ted' of course knew exactly what we would do. His 88s had now been joined by several mortars and the road ahead was receiving some direct hits so, Bob, foot down now!

The first 150 yards were covered at about 25mph until the incline slowed us to about half that speed, and it was this that saved the cement because 'Ted' in his wisdom, had worked out our approximate speed and set his sights accordingly, so the shells were now bursting way out in front.

It was then decided that to avoid becoming sitting ducks more cement had to be dumped, and so as our load lightened so the speed increased.

To add to this factor of course were the numerous bends in the road and, in retrospect, I wonder if 'Ted' was deceived into thinking that the bursts from the cement bags were some of his shells dropping on our tail.

The main thing was, we survived as did at least 1 dozen bags of cement. It cost the Germans quite a bit in manpower, ammunition and loss of prestige and as a result a bridge was built which eventually, probably, helped to shorten the war.

As a simple Royal Engineer I could never understand the stupidity of war. How easy it would have been for that (or another) gunnery officer to take up a position on that ridge, with glasses, and plotted every gun position as it fired instead of sitting in fixed positions firing twice a day with all guns and expending valuable ammunition at no fixed target!

Destination reached and while bridging stores were being assembled on the home (launching) bank, two teams of bricklayers and concretors started work on the far bankseat. It was midsummer and very hot and sticky so Bob, in his wisdom, divided the work into two shifts with the midday hours avoided.

Most of the time was taken up by the brick and concrete work and almost a week elapsed before launching could be started. The bridge itself had to be (as mentioned before) strong enough to carry the heaviest loads of the Army and so was a massive structure of triple double construction and over 200 feet in length.

Building it was quite enjoyable because of the absence of 'Ted' with all his brass band support, and of course unlimited friendship from the natives with their wine supply. The bridge and associated works were completed about the 17th August and named, naturally, Albacino Bridge.

Now the reason for our labours and sweat started to show dividends. Traffic over the completed bridge started to swell from a trickle to a flood with the Divisional Signs of at least five divisions easily recognisable. Guns, tanks, trucks, of all sizes queued to get over and it was now obvious that things were happening and the next push up the East Coast was coming.

Soon it was another rush to move. Sassoforata had been cleared and 'Ted' had blown the next bridge. The problem now became how the hell to get through that jungle of traffic to get to it?

It took a small convoy of DRs and redcaps to achieve this and when the bridge area was eventually reached it looked like fair day and Derby day combined. People were camped everywhere just waiting to cross that river, the Sentino. Some were doing the usual brew, others just 'kipping' and performing the normal functions of life but, unlike most scenes of days gone by, now they were in their thousands. I well remember saying a silent prayer. 'Thank God Mutt & Jeff are not about!'

It was to be a 130ft double double, quite a structure, and eventually called 'Flappe', after the flaps and pressure on us to complete. It took just over six hours, surely a record? Total completion was achieved in 12 hours flat and immediately that great convoy started to cross. What a different war this had now become. The comparison between this and Tunis was unbelievable. Whereas then we were bogged down to creeping about at night-time in small groups, here were whole divisions, all eager to get forward to have a go at 'Ted' as if it was all a grand cup final.

Now followed a series of moves, sometimes of over a dozen or so miles at a time, but the one good thing was, the move was always north and therefore always nearer to home and the day for 'Ted' to say 'Kamerad!' Most of the moves finished with a bridge to build or an area to clear of mines but we were always ahead of that massive convoy.

Towards the end of the month it became obvious that Jerry was beginning to dig his heels in and show resistance. The occasional shell turned into a dozen or more fired as a group and the heavy bombers started running by night again. Mostly anti-personnel bombs again, which were obviously aimed at morale busting. Was this the start of the 'Gothic Line?'

Our forward movement over the next few days started to slow because of the many strong points 'Ted' had established, all of which were protected by barbed wire entanglements and minefields. The wire itself was reasonably easy to clear when it wasn't mined or booby trapped, but the minefields were a different matter. Each had been carefully prepared over a long period and were well protected with a liberal scattering of anti-personnel mines and anti-lifting devices. Many Sappers died or received serious wounds from these devilish devices. Some reports were being received to the effect that the Germans were even booby trapping their own dead. These reports were going the rounds some time ago and as a result, the German dead who lay in most places where he had resisted in any strength were left lying where they were, instead of receiving a decent burial. One result of this was that instead now of seeing German corpses with massive and messy wounds, the majority were washed clean of blood and gore by the heavy rain showers received mostly by night. It was a very weird and unsettling sensation to see into a head containing clean bones and no flesh. The daytime extreme heat made things very unpleasant indeed, with the flies and other nasties multiplying a hundred fold.

It was at times like these, with the addition of heavy shelling now taking place and heavy bombing by night, that one wondered just how much the human mind could stand. Time and again men cracked through no fault of their own. The absolute limit of human endurance had been reached and there was no way of preventing it. Only by removal from that never ending carnage could any relief be achieved.

If anything the Allied barrage was growing in intensity and coupled together with the bombing and strafing taking place all round, it was obvious that the stronghold of the Gothic Line had been reached.

When the guns were laying down a barrage overhead, one's thoughts turned to those long convoys of 3.7, 4.5, 5.5, and 7.2, not forgetting of course the finest British gun of all, the 25 pounder, and the sweating and swearing gunners crossing our bridges. Were these the fruits of our labours? Gunners being maimed and killed and ourselves being driven insane with the noise of it all?

It was at this time that we suddenly came under command of 46 Div., The Oak Tree, an old friend of the North African days and a move which always meant a very active spell was about to break.

Sure enough there followed days of continual movement with numerous jobs of mine clearing, river crossing, booby trap clearance etc., etc. There was hardly one night spent in the same area and it was obvious from all the activity of guns and aircraft on both sides that a continual attack was being maintained. One particular Unit who appeared to be on front line duty for long spells were the Hampshires and judging by the amount of replacements going in, and wounded coming out, their casualties must have been very heavy.

On the last day of August a message came in from the Observation Post that several large German guns could be seen taking up position across from the Div. front. Later on that day they (the guns) began to range up on the cross-roads slightly to our right and how right the O.P. was, they were big stuff indeed and were causing chaos at the cross-roads. Surely there would be a strike against them soon?

By nightfall it was artillery only who took them on and, because of darkness, the RAF had missed their chance. This was to prove a costly and hard lesson learned.

Just after midnight their barrage became murderous and impossible to withstand, so it was decided to evacuate our semi ruin of a farmhouse. Unfortunately it proved too late and after several salvoes of shells, pitching all around, we took a direct hit. Total collapse of house. All men under rubble. Non casualties digging for survivors, many stretcher cases. One death known – young Sergeant – saw Eddie and Michael stretchered away – total chaos – shelling continues.

Daylight saw a sorry mess with trucks from various Units hit, with their human cargo, by shellfire. No buildings were left standing in the area but then the RAF started to find 'Ted'. A continuous stream of Marauders kept up a never ending bombing run on the Gunner positions until, again, the world had gone mad and all sanity was lost. Was it possible to feel sympathy for the ordinary German soldier lying screaming under these bombs? Men who, perhaps, had been conscripted into the army against their will and were now being pounded out of all sensible feeling. Where were the people who had caused it all? Certainly not under these bombs, but surely their turn was to come!

The big guns were silenced.

No respite from the job in hand and forward once more where a bridge across the next river was urgently required. The area was under shellfire and so no 'Derby Day' stuff here. Everyone seemed well and truly under cover and appeared to be adapting the now recognised policy of waiting for the RAF and Artillery to take the sting out of 'Ted's' resistance, before making any advances. The bridge was one requirement before any forward movement could be attempted, so forward the Sappers again.

This time a triple single over quite a span but fairly straight forward construction, apart from the shells whistling close by which, fortunately, did not cause any casualties among our Section.

The name of the river – Apsa which from memory was the first one not ending in 'O'. Why, I wonder was the change from male to female and how could a river have a gender? The name of the bridge was not recorded, probably because of all the running and ducking going on there wasn't time to write a sign.

Look around the mountains, in the mud and rain
See the scattered crosses, some which have no name,
Heart break and sorrow are all gone
The boys beneath them slumber on;
They are the D-Day dodgers who stayed in Italy.

CHAPTER THIRTY ONE

THE PAPER WAR

There should be mention here of the propaganda war that was taking place on both sides. All cleverly done, particularly by the Germans who, no doubt, devoted a great deal of time and machinery into this aspect of war.

A lot of it was lies, and then again much of it was based on the truth but really stretched almost to breaking point.

'Ted's' information sheets were delivered by, mostly, small calibre shells which must have been especially designed so that when they burst high above a troop concentration, the small amount of explosives contained in the shell would scatter the leaflets without damaging them.

The British system was totally different in all ways. Firstly the method of delivering was always by aircraft. Pamphlets and papers dropped from a fair height and well scattered but unfortunately if the wind was in the wrong direction we received most of them. The thought occurred again, 'Thank God that this is not chemical warfare!'

These British papers were two types usually, one of which was printed in both English and German and was worded to the effect that 'This German soldier is unarmed and wishes to give himself up to the Allied forces etc., etc.'. In other words a 'safe' conduct into captivity. I wonder just how many 'Jerries' were shot waving these bits of paper? It would all depend on the amount of shelling and shooting that the British soldier had been receiving at the time, and just how many of his mates had been killed or wounded during the previous period.

The other was a complete newspaper of approximately the size of today's small daily papers and had news and happenings of the war from all fronts and parts of the world. There were always a liberal amount of maps of war situations which obviously told the German soldier just what a bad position his country was now in. During our 'off duty' breaks we would spend hours learning from these just how the situations were on the Russian and Pacific Fronts, they were far more up to date than our own news sheets and I wondered here 'was the priority of this, right?' Was not our morale just as important as 'Ted's'? Of course, there was always the fact that we were going forward while he was retreating.

The German system was pure propaganda and consisted of numerous leaflets aimed at disturbing or even breaking the morale of the British soldier. The amount and different types received became so numerous that I began to make a collection and eventually, having received permission, sent both German and British examples home to my local newspaper editor. They received quite a 'blow-up' on the front page under the heading of 'Local man in Paper War', followed by a graphic description, so much so that dear old Mum was being stopped in the street by all and sundry and held in long conversation about something of which she knew very little, but of course, loved every minute of it. They are now in Cardiff Castle Museum.

Several types were aimed at the Jews and just how they were running the country back home while you - The British Soldier - are lying in the mud and blood of Italy.

One depicted a large dining table absolutely laden with glorious food. Seated alternatively with beautiful 'English-rose' type girls were fat bloated Jews, and overprinted in outline on the table was a British soldier lying badly wounded with blood pouring from a head wound, and words to the effect of 'Look at the Jews in London enjoying your food and women'.

A few days before that he ('Ted') had forgotten that he had been telling us that 'London had been completely obliterated by German bombs'.

Another regular receipt from 'him' was one which, at first, caused some upset and annoyance, particularly amongst the married men. 'Are you *sure* you know what your wife or sweetheart is doing while you are lying in the trenches?' Now, in the cold light of peace, this appears to be clever wording or even amusing, but this was an entirely different matter to those men, living as they were on biscuits and 'Compo' rations mostly, and probably having been away from home for a couple of years knowing that our country was full of Yanks loaded with money and lots of goodies to give away. The air usually turned blue with ff's and a few 'German bastards' thrown in. I can imagine the treatment a German would receive if he came in then waving a piece of paper.

Propaganda against the Yanks was always a favoured subject, aimed, obviously, at causing bad feeling between the Allies, but naturally little notice was taken of the rubbish.

One more German pamphlet depicted an open topped 1938 sports car with a young man and his girl parked in a lover's lane.

How long since you had your arm around your girl in a leafy lane? Instead you are here in the blood of Italy with your arms around your rifle, read this caption.

The Yanks magazine *Life* was regularly received in beautiful colour, but just one sheet and on the reverse side *Death* with a British steel helmet on a skull.

Typical German mentality which, for sure, did very little good and must have cost him a good deal.

Enough about propaganda, it's time to get this war finished!

CHAPTER THIRTY TWO

A NINE DAY HEAVEN

For some time rumours had been circulating amongst the Company's 'know-it-all' boys that groups of the Section were to be sent to Rome on nine days' leave. That's just not possible, was the natural reaction. How, in the middle of all this bloody killing could anybody just jump on a truck and land in a beautiful city, where nothing went wrong, your heart stopped pounding and your stomach emptied of butterflies? But it did happen. Heaven indeed with only one blot on the landscape, but in the meantime, things were still happening here.

Autumn had arrived and with it those cold wet miserable nights again when all clothing became saturated with no chance of drying out even if it did stop raining.

On the 1st September a 5am start to a journey was made. The move took us through infantry and tank positions to where a series of hillside tracks had become virtually unrecognisable as such. They were now just a quagmire where everything mobile ceased to be so. What vehicles had succeeded in getting to this point had now become completely bogged down and, because of a serious setback on the ridge overlooking the area, where 'Ted' had pushed the 56th Div. (The Black Cat Div.) back some distance, he now had observation over the area and was acting accordingly. Almost continuous mortar and shelling was pounding the area and again life had turned to hell.

Our orders were not to bother with the dozens of stranded vehicles now being rapidly turned into scrap metal, but to form one track which would be usable by all the new trucks now arriving.

A daylight job proved impossible because of the concentrated shellfire so Monty's Moonlight was laid-on and eventually some sort of track began to emerge.

On the second night of this work it became obvious that our task was being made possible only because a very strong attack was being made to recapture the high ground to our right. This attack must have eventually proved successful because the heavy shelling gradually died away and work went on until dawn on the track, when completion was reached.

A new form of warfare, for us anyway, developed during that night. German aircraft dropping phosphorus bombs. On impact they burst and scattered what can only be described as a liquid fire over all and sundry.

The wounds from these caused untold agony and many British troops died a very painful death.

My next diary entry reads – Sun 3rd Sept. 1944. 'The war is five years old today – are we all going mad?'

That day it was a further move forward past the area of the scrap yard and newly made track. Here the evidence of what went on was everywhere, numerous bodies and what remained of bodies were scattered all around. What a mad world!

There is no doubt that this area was well and truly the 'Gothic Line'. Defensive positions were everywhere and 'turfing' the Germans out of them was Johnny Gurkha. He is a magnificent soldier who, surely must be one of the world's best. How would Britain reward them after the war?

It was a minefield clearing task which I suppose is about the worst job we are called on to do, but on this occasion no casualties to our immediate personnel thank goodness.

The battle for this part of the 'Gothic Line' grew in intensity over the days to follow, with heavy bombing raids being carried out by both sides, Allied by day, German by night with now his phosphorus anti-personnel and H.E. Can one get used to this?

The answer to that question must always be no. One reads of battle hardened troops and such rubbish but, although they learn how to protect themselves (say) by digging a foxhole at the right time and place, the battles get worse as the time goes by. Every bomb and shell falling close by is registered in the mind and, depending on circumstances and personal stability the day of breaking is bound to come. I very often thought that my sanity was saved only because when 12 men plus one (One Sub) were lying in a terrified heap as they often were, somebody had to give a lead and, at least, pretend to be less frightened than the rest.

For the remainder of that awful month, during which we hardly ever had a dry shirt to our backs, the battles went on all around in absolute zero conditions. Morale was very low because there appeared to be no end to the pounding of high explosives, the endless mud and rain, and the emotional tasks entailing life risking situations.

The diary notes from here read that the navy had added its weight to the daily (and nightly) barrage. Also between Allied bombing raids during daylight hours, the Kitty bombers had started to appear regularly. These pilots deserved recognition for bravery. As they dived low overhead to strike they received a terrific barrage of German 20mm flak and machine gunfire, but they dived through it all to make first a bombing run then a continual circuit of strafing until all ammunition was gone. Gentlemen I recognise and salute what you did, the life of many an Allied soldier was saved through your bravery.

After some progress on to further high ground there suddenly came into sight the three peaks, so easily recognisable from the postage stamps of the small boy at school, of San Marino. This, as far as we knew, was a neutral state but it soon became evident that someone was abusing their neutrality, because a series of air bursts could be clearly seen in the sky above.

Several more days of progress, slow and costly, towards the neutral state, and now our 25 pounder shells could clearly be seen bursting over the boundary. That could mean only one thing, 'Ted' had broken the neutrality and was being chased for it.

The task now, right on the boundary, was a bridge over the Ausa river (feminine again?) a fairly wide one of some 200 feet and once again would call for night working because of the situation. One very unpleasant feature here was the presence of many a dozen dead cows and horses. The reason for this never became obvious but the smell of rotten flesh and gas filled bodies was almost unbearable. The 'know-alls' said that 'Ted' used a lot of horse transport, and cows for fresh milk and food. They were abandoned here because of having been overrun by one of our attacks. I wonder!

Monty's Moonlight was called for again and proved invaluable. Panel pins could be seen to be hammered without hitting thumbs first so, if nothing else, our dear General was indirectly responsible for cutting down the number of 'f's' flying around by about 99%!

Rain continual rain caused complete saturation again. The diary says 'too wet to moan now.' But of course, no one listens to the moans anyway – because they are wet too!

A crawl back to a saturated bivouac to be greeted by a wonderful clerk from HQ with the words that I just could not believe.

"You have been selected for 9 days' leave in Rome."

"Repeat please," and again, "Repeat please," until at last it registered!

How, when, where were the questions. How do I get dry? Where do I get transport? When do I leave this mad world etc., etc.? It was all so unbelievable!

"You leave in one hour," was the answer, "and if you are not ready, the truck leaves without you because it has several pick-up points where people are waiting."

I could leave as I was, which was saturated and mud covered, in one minute was the answer. So, discard the wet clothes, on with the (damp only) ones of the previous day, wash the mud off body and face and grab shaving kit etc., and ready well in time.

7.30am. Several of Sub-section One had been selected to go and soon we were bowling merrily along to Company HQ, having left pleading requests behind to 'dry out' the discarded wet clothing (at least hang it up in the 'bivvy') and, whatever you do during absence, make sure that our kit goes with you when you move. This was made under threat of dire consequences of course if not carried out, but promises of a yard of spaghetti from Rome if achieved!

Here it must be stated that the intention was, when Rome was reached, a further journey of some 130 miles south (by hitch-hike) would bring me to the slopes of Vesuvio, and I wonder what? Time, of course would be an important factor but, what the hell, one or two days would do at Trécasé, and were we not out of the mud and bangings of that mad world?

Company HQ reached, then on to CRE for final pick up. Then came the typical disorganisation which made the modern soldier so browned off with the Army. No-one had ordered the transport from here on, and there were still several hundred miles to go.

All morning we sneezed, coughed and cursed in damp clothing in a wet tent until just before midday when a '3-tonner' was provided. This was the first day of leave, so we were already down to 8 1/2 days.

On the road to Ancona a bit sharp before anyone changed the plan, and then south down the Adriatic coast. Familiar places began to show up but with a difference already. Civilians had now begun to return to their homes and clearing up was rapidly being carried out, but it was an almost impossible task because most towns and villages were absolutely 'gutted'. At an estimate, about 90% of buildings were shattered and lying in piles of rubbish, roads and streets were cratered, water and other services were non existent and one could not help but feel sorry for our former enemy. Without any doubt whatsoever, it was certain that the German bastard had deliberately used the 'scorched-earth' policy right throughout Italy and destroyed all he possibly could. Evidence began to emerge later in the campaign of terrible atrocities carried out by the Boche on the Italian people. The thought of this sort of thing happening back home brings a shudder to one and all. Thank God he did not cross the channel in 1940! On reflection, of course, he must have known that there was an 18 year old Sapper waiting for him on Dover cliffs, armed with a rifle and bayonet. But, of course, he didn't know that I couldn't get into that hut to telephone a warning, because it was locked. Perhaps if he *had* known...?

Travelled the rest of the day south, slept night in back of 3-tonner, no beds of course but the diary doesn't say that. What it does say is 'Ear drums ringing from lack of bangs!'

Down to Foggia and across to Rome which was reached late afternoon - 7 days left, and the return journey to be allowed for.

Rome will not be described here. It was, and is the Eternal City and a good guide book will tell all. Don't buy one off an Italian, he will swindle you 100% if possible. We soon found that swindling in all its form was just a game to them, a way of life when honesty was not even considered.

Kit dumped in Rest Camp on outskirts of city, a quick look around, slept night and at crack of dawn out onto the Naples road – thumbing a lift.

Lots of Yanks coming and going on leave, so within minutes was on the way. Several changes of transport en route and then Trécasé.

On the long walk up from the AutoStrada, a call was made into the casa (home) of a friendly Italian family, well remembered from the previous stay. The best vino soon flowed in a welcoming manner but there was, somehow, a strange atmosphere about them which did not come over too good. They wanted to know all about the war up country of course, etc. but during their conversation the words 'prigiaoniero Inglese' came over loud and clear and occasionally the word 'Carla'. They were talking about an Italian prisoner of war in England and, I felt sure, my relationship with Carla but, let's see, without jumping the gun.

The welcome at 161 via Regina was like that to a son home from the wars. Mamma cried, Luigi said his piece, but in broken English now and, of course, the vino flowed. These were the only two at home at that time, but listening carefully to their dialect (Neapolitan) it was obvious that things were not quite right.

The young girls came next, and eventually Carlotta. Surprise and, I think, some anxiety showed but only the words of welcome were said.

An excellent evening followed with non-stop talk, non-stop vino flow and spaghetti Neapolitan by the mile, or was it kilometre?

'Sloshed' to bed, an unconscious night when nothing and no one went bang, and a return to a conscious existence about mid morning – black sweet coffee!

Then, and with a shock, the thought occurred, no beautiful long black hair draped over the face to wake up Leonardo! The reason was revealed by Papa that evening.

Before my arrival on the scene for the first time, an old Italian custom had been faithfully observed and that was to promise the eligible daughter's hand in marriage to someone of Papa's choosing. In this case it was the son of his best friend.

All this Papa explained to me in slow and loud Italian, with the appropriate hand gesture thrown in.

This young man had apparently been called to the forces early in 'la guerra' (the war) and, as a Tenente (Lieutenant) had gone to North Africa to 'faré guera con l'Inglesi' (to fight against the British) and had been reported killed. Heartbreak all round, said Papa, but after a couple of years Carlotta was now over it. When she met you she was 'overjoyed to know that you would marry her and portare a l'Ingliterra (take her to England!)' Christ! Steady on old boy! That's a bit heavy isn't it? Just because the old hair is draped across the face of a morning and...

'But,' said Papa, in recent weeks the Tenente had been declared a prisoner of war in England and would soon be returning home.'

"Now!" said Papa, "the big upset has occurred. There is no doubt in my mind what Carla should do, and that is to marry the son of my best friend, the Tenente. Please do not take offence because to me you are not only like a son but a very fine man and a very brave soldier fighting to throw Tedeschi out of my country etc., etc.!" (He obviously didn't know me!) But this is the Italian way of speech and, when spoken in their language it comes more naturally off the tongue, or should that be the shoulder?

Please remember that this (one sided) conversation was all in Italian and, by now, I was flapping a bit trying to follow the gist of it all!

Then came the really bitter bit.

"Carla has decided that she wishes to marry you and nobody and nothing else will do!" Christ! "Mamma and the rest of the family are undecided so tonight we are going to have a discussion and decide."

It appeared that my opinion wasn't being called for but somewhere there was an alarm ringing! But let's see!

After the evening meal and removal of enormous quantities of vino from larder to stomach (I never thought it possible to drink so much without sliding under the table, but to them it was everyday stuff) and then Papa opened the bowling!

It must be explained here the absolute difference between a family conversation in England, to that of one in Italy. As is well known the Italians have a gesture to describe all situations e.g.: hunger, evil, good and a hundred others, and these were used to great effect particularly when the body temperature was rising as it always appears to be.

In England the same situation would probably call for an armchair chat over a cup of tea, and a few expressions such as 'steady old girl' etc., etc.

This present discussion was one from which I was left out altogether because, firstly it was all in their local dialect, and this can vary from district to district, as with Geordie to

Cockney, and secondly what was there for me to say without putting my big foot in it?

The arm waving and rapid conversation went on for a very long time, and it was obvious that Papa and Carla were quarrelling which, at times, became violent and tearful.

Eventually, with decisions made, peace reigned and after the family drifted off to bed to leave Carla to explain to me just what the results of all that were. I settled down to hear, in perfect Italian, that 'Carla loved Leonardo more than anything in the world etc., etc. Mamma and Papa had pointed out to her that by marrying me she would not only split from her family but would cause a great upset between Papa and his best friend, the son of whom was writing home regularly to say just how much he wanted to marry Carlotta etc.'

Christ! now the alarm bells *were* ringing!

That night the subject received a lot of thought on what action to take by yours truly. There were several considerations to face:- 1) Don't cause a family split by encouraging Carla; 2) Stay friendly to all and show appreciation of their friendship and kindness to me. To do this meant a break with Carla, gently, and over a long period if necessary so, action young man!

The following day they received the explanation that I would be leaving tomorrow – because it was only a short leave, and someone had to chase Tedeschi out of their country etc., etc.

Goodbyes were said amongst tears. Real ones from C but doubtful from Mamma because, of course, she just had to back up Papa, and I was on my way knowing really that this was goodbye for good. Enough said on the subject but there was a sequel of sorts to follow.

Some six months after this episode, an Italian solder stopped me to ask 'was I Leonardo, and had I been to Trécasé and did I know the family Cirillo etc.?' The answer yes brought a hug, a hug mark you and a letter, by hand, from Carla. Apparently the soldier was a 'cugina' (cousin) from the same village and had been pioneering (labouring) for me for some time, and had just returned from leave to Trécasé. Sort that one out!

The letter bore all the hall marks of a broken heart and questions of why and why not etc. Time is a great healer and wasn't there a Tenente looming large somewhere, so I decided to leave it at that.

"Please tell your beautiful cousin that I think of her everyday and will see her again one day."

But the decision was made and I knew that I never would!

Could I just take five minutes of your time to say the final word on this?

A year ago my wife and I toured the whole of Italy and I made the point of taking her to Trécasé. She knew the story and was delighted when most of the villagers, when they knew who we were, turned out to give us a tremendous welcome. A slap up meal followed at their brand new restaurant with the manager acting as host, and then the questions.

Carlotta had died the previous year. Her husband, an ex-Tenente, still lived in Rome with their two children. Luigi was a doctor in Naples. Mama and Papa had lived into their 90's and had died recently.

161 Via Regina was still there with a new family of course. An invite inside was agreed to and, surprise, surprise, although there had been major alterations made, my old bedroom space was still there, where the beautiful long dark hair draped daily.

Goodbye Trécasé. Or was it? In a small town in the heart of Wales there is a house called Trécasé!

CHAPTER THIRTY THREE

RETURN TO WAR

And so back to Rome. Only a couple of days here, so not a lot of time to gain much appreciation of the place. First impressions were of a city, big, beautiful, smelly, costly, extremely so, and over populated by Yanks who seemed to be everywhere. The small boys of Rome had developed a few dozen, so called, English words and followed anyone in Allied uniform with these wonderful words "Cheeps Joe? You wanna meet my sister Joe? You wanna nice clean girl?" and even, "You wanna nice clean boy Joe?" Yes, they were here, too, not very much different to the Casbahs of North Africa.

A guided (and costly) tour of this city and it was time to take the road north again.

It was now early October and as we travelled the colder weather could be felt. It was time to give up KD and back to the old battle dress again!

Slept the night in a truck near a small village and by the next night was in Rimini. This was a fair sized town but had received a tremendous battering by both sides. Stayed the night again here, then next day on to CRE.

My diary entries here become a little hazy and to be quite truthful so does my mind because of the awful things that very suddenly brought us back to life, or nearly death.

There is a distinct recollection of staying at No. 2 Section and then on to HQ or was it vice versa? If it had been vice versa then things would have, perhaps, been better for all.

HQ was in the town of Santarchangelo and No. 2 Section not far away. During a chat with the local infantry unit, we learned that 'Ted' had the whole area under observation from the high ground 'at the back'.

"You will be very lucky to get that truck through in daylight!"

Thanks very much for that news and welcome back from leave!

The next memory is of being outside of No. 2 location farmhouse with the truck against the wall away from 'Ted' and out of sight. Here, my old mate of Fordingbridge, Jimmy W, was running the stores and for sure we would qualify for a mug of tea.

Jim was pleased to see us and got a tea dixie on the boil. A long chat of Fordingbridge and Betty and Molly so and so, tea made with Jim carrying a whole trayful across the room when 'Ted' hit us!

He had obviously followed our journey along the lateral road, seen us stop at the farm and decided to spoil our tea party.

The first shell was a big 'un. It landed in mud across the road, and the picture I saw was huge clods of earth coming through the air and at the same moment old Jim trying to dive under the table without spilling the tea. How he achieved it will never be known but there he was safely underneath and half full mugs on top, ready for supping!

The tea tasted of nectar until that big boom in the distance said that another one was on the way.

This one took half the roof off and the tea now tasted of plaster and dust, but nobody hurt yet!

Then came a saving factor. Trucks belting past at full speed and so attracting the 'Ted' gunners to a bigger target.

Officer i/c No. 2 Section advised us to stay the night in HQ as they were in the town and therefore not an individual target!

That was one piece of advice, in retrospect, which I wish had never been taken because what followed was judged up to then my worse night of the war. This is said with all sincerity, even though there had been awful nights, bloody awful nights before, such as Medjez-El-Bab and the Sangro etc., etc.

The shelling was intermittent but by very heavy calibre stuff and seemed to go on for hours. The shells landing were, I guessed, about 210mm, heavy for a mobile type of war but, his favourite when the object was to destroy a target. This he was doing very thoroughly to that town, district by district.

HQ billet surrounded a concrete courtyard with various small buildings attached, and it was in one of these that the returning leave party was sleeping on the concrete floor.

Was the word sleeping used? Such a thing wasn't possible with all those express trains roaring past. Then it happened. One or two pitched very close with the shrapnel crashing against the wall until the thought was 'one more and it will go'! Then came the direct hit!

How does one describe such a thing? I was in a complete daze but became aware of several things. The roof had gone and one wall, there were plaster and bricks covering everybody, and breathing was nearly impossible because of the thick dust, but, although stone deaf from the blast I was still alive and in one piece. Thank God was the reaction, until I saw Syd. He was lying half propped against the wall but in a terrible state. The shell splinters had ripped off some of his clothing and caused a wound from which I knew he would never recover. He was conscious but could not speak. His eyes were saying please help. What could I do except call for help? Little did I know then that others had died too.

The next chap needing help was Jim, he was sitting in a heap against the wall, but alive, with head bent forward and hands clasped in front. A quick feel of him showed no wounds but he was completely paralysed. Hands held so tightly together that they would not come apart and the whole body rigid. God above! Was this the Jim I played soccer with who was always the first choice for the Company team in nearly all sports?

As you will realise by now, we were all in a state of shock but my main concern was just how was our Sub. faring, at least those who had come on leave with me.

Out into what was left of the courtyard only to see stretchers being carried, occupied, in all directions. The thought through the haze was 'how were people still alive and able to do this?'

Somebody was yelling at me: "Bert is dead, Charlie will never live after these wounds!"

I knew then that this wasn't real, it was just happening, and yet those express trains were still passing closely overhead!

Things started to make a little sense after a while and I guided the stretcher bearers to Syd who by now, thank God, was no longer conscious. My stupid mind was asking how could they move him without parting the torso from his legs, the wound was that bad.

The official figures afterwards said nine casualties but this was wrong. A count by the 'other ranks' of lads we knew revealed seventeen gone altogether.

The aftermath of this night's shelling was to affect almost everyone in the Company. Chaps who were so well known to us all, were gone. Bert was the Sgt. in charge of motor transport, a finer bloke would never be found. Friendly to all and yet very efficient at his job. He could always be seen on that motorbike when the Company was on the move. Charlie was happy-go-lucky and a typical Sub-section commander whose blokes would follow anywhere.

With the two lost of No. 1 Sub-section the total gone of the original 12 plus 1 was 9. Just 3 men and myself were left, all the others were replacements. Some of the replacements had been replaced!

Syd had come to us in the early days from the Paras. Had taken a 'bashing' somewhere and had been transferred to his trade as a 'chippy'. One of the best!

Jim's case could not be understood. Here was the finest all-round sportsman with the highest of standards for fair play. Common sense was part of his make-up and he was always one of the first to follow on when the order was given. Putting him on to that casualty truck on that terrible day, so many years ago, will not be forgotten ever.

Forty years later at a Company reunion, one of the three survivors, Bob L was telling me that he had been to visit Jim. He was in a Mental Hospital where he would spend his life.

Speech had not returned in 40 years and he was almost completely paralysed.

By a strange coincidence at a Chepstow old boys reunion, I had a yelling conversation with my old mate 'Pin' Richards. Yelling, because I can hear with one ear only, and that's not very good. (Pin was wearing an NHS hearing aid in both ears.)

"How and when did you become deaf?" was my question.

His answer, "At a little place called Santarchangelo on the Adriatic coast of Italy. 'Ted' gave us a hell of a pasting overnight. It was our worse night for casualties!"

His was a totally different unit to ours. 'Pin' suffered three severe wounds on separate occasions, which included the loss of one eye and total deafness, but still insisted on serving his country. It would be very interesting to know just how many casualties there were in that place – could it possibly mean Saints and Archangels?

The day after the German attention to the Company they were all sent back for two days to San Marino to 'sort themselves out' and get ready for the next 'push'.

But not No. 1 Section, they had not been in the shelling because of a job 5 miles up the road. The blokes with me from No. 1 who had been on leave and mixed up with the shelling just had to grin and bear it. We did neither, no one grinned and everyone moaned like hell, but then war has no sympathetic ears.

There were road repairs to be done in the area and these had now become very urgent because of the spoiling policy 'Ted' was using. Every road and track had been cratered by what must have been powerful bombs dug into them so causing devastation which took days to repair.

The river bridge was blown too and although the infantry had managed to get some chaps over, their situation was desperate. No supplies, no tank support, and therefore no help until a Bailey could be built. It had to be a night-time job because of the presence of those 210mm, and the area being overlooked by (his) high ground.

It was double-single construction and quite hefty to complete in one night. 'Ted' didn't help matters by dropping his 210mms all around the place but come dawn we were away, job done. The tank men had to use smoke to cross. This hid the bridge but alerted 'Ted' to something going on, and he rose to the occasion by laying on a 'stonk'. This as usual, was a blanket type barrage using mostly 88mm, and mortars.

It was the next day that we learned from our Italian map, the name of the river. It was the Rubicon. Naturally the bridge was called Caesar's crossing.

CHAPTER THIRTY FOUR

THE LOMBARDY PLAIN AT LAST

For about six days after this, the main jobs were to get the roads open, because the Army were now across the Rubicon, and pushing hard to capture the next line of hills which, the map told us, was the last high ground before the Plain of Lombardy.

Surely once on that huge plain (the Po Valley) with no high ground for 'Ted' to have the sighting advantage, it would be a racing ground for the tanks right up to and over the Po. Let's wait and see!

The first move took us nine miles into the foothills, and every mile had to be fought for by infantry and tank. It may sound corny now, in these days of peace so many years later, but those infantry chaps were magnificent. Not many volunteers amongst them, I should imagine, and many white faced and new from England but I salute everyone of them. Their many graves along the roads tell the story.

If anything 'Ted' was getting more and more stubborn to shift from those positions and his delaying tactics were stretching us to the limit. River crossings, minefields, booby traps, road cratering all added up to days and nights of dirty and dangerous work.

The infantry were again reporting numerous booby traps of all descriptions.

Houses exploding in their faces, trip wires in the dark killing all their patrols, and Schu mines by the score caused numerous casualties. This was a dirty enemy we were up against, a bastard in every way who would stop at nothing to kill and maim.

Sorry to carry on a bit, but my hackles still rise when I see again those 19 and 20 year old lads whose lives were shattered by this bastard. These were not Nazis. These were German,

every one of them German. A nation of people blindly
following an ambitious madman who hoped, as they all must
have done, to conquer Europe and more. They were still
attracting hate from nearly all the nations of the world although
beaten on all fronts. Russia and the Western Front together
with the Italian front were advancing all the time but still he
persisted in his killings and atrocities. It was the supreme
sacrifice, made by those 20 year old lads, that would be the
only thing to stop them in the end. Apologies again!

It was during one of these booby trap periods that Johnny
Gurkha sent through to say that casualties were becoming
numerous from mines and booby traps, could the Sappers help?

No. 1 Sub. was detailed and after abandoning the 'White'
some distance behind Johnny's line of advance, went forward to
be met by a British Major and several dozen of his blokes held
up by what was obviously a scattering of Teller and 'S' mines.
These were slowly and very gently cleared by the lads,
followed and guarded by, at a safe distance, a few dozen
Johnny G's full of curiosity to see how the job was done by the
experts.

It was now that we came across the booby trap. A German
Paratroop helmet planted firmly in the middle of the road by the
retreating Germans who had not cratered the road here, but
were hoping that the stupid English would do it for them, and
kill themselves, by moving the helmet.

How to tackle it was the problem. It had to be done by
myself of course, and we had worked out a 'drill' for this type
of job and carried it out successfully on many occasions.

This one was somehow different. Clearing everyone back
for 200 yds, the 'drill' was put into motion. No loose surface
of the road near this trap. No visible wires of any kind. No
sound of a mechanism from it. What the hell?

There was only the last (almost) resort left. Signal cable
rolled out of reel for about 200 yards, the recognised two-loop
clove-hitch around the helmet and a gentle retreat to where all
and everyone were holding their breath.

A good tug brought the helmet rolling towards us. No smoke, no bang, no nothing except one embarrassed Sapper NCO and a whole crowd of G's grinning all over their faces! Some stupid German, in his haste to retreat, had dropped his helmet off the back of the truck. How stupid can one get? Some you win, some you lose, I was happy not to lose this one!

Another move forward of quite a few miles, this is becoming very morale boosting. Every mile is one nearer home and one nearer the occupation of the Fatherland. He has caused two world wars and a whole series of butchering and destruction and must *never* be allowed to do so again. This time the politicians must listen to the people.

The geography of the country was now changing rapidly. The last foothills of the Apennines had indeed been reached and from the position now taken up, the panorama was one of a vast flat area as far as the eye could see. What a pity that we were there to do something other than admire the scenery.

A very large town could be seen way over to the right which had to be, according to my now very tattered and extremely small scale Italian map, Cesena.

The map shows Highway 9, one of the main arteries of Italy at that time, running obliquely from Rimini on the coast, following the line of foothills on its left and passing through a series of large towns en route to Milan in the North. The first of these was Cesena, for which the scrap was about to start.

The geography of the country had now swung firmly in our favour. From these hills the towns on Highway 9 could be clearly seen, so giving our OP's and Artillery a much better advantage. To add to this, the country was absolutely flat and, speaking as a Sapper with little knowledge on the subject, perfect for tank warfare. There were two big snags to making this a rapid advance to the north. One was called 'Ted' and the other a series of rivers any one of which would now, perish the thought, become another 'Winter Line'.

Not that! Surely not that again! Bogged down in snow mud, muck and blood for six months!

Surely this was now open country where he just could not make a stand. We shall see!

The first river between us and Cesena was the Savio and, after, a couple of pleas from several Infantry Units, who all wanted a bridge, the move forward again was on.

Then something very unusual happened. Instead of cracking on with the bridge, and under cover of darkness, we were ferried across the river in all sorts of water transport. My gang were in waterproofed Jeeps of all things, but what was the reason for this move? Surely the river bridge must be more important than all this ferrying business. Once again ours is not to reason why, the other ranks, the blokes on the ground doing the job are told sweet FA. The 'Planners' up top are too busy to take time for explanations, so, follow me lads!

This time it was something different. No river to bridge but a road repair which was incredible in size, particularly in its length in the dark. The whole road seemed to have been destroyed by 'Ted' in his retreat. There was just nothing left of it. He must have used tons of explosives and gone to great lengths to achieve this. But why, when one night's work by a party of 'good' Sappers could put things right. He wasn't thinking on our lines obviously. Just as long as he could cause delay I suppose he was 'happy'.

There had been no forward movement of troops from this point on, and although we were assured that some infantry had crossed the gap in order to establish some sort of bridgehead, the order was 'no noise - muffle everything!'

The reason for this soon became apparent. Instead of a few guns booming in the distance and the subsequent shells whistling around the ear, it was the burr burr-pt of his Spandau machine guns. Tracers were coming in bursts from the front and to the right.

It was to be a Bailey but, with the approach area and the far bankseat being hard road surfaces it should not be much of a problem, at least, that's what the 'boys in the office' would think. It's only when you're actually on the job that the real problem can be appreciated.

It is very dark, the bankseat area is one mass of demolished rubble, and reports from the far side say that it is in an even worse mess over there. And there's 'Ted' of course. How could we be without him at this stage of the war?

Stores were late in arriving and had to be carried quite a distance because there was no possible way of bringing noisy transport up to the job. Many a prayer of thanks was said because, mainly, the structure was relatively small.

The news was now circulating around the blokes that this road was absolutely vital for the attack on Cesena within the next few days. Also that several bridges were wanted urgently across the river which we had been ferried over, the Savio.

Further stories made the rounds too, that our sister (or brother?) Company had attempted to bridge but had been severely shelled with heavy casualties forcing them to abandon the attempt. Not exactly heartening news when it was understood that that would be our next job.

The night was moving through the small hours and it could be sensed that some panic was setting in. Order was that this area had to be cleared by daylight at all costs because firstly, 'Ted' would give you his undivided attention and secondly The Enemy must not suspect activity from this quarter!

As the stores were being unloaded and brought up they were immediately built into position and return journeys made, but, panic as much as humanly possible, completion wasn't to be and, timing things to the last possible minute, Bob called a halt, so allowing time to get back across the river before daylight.

This included camouflaging the structure too, something which had been allowed for and involved vehicle camouflage nets and shrubbery of varying kinds. Job done before daylight and a 'high tail' across the river, seriously hoping that the remaining Infantry were OK and out of sight.

The weather just has to be mentioned again. It was rain, rain, continuous bloody rain. Saturation point had been reached days ago with the only consolation being the fact that an old farmhouse had been commandeered as a billet, and everywhere dripping clothing of all types could be seen. The organised Subs (like ours) usually managed to keep one bloke back on the farm to do all sorts of things. Most important of these, of course, was to try to dry out the clothing by lighting fires etc. Without this system, and without doubt, influenza, pneumonia and any relative condition would have taken their toll.

Returning to the bridge on the following night, early of course, the disturbing news waiting from the infantry was that 'Ted' had suspected something was happening in the area and had mortared virtually all day. Thanks a million – now what?

Bob had the 'brilliant' idea of a distracting party and called for volunteers. How could anyone volunteer to shoot off flares and make a general commotion, so making 'Ted' concentrate his fire on to them instead of the real target? But they did and a quick plan was worked out just how to do it. Any Sapper reading this will appreciate just what we did with gun cotton, primers and dets, Cortex, F.I.D., flares, etc., etc. from a *very* safe distance. The plan worked (thanks Bob) and 'Ted' replied accordingly. The bridge was finished well before dawn with only a few bursts of Spandau over head and, for sure, these were only guesswork from a nervous Fritz.

From here on things were being done in a hurry. People were panicky because the attack for Cesena was looming large and no one had managed to get a bridge over the Savio yet and, naturally, without one the push was just not on.

Various ideas, apparently, were dismissed such as getting infantry across by boat and ferry to form a bridge head (this was considerably lower down than our initial crossing of previous nights) but was ruled out because of the risk factor, 'Ted' was close in strength. Montgomery was obviously gone, a thinking man was now running the show.

The solution arrived at was a 'silent' construction Bailey, of course by night, and by day a heavy smoke screen would be put down to hide it. Christ!

That night the last few years of experience and lessons learned the hard way proved invaluable. Panel pins were greased, adjustment fittings (such as sway bracing) were well oiled, hammers (mallets) were muffled where possible and swearing was kept to an absolute minimum (you had to be deaf to believe that) but 'Ted', of course, wouldn't know an 'f' from a 'b' so things gradually took shape and the job was completed by the first light with very few casualties, except for sore thumbs when the head of the pin couldn't be seen in the dark!

The attack on Cesena went in on the following night. Detail will not be discussed because, primarily, we were not involved in the actual fighting, our part was done. But to those Infantry and Tank lads who were, I once again salute with all feeling because the amount of shelling, mortaring and machine gun fire he threw against them just had to be seen to be appreciated. How any survived was incredible but, survive they did, and with two days' heavy fighting forced Jerry to back up.

Promotion. That was the word from HQ. You are promoted again and posted to No. 3 Section.

If the truth was really known this is just the thing that I did not want to happen because mainly it would entail saying goodbye to all the blokes around me, who I had grown to know so well over the past four or five years, and probably meeting and soldiering with blokes never seen before.

The only two consolations in mind were 'You were in No. 3 originally so there must be blokes left there you knew in 1940/41 and, after all, you are a Regular with several years yet to serve, (four in fact at that moment) and this will help your pay and career.'

So be it. The move was only several miles down the road but the thoughts regarding strange faces were right, No. 3 Sub. of No. 3 Section were all virtual strangers except two, so stop moaning and settle down to it! OK, will do!

The day after arrival was moving day again. The 'front' had moved on following Highway 9 from a line with Cesena at the centre, to the next river line, the Ronco.

From our position on some high ground well to the left of the highway, the city of Forli could plainly be seen. From that distance it looked fairly large and well spread out, but of course well occupied by 'Ted', who, it seemed, was once again digging his heels in. The whole area, including the city, was covered in shell bursts with a smoke cloud hanging over it. It had been raining continuously for days and as a consequence there had been no air activity, but now the RAF took full advantage of the sudden improvement in the weather. Huge groups of medium bombers kept up a continuous run over the area, but what the targets were it was impossible to see because of the thick smoke covering all. At one stage a group of Mitchells dropped a whole load of HE on the road area immediately in front, but I'm damned if it could be seen what their target was, even with borrowed binoculars.

November was fast approaching and with it a further deterioration of the weather. Colder and wetter, if that was possible, but all adding to the misery of the conditions, and very ominously beginning to bog things down again and so pointing to another winter of mud and blood. Please God take a hand and *do* something!

The 1st of November 1944 brought a vicious counter attack from 'Ted'. His infantry attacked in strength, and at the same time he laid down a very heavy barrage of Nebelwerfer (Sobbers) fire and artillery using 88's and heavier calibre stuff.

It was, again, one of the worst days experienced, resulting in our sister Company losing a good many chaps killed and wounded and with ourselves diving in and out of mud filled ditches causing alternate bouts of laughing and crying (this *had* to be experienced to be appreciated). Laughter when the shelling ended and the words of the 'joker' (so-called) ridiculed him for being a bad shot, and crying when it became so bad that you knew 'my turn is coming' and your whole being was screaming internally.

Cpl. Frank P died this day. It was the terrible death of a close friend and, with him, quite a few boys wounded.

Just how does one carry on when someone you know so well is mangled to death and others have limbs taken off? Where was all this madness leading us to? Were any of the originals going to survive what this madman was doing?

As the next forward move was made, which, by the way, involved filling in road craters which the bombers had caused, we became aware of the terrible stench coming from the materials (brick rubble) being used and it was only then, after close inspection, that it was realised that bits of human flesh was mixed with the rubble. Obviously the demolished house where it came from had been hit by bombs or shell fire. Someone suggested booby trap, but of course there were no means of telling because of lack of uniforms. Just get on with the job was the order!

There must have been some stiff resistance on the outskirts of Forli, probably tanks dug into cellars or similar. 'Ted' was fond of this and knew just how hard it was to shift him, but the RAF now had the answer, rocket firing Typhoons!

What an awe inspiring and frightening weapon. Just to witness them from fairly close range was bad enough but, to be on the receiving end would be a nightmare beyond comprehension.

In this case they came in numbers and seemed to patiently wait their turn, select their target and it was goodbye Mr Chips! The wonderful thing about it all of course was the fact that there was nil interference from the Luftwaffe. How different from North Africa, which has probably been said before but is well worth repeating.

Cesena was now being 'civilised' by our base Units, and there was even a rumour going the rounds of a cinema unit being set up there. Let's hope for the future!

Forli city was now 10 miles further north-west along Highway 9 from Cesena and, from reports coming in, 'Ted' was falling back and leaving the city in ruins. This would probably be right because I'm sure our bombing and shelling added to the mess.

CHAPTER THIRTY FIVE

FORLI AND FAENZA

From here on in this tiny piece of the war, the writer will concentrate on incidents (true incidents) of interest as opposed to bridge construction and mine warfare, because there is a danger of the telling of those facts, dangerous as they were and each one unique in its happening, becoming monotonous and boring.

Briefly, several more rivers were bridged before 'Ted's' Winter Line 1944/45. (God! How many more winters?) This was on the Sentio, a small river but so positioned and with man made flood banks so as to give 'Ted' some very good ready-made defences. Rest of that later.

The Montone and Lamone were two of the rivers well remembered because of the difficulties experienced in their crossings but, as promised, the monotony will be dropped to concentrate on incidents.

By the way, and before so doing, the previous river, the Savio, suddenly decided to do a Sangro on everybody. The level rose very rapidly, obviously caused by the heavy rain and caused several bridges to be washed away, so it was standby for action!

Fortunately, nothing happened to 'Spean' Bridge so, flap off again!

After a few more days of pretty hectic scrapping for Forli, 'Ted' was forced to abandon it, and once again I salute the Infantry and Tank blokes who took part in the battles. They were beyond praise. The British 4th Division was one of the Units taking part in the battle and here happened just one little incident which is forever present in my mind.

It concerns the British lady. In this case, a woman of outstanding courage and calm common sense with a very strong sense of purpose and duty, and you won't beat her in any language or nationality!

It happened in Forli. The situation was one of devastation, despair and total chaos. German heavy shells, mostly phosphorous, were crunching in every few minutes, causing one and all to shelter in whatever ruined building could be found.

Some *bright* spark (repeat) some *bright* spark had decided that our dwelling house should be slap bang in the centre of Forli, an obvious target for 'Ted', and not some quiet country cottage with the dark eyed maids in attendance and loads of vino of course, on which 'Ted' wouldn't waste his shells.

The road to the next town, Faenza, had been badly cratered and sure enough my gang had been detailed to make good, 'best you can', no transport available, road under observation!

Try to picture the scene, 12 men plus 1, sorry, should there have been the word brave in there? Carrying picks, shovels and all the other Sapper essentials to do a good job, virtually crawling down the street of ruins, diving into a ruin every time a 210 mm came crashing in, when a well-educated English female voice politely asked, "Tea gentlemen?"

Was I hearing things? Must have been, but it came again and sure enough there she was, tall, distinguished like an angel, standing in a partly ruined building, teapot in one hand and a plate of biscuits in the other! Yes real freshly made English tea (or whatever) and biscuits.

She, it transpired was the General Officer Commanding 4th Div's wife, and had taken it on herself to come out 'to see what she could do to help the chaps up front!'

That 10 minute break (or was it 20) was a real morale booster and all felt better afterwards. Oh! for a few (or many) more like her. Things would have been vastly different for sure!

What happened at those craters afterwards was purely incidental.

In this next paragraph, time has been taken to describe just what devastation a thing like shellfire, or its equivalent, can do to a person's mind. No names will be mentioned for the sake of the person concerned, and what happened to him afterwards was never known to me, but if the people involved in the incident do happen to read this they will know to whom this refers.

Still in Forli, still getting the shit knocked out of us, sorry, still trying to repair a devastated road, which 'Ted' must have really enjoyed making a mess of.

The Section's 'building' was large and almost roofless with the stores some 100 yards down the road.

The next crater repair job called for a winch truck, but when driver 'B' was called for, he was nowhere to be found.

While signing for stores for the job and asking Fred (Stores) if 'B' had been seen, a negative answer was received but a nod of the head to indicate behind him told a lot!

On investigation 'B' was found lying in the centre of a 'burrow' of 150 pounder tents, absolutely petrified with fear from the shelling.

The advice he received from me was to get to the M.O. immediately and Fred to see he did. He was never seen in the Company again!

That man was, in England prior to coming overseas, a well remembered sarcastic and boastful individual. Fear does some strange things!

Another little incident which may now seem petty in the cold light of 50 years of peace, concerned yet another crater on the road to Faenza.

'Ted' was close so night work only. The gang were busy with picks, shovels and 'what have you' when someone said, "Look out of the way here comes a Churchill!" Sure enough this huge monster came looming out of the dark from the Faenza direction, parked itself on 'our' crater, settled down comfortably swung its huge gun around and bang!! We all fell over, it was nothing less than a Tiger MKII, the largest and most fearsome German tank of the war.

Now that monster had to be seen to be appreciated and we were viewing from 20 yards, off the ground of course!

Now what do you do with picks, shovels and a few rifles against that!! Nothing, was the sensible answer, and after about a dozen rounds he retreated whence he came. Not that the retreat was caused by No. 3 Sub. of course. This was probably one of the devils shelling Forli.

The wintry days were turning nastier all the time and the occasional snow shower could only mean one thing, the winter was fast approaching.

After several more days, endeavouring to keep the roads open was proving nigh impossible; firstly because of the weather conditions, and secondly the state of the roads from German demolition and the weight of traffic, particularly tracked vehicles, on which we moved forward to the Faenza area.

Here was another fair sized town, as seen from a distance, but 'Ted' was still in occupation so no one took a joy ride in to see.

Some roads had become so bad in the area, and because they were not really leading where battle conditions required them, new tracks altogether had to be made from scratch. One such was the track known as the Lamone Road which became famous through a BBC broadcast. The reporter describing it as a 'drunken track being constructed by thousands of British, New Zealand, Indian and Italian troops. The weapons of peace, the pick and shovel, are winning the battle for Italy!' At the height of this work a minimum of 200 trucks were being used to cart and dump rubble, a headache for any organisation when consideration had to be given to supply of trucks, materials, flow and return, in waist deep mud, and of course 'Ted' who was always interested enough to send the occasional firework over. Thank goodness that the Luftwaffe was now virtually kaput!

One or two smaller bridges were built about now but as promised, although important to 'the man on the job' will not be detailed.

The building occupied by No. 3 Section was a fairly large house some distance across the fields from Faenza, with an outlying farm which No. 3 Sub. promptly commandeered.

The only habitable room was above the farm machinery store, access to which was via a wooden staircase, and No. 3 settled to a life on a dry wooden floor for a change. This was really a place where clothes *could* be dried out by an organised bit of thinking.

The usual guard of a night was mounted, by shifts of course, and it was during one of these shifts that the bloke on duty woke me to say that he could hear muffled voices.

Decision time, was it worth getting out of that comfortable stretcher? But because no one wanted their throats cut in the night, it was decided to investigate.

A good tour around the place, tommy gun at the alert, revealed nothing.

On the next night, and a different bloke on duty, the same thing happened but this time I feel sure that there were female voices too, he said. This called for a full investigation because this bloke was a sensible level headed guy, not prone to talking nonsense.

Nothing found that night but at the first chance during daylight hours we did a thorough search of all the farm buildings. On one side of the house a layer of sleepers were discovered in such a position that it was obvious they formed the cover to an underground cellar or similar.

The blokes were alerted while the boards were lifted. Hiding down below in two basement rooms was a whole Italian family. Father, Mother and two daughters, all absolutely petrified of being shot. Real country peasants who had been told by the retreating Germans that when the English came they would all be shot because of being former enemies.

Within two days they had learned just how wrong 'Ted' had been, because now they were sharing our rations and we their stored vegetables and, of course, vino. Mamma was doing our washing with gusto and the daughters were cleaning the place in general.

Of an evening it was talking and even singing time with the vino flowing of course and things becoming very friendly.

Mamma and Papa were middle aged, which of course to us seemed quite old, but the two girls were in their teens and both very attractive, as most Italian girls are. Bruna and Valeria, 16 and 19 respectively, both very shy having had little contact with men before.

So that's the build-up to the incident about to be related. In my mind there was a danger of things getting out of hand, particularly when the vino was in.

The one chap who posed the biggest danger was Paddy, a big raw Irishman, straight from the bogs of Ireland and when a few drinks were in, his thoughts and talk was always women. What he would do etc. when he got his hands on one for the first time in x number of months (or years) even!

To be fair to the rest of the gang, who had only been known to me for several weeks, they all appeared quite decent and reasonable blokes, but this Paddy bloke was a different matter. He reminded me very much of Monka, remember 'Monka' from Chepstow?

Perhaps I was overdoing it a bit, but of a night time, when all were kipping down, the stretcher would be placed strategically across the open doorway so that anyone leaving the room just had to step over me.

On the third night, someone stepped over and by grabbing him by the leg it was ascertained to be Paddy. "Going for a piss," he said, to which the reply was, "Be back in 5 minutes!"

5, 10, 15 minutes went by and no Paddy, so by now I *knew* that something was afoot. Down the stairs quietly into the machinery room and there very unmistakably was the sound, across the room of violent sex taking place. Christ! This is trouble now! But switching on the torch there appeared a sight never to be forgotten! Paddy in the altogether and belting away at the female form in front of him, who was bending over and studying the contents of a wheel barrow in the dark, Mamma!

Have you ever heard an Irishman swear when interrupted in such an operation. It's an education!

Mamma could not look me in the eye again for days, but somehow my washing was getting an extra scrub and the vino glass was always full!

The New Zealand Division was now in the line and we were attached for all the engineering work they requested. What a fine bunch of blokes they turned out to be, and how friendly towards the British, particularly the Maoris whose average size was about two stone heavier than us.

Christmas was fast approaching and word passed around that the 'Kiwis' were holding a party in the part of Faenza now occupied by them. No. 3 Sub. were invited by the blokes for whom we had been clearing mines for the past several days.

Was that a party! They had each and every type of booze and (God knows how) about a dozen or so Italian women. After two or three glasses of varying taste and colour vino, no one worried about who the women were, or where they came from. I well remember that before first light I had married one of them! Wonder what happened to her?

One effect the booze had, and this has been said before, it causes a dulling of the senses to such an extent that even when the shells were flying, no one seemed to worry too much. That morning He removed half our roof and broke every window in the place but within hours a semi drunken gang had it all waterproofed and ship shape again and no moans either. What the hell! It was Christmas after all.

The attack on Faenza seemed to be growing in intensity all the time, after a particularly heavy British barrage which involved, just afterwards, No. 3 Sub. clearing a track of Teller mines. It was with very heavy hearts that we found the whole area full of dead troops, not only German but very many

Maoris. What had gone wrong? Had that barrage fallen short? It was a matter never to be explained along with a great many other mysteries of the war. The next two days were mostly spent burying people in temporary graves.

It was about now that the Infantry holding the forward area to the north-west of Faenza were repeatedly calling for better means of access to their positions. The poor devils were dug in mud and muck of all sorts with 'Ted' doing his best to add to the misery of it all, but no means at all of keeping them supplied by road of the necessities of war.

The decision was that a new supply track had to constructed from the existing road to run the full length of this front line position, so forward No. 3 Section!

It was quite a hazard even getting to the track because the 'Up' Route was under observation by 'Ted' who kept his gunners very busy trying to upset everything.

The construction of the track was to be a mixture of Somerfield Track, sleepers, felled timber etc., sufficient to carry Jeeps and personnel only.

This was all very fine and no doubt essential, but no one warned the construction gang that this was absolutely front line stuff. The first inkling of this occurred when unloading stores off the White, a Spitfire came diving in with all guns blazing. At the very first second it was thought that we had been mistaken for his target, but then it was realised that although he was firing from directly above, his target was a Jerry position several hundreds yards in front. Once again my hat comes off in salute to that pilot who appeared to have every manner of missile in the book thrown at him and from all around our position, it was just unbelievable. He survived by a miracle only.

As work started on the 'home' end of 'Xmas Track', as it was eventually named, it became gradually clear just what and where the position was. It ran the length of a ridge overlooking the Lombardy Plain and from there our heavy machine gunners had a commanding view. The trouble was, and here I draw breath and wonder, even now, about the stupidity of it all, the track ran *in front* of these guns and the officer i/c would call a five minute warning when they were about to fire! Can you imagine a more ridiculous situation because, naturally, 'Ted's' gunners would reply and usually his 88's would join the fun!

Our very sensible gunners were dug into deep and very sensible gun pits, but where were the very intelligent Sappers? Running around like scalded cocks looking for holes to dive into, and seldom finding one of any depth.

This stupid situation carried on for a week or so, and then because the front line moved forward slightly the whole thing was abandoned. It was high level planning at its peak! Surely the track, very little used by the way, could have been sited behind the guns or some other alternative. Some casualties did occur amongst the lads, the closest and most upsetting to our gang was that our good and faithful driver, Ted, lost an eye during one of these shoots. A very good chap who received an MM for his bravery (putting up with us mostly) but no track was worth suffering loss of life or limb.

AUTUMN/WINTER LINE 1944
SPRING OFFENSIVE 1945

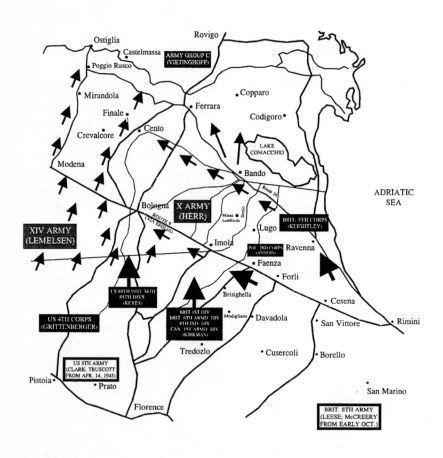

    Main attacks by 8th and US 5th Armies
          September/October 1944

          Attacks by 8th and US 5th Armies. April 9/22

CHAPTER THIRTY SIX

THE SENIO

The weather was, if possible, deteriorating still further. Snow showers were an almost daily occurrence and slowly but surely things were beginning to grind (or squelch) to a halt. The Italian mud was taking its toll again, just as in previous years, and it was now, for sure, that the Winter Line would be on the River Senio.

Up until that time we had not seen this new river but some of the chaps had been up on 'recce' and reported back that it was a 'one off' and would be unique in the world of bridging. (So more of that later).

All sorts of queer things now started to happen to the Company. Firstly we were withdrawn from the forward area, and for a fortnight carried out light training and rest (from it all) some 20 miles behind the shooting area.

There were cinema shows in Cesena and even a canteen where tea and cakes were the order of the day.

A lot of the Company were given seven days' leave in Rome and, rumour had it, that everyone else would do so in rotation.

Over the next few weeks, varying types of new training methods and ideas were carried out. One of these was the boring into and demolition of the flood banks of a river, then an assault crossing and blowing t'other bank. This was ominous, could this be a dummy run for the Senio? No one said a word but, someone, somewhere, knew what was coming!

Then there were the 'Funnies'.

These were all types of experimental equipment, mostly RE developments, using tanks as vehicles for crossing rivers and ditches without exposing personnel to enemy fire.

One very useful piece of those 'Funnies' was a Churchill tank fitted with two arms of bridging equipment on top so that when the tank was positioned in the river or ditch, the arms

308

could be winched into a position forming a bridge over the gap but, again, more of that later. The name was 'The Ark' and was well worth remembering.

Another one, called 'The Toad' used an Assault Landing Craft mounted, again, on a Churchill and was apparently used later in the campaign for the Po crossing.

Then suddenly it was Rome. Yes Rome, somewhere I had seen very briefly before but then my mind was thinking of other things. This time it would be Rome and nothing but Rome and no such silly thing as women would enter into it but, on second thoughts, who the hell wanted to spend days (or nights even) looking at statues etc.?

It was truck to Rimini and then train, yes train, to Rome. The Sappers had done well rebuilding the track for the whole length of the country.

Rome again was impressive but, as before, marred by small boys who appeared to have numerous sisters and dozens of cheap (chip) shops around the corner.

A pattern was soon adopted of how to spend the days, which was mostly viewing, eating and drinking. But for the nights, it was every man for himself with no questions asked and no explanations given. Please remember that I am now a respectable grandfather who, because of the passing years, can only dimly recall those nights in Rome!

Some types of food were available in the bars and cafés, the favourite of which were eggs, mushrooms and Asti Spumanti. The latter being so ridiculously cheap as to be on a par with lemonade.

And so the Roman days were passed and soon (or nearly so) forgotten on the return to the business in hand.

As will be realised by now the whole idea of this period was resting the troops and some training in readiness for that big attack which must come when the weather improved.

Several items of interest happened during that period of preparing for the big day, one of which brought contact with the troops of South Wales and even my home town area.

During one of the visits to the Cesena canteen, the unmistakable South Wales accent was heard, and enquiries made, resulting in the knowledge that the Royal Welsh Fusiliers now held the front line position on the Senio.

They were very generous in their invitations to drop in and see them if passing by. Not if I could help it was the reply because of the fact, as they said, that the last 100 yards or so would have to be covered in a crawling position or preferably by night because 'Ted' was only 38 yards away across the river and, not only did he have listening devices but periscopes too! Periscopes? Yes periscopes!

A word of explanation here, slightly out of sequence but, essential to the story.

Some time later the Section were well forward and, once again, running through various 'drills' of what to do on the coming assault on the Senio. During this period No. 3 Sub. were sent to clear an area of mines leading right up to the Senio itself, obviously the area where the crossing would be attempted.

The clearance job turned out to be much bigger than anticipated and, as a consequence, several nights had to be spent bivvying in a local ditch.

It was surprisingly quiet for a front line area because, I suppose, the Allied forces were content just to build up for the big day and 'Ted', knowing by now, surely, that he was a beaten man, content to sit quiet without stirring things up, and this is just how it turned out to be.

The chance came during that period of paying the R.W.F. a visit and what transpired to be front line warfare really was an eye opener.

They, the Welsh lads, were dug into the home bank with foxholes, gun pits and all manner of communication trenches reminiscent, surely of World War I. The bank itself was a huge affair and of course matching the one on the other side. These banks were man made because of the low lying land in order to prevent flooding which, memories of the Sangro, occurred most winters. The top was used, in peace time, to drive bullock carts along, and naturally widened considerably at the base for stability. This gives you some idea of the task required on the great day because both of these banks would have to be blown away and gaps made for an assault bridge before any progress could be made in the way of tank warfare etc.

Looking through their periscopes it could clearly be seen that the water was less than 20 yards wide, but depth unknown. Now the training and demonstrations of 'The Arks' began to take shape. So that's how some of the assault crossings would be made!

The Boyo's took great delight in explaining 'normal' everyday life in their 'holiday camp'.

Very little firing took place between them and 'Ted's' positions on the far bank. *He* was well and truly dug in and would take a lot of shifting. Most sightings were done by periscope and an almost friendly atmosphere existed.

For instance an occasional shoot would be called for and a Sherman tank would climb the bank, take up hull-down position and fire a few rounds into 'Ted's' position. Within minutes, and they swore this was true, a target would appear from the German lines for it to fire at!

On other occasions a young German soldier would climb over the top, wander down to the river, unbutton his fly and not to be crude about it, have a piss! Just 20 yards from a hundred guns.

Their favourite story was Loopy Lofty.

This character apparently was a giant of a German (must have been seven feet tall from their description) who appeared every morning just after first light and proceeded, very calmly and professionally, to perform cartwheels, handsprings and various other acrobatic feats along the top of the German held bank. All this received rapturous and well earned applause from the Welsh lads, to which 'Lofty' would bow in appreciation (after all he was risking his life!) and to the calls of

"Encore!" he would wave and shout "Auf Wiedersehen!" That story sounds as tall as he was! They also added that, "There are no *good* Germans, but at least this one was likeable and entertaining."

Jumping forward a little with this story of gory warfare with paid holidays, it was about now that the decision came to rest the British troops until the time of the big push. So the RWF were taken out and, the same as last winter, a crack Italian Regiment was brought in to hold the line.

Once again it was pantomime time to watch them come in. Armed to the teeth with all sorts of weapons, guns, knives, grenades, bandoliers of cartridges slung over every available shoulder until one wondered just how could they run backwards with all that weight! The impression one gained was that the Senio would be crossed tomorrow and Berlin entered within a week but, instead what did these wonderful brave soldiers do? They shot 'Lofty!'

Apparently one day after arrival 'Lofty' appeared and about a dozen guns opened up. 'Quel la Guerra!' (that is war!)

It was about now that dear old Mum wrote to say that Dad was seriously ill, and within days another letter followed to say that Dad had gone. Poor old boy, apparently he had suffered with cancer for some time without complaining and Mother had not said a word about it to me. She didn't want to worry me, was her explanation after the war.

Brother was away in the RAF, so an application for leave on compassionate grounds was made, only to be told in no uncertain terms, "That is not possible, you are needed here because we have no replacement!"

End of story.

My parents will always be remembered for their guidance, love and kindness to me. They are buried together under the word 'Reunited' and receive visits several times a year from a grateful son.

CHAPTER THIRTY SEVEN

THE FINAL BATTLE

Winston Churchill's words to Field Marshall Alexander: "This great final battle in Italy will long stand out in history as one of the most famous episodes of this 2nd World War."

So history was about to be made and No. 3 Sub. of No. 3 Section was to play its small part in it.

Every word of the events is exactly as it happened and although it may sound an unlikely tale in this day and age of peace, the history details of the Italian Campaign verify its authenticity.

Unfortunately my diary could not be made at the time, because of circumstance, but completion was made as soon as opportunity occurred afterwards.

A good many years later I was asked to give a lecture at the Royal School of Military Engineering, Chatham, to a class of student military Clerks of Works. The subject was 'A Sappers Day in the 2nd World War' and I chose as an interesting series of events the 'Final Battle for the Senio'!

After the lecture, and during question time, it transpired that a lot of the class just did not believe what they had been told until a senior instructor at the School came forward and said, "Every word is just how it did happen, I was there!"

He happened to be a fellow NCO in my Company at the time who was well known to me!

Eric! If you are reading these words, please get in touch!

For months the build-up of stores and materials of all kinds had been taking place. There were dumps everywhere of all the things required to make modern warfare. Enough, it could be thought, to take an Army the size of this one right through to Berlin.

It was early April '45 and the Italian weather had cleared beautifully, and here it must be said that, for once, the people in the 'top office', the planners, had got it right for time and weather. The training and preparation beforehand was to prove invaluable, so what are we waiting for?

April 9th arrived dry and clear. We had been withdrawn some distance back from the actual banks of the river and had selected a small valley as a waiting area. 'Ted' had to be softened up first!

The river was well in sight and here it must be pointed out that all Italian troops had been withdrawn from the area before today and the line was now held by the 8th Indian Div., our old friends from the 'Y' Div. experience, remember? They were well experienced and good troops but, Oh! Where were the Welsh boys, or the Geordies, Cockneys or Scouses of Blighty?

At 2.30pm the first heavy bombers appeared. B24 Liberators, and stretched as far as the eye could see. Hell! Where did they all come from? Many prayers were said about getting their target right and then the world went mad! They dropped a complete carpet of bombs, destroying everything above ground level on *both* sides of the river.

Then the guns opened their barrage. 1600 guns on this sector and all firing 'intense'. The Bofors AA even joined in until all minds were saturated with the intense noise. Nothing was making sense and no one could survive it seemed.

This barrage continued for a full 20 minutes and then the air was filled with fighters and fighter bombers of every type. Machine gun fire, rockets, canon and bombs all rained down on the river. God help the receiving Germans! Was it possible to feel sorry for them?

Then the heavy bombers again, mostly fortresses this time and all dropping anti-personnel bombs. The world was going further into the depths of depravity, and yet there was to be no respite. Just as soon as the bombers finished their onslaught, the guns took over again. The ears were now jumping with jagged pain and even stuffing in bits of rag made little difference, it was far too late.

The instinctive thought came that any personal items of importance should be carried somewhere on my person, just in case! As things transpired, it was only by doing this that my diaries survived!

For the remainder of that day, the terrible onslaught continued for what must have been the highest concentration of high explosive poured on to a small area of ground of any attack on any battle front in history. From 2.30pm until 8.00pm it was one continual scene of destruction until the attackers, the men waiting to cross that river, were reduced to almost nervous wrecks.

At 8.00pm there appeared on the scene a weapon capable of human destruction on a massive scale, the 'Crocodile'. A Churchill tank, with trailer, capable of throwing flame much further than the width of that river. Many dozens of these lined up and poured continuous flame onto any wretches that had survived the other forms of death.

Their job done it was now the turn of No. 3 Sub. and, in a totally deaf silence, we went forward to carry out the 'drill' practised a dozen times before.

With earth augers (6 dia) and extension arms, holes were made into the soft soil of the bank to the absolute depth it was possible to reach – that is 3ft plus 9ft = 12ft. A series of holes were made on either side of the home bank (in total darkness of course) and each one packed with prefabricated metal sleeves filled with ammonal. When completed, all holes were then linked up with the primary and secondary means of detonation.

Right up to that moment everything had gone like clockwork and the actual physical assault across the Senio was about to begin when in stepped 'Mr Chaos' in the form of Johnny Indian!

The assault troops of 8th Indian Div. were forming up, they appeared from nowhere and in no time were everywhere!

How on earth does one explain to 500 Indians in the dark, none of whom appeared to speak English, and in whispers of course, that the bank on which they were now lying was about to erupt?

Eventually the message got home through their officers and once again all was ready to blow. It was realised by all concerned in the assault bridging jobs that just as soon as that terrific explosion took place, two things would happen. Firstly, 'Ted', knowing that a bridge had to be built across the river would now know the location and would act accordingly, and secondly it would signal the 'Arks' (remember them?) to do their job.

Crater made successfully and bang on time those lumbering giants appeared, three of which had been allocated to the bridge area.

Here is where chaos again took over from the planned 'drill'. 'Ted' by now was very interested in the proceedings and had begun to lay down a 'stonk' from some distance back.

One of the first casualties, as it lumbered over the bank was one of the 'arks', so leaving two to be shared by ourselves who now had to cross over in order to blow the far bank. A small bulldozer (armoured) was now enlarging our crater in readiness to launch the bridge, all very organised up to then.

The orders to the Indian Division were to storm across the river and form a bridgehead on the other bank. This they were determined to do, except that no one had told them that one of the 'arks' was for the use of the Sappers' building the bridge.

We were 12 men plus 1 at that moment. There were 14,000 of them, none of whom, it seemed, spoke English and all were massing to cross on the back of the two Churchills.

It was pitch dark and 'Ted' was doing his best to interfere with the chaos. Will someone tell me please that it's all a nightmare and that it is not millions of black faces on a dark night ready to shoot any white men.

Eventually we crossed and, after establishing the appropriate site for the bankment, received another shock. Right at that point were German positions, all hollowed out of the flood bank and well and truly surrounded by thick concrete roof and walls.

There was no alternative but to demolish, and so a little extra ammonal did the job.

At last things were shaping up and the bridge building started. It was now that one other problem came up. Again, from nowhere, large bunches of German prisoners began to appear, all eager to give themselves up and to get across that river away from all the bombing and shelling. They said that thousands were 'kaput' and many more 'krank' (sick) in the head from it all. This was not doubted for one minute!

It must have been 3.00am before organised building really got underway and 'Stirling' bridge began to take shape.

'Ted's' artillery and mortar crews were still capable of staying in the competition and kept us well informed of his displeasure at our crossing of his river.

First light came with the bridge almost complete but, very fortunately, because we were now working at a low level, the area was not under observation.

Already queues of trucks were assembling to make the crossing and *'Derby Day'* was again making an appearance.

This we now know was his last battle, he could not possibly stand any more of this, particularly with the Russian and Western Fronts closing in. And, as time will tell, so it was, he was unable to make any further stand in Italy.

Back to the job in hand, the approach and exit roads were completed and traffic began to flow across before mid morning.

To give you, the reader, some idea of the intensity of this battle, here are several quotes by John Ellis in his book 'The Sharp End'. He says in the chapter 'The Fighting Man in World War II':

"The most concentrated fire-power of any war was during the battle for the River Senio in Italy when, as the Polish Commander wrote, 'a section of the Artillery expended 170,000 rounds in four hours. Apart from 1,100 pieces of artillery there were mortars and AA guns all on 'intense' fire. If the barrage had continued any longer, besides being already deaf, we were all bound to go mad.'"

John Ellis also states 'that during the crossing the 8th Indian Division (remember those 14,000 black faces?) lost all four Company Commanders in two hours'.

He continues with the Report from the New Zealand Divisional Commander.

"We (the Kiwis) used as many guns as the whole 8th Army had done at El Alamein.

"The sound was of whole trains being driven at speed overhead and raining down on the river bank."

CHAPTER THIRTY EIGHT

THE END OF IT ALL

We were stood down, well satisfied with a job well done in a chaotic situation. Time for a brew!

Then it happened, and it is at this point that my physical interest in the war ceased to exist. My diary was brought up to date a good many days later.

As the traffic began to flow across, there appeared from the direction of our lines what can only be described as a 'fleet' of four engined bombers, mostly Liberators, and they filled the sky.

"They are," as Bob explained, "the Americans come to help and their target is the next river line, just in case he feels like making a stand. In order to guide them our 3.7 (AA) will put up a corridor through which to fly."

What a sight to see, all those bombers going to do their deadly work, until suddenly it was realised that they had got the wrong river line and the carpet of bombs was falling on both banks of *our* river. At first they were well downstream, in the Polish sector, but soon travelled the complete length of our front and carried on into New Zealand territory upstream.

The chaos and death caused must have been enormous and it was at this point that I took no further interest in proceedings.

There is a dim recollection of terrific bangs going on all around, and of clods of earth being thrown about, a truck on fire and someone shouting that the bridge was hit, then by some turn of fate, I was in some sort of vehicle, lying down, and travelling over a very rough road. That is the total recollection of those mad minutes. The next episode of consciousness was waking up, on a stretcher, on the grass of a tented 'Forward Dressing Station'. A doctor (Colonel R.A.M.C.) was bending over the stretcher and talking to me with a very serious look on his face. It was then I realised that not a word was reaching me and, in fact, *everything* was dead silent. I was completely deaf.

It was now that panic set in for the first time and my hands went racing all over my body feeling to see what was missing. It was then the Orderly came over and tried to explain but finished up writing down the words. "You have been unconscious since yesterday, the M.O. is dealing."

From then on it was a series of journeys by road, in total silence, until arriving at a building which, obviously, was a permanent hospital.

Being dumped, next, in a cell-like room with white washed walls and no windows, and not being able to hear any answers to my questions was becoming very alarming. Was I, at 23 (and 6 days) years old going to be deaf for the rest of my life?

Being made to lie in bed was also alarming, so much so that when the Orderly next appeared he received loud pleas from me to get up and wander about the place, because I felt fine and quite capable! He left for a while, and on return gave the OK.

It's here than an explanation is due as to what happened because, at that moment, there was no real answer to just what I was doing here.

The M.O., a South African (his Springbok badge and orange flash said so) visited next morning and carried out a thorough check of all and everything. He explained, in signs, that all would be revealed that day in writing.

That sheet of paper took a long time coming and when it did was in type on official paper under the address:- No. 7 BPC. Assisi B.F.P.O. No. X.

What it said was:-

'You are here to rest and to be rehabilitated back to normal life. Your record shows that you have been in 'forward areas' more than 20 months which is maximum.

'We are told that the incident of your being carried out of the 'battle area' was caused firstly by American bombing, so causing the Germans also to lay down a barrage, and it was one of their shells which hit you in the blast but not, fortunately, shrapnel.

'Unfortunately your hearing has been damaged, but it is hoped that in time it can be partially restored.'

So that was it in a nutshell. What 'Ted' had failed to do over the years, on his own, the 'Yanks' had now helped him to do!

As you can imagine, emotions were now running high. What was all this rehabilitation business about, and what was this 'resting' nonsense? What about the war? How was that going? How was No. 3 Sub.? Surely if I was knocked about, how were they? What about everybody else? I well remember one truck burning with blokes inside it, so surely there were others!

That was by far the worst part of those days, not knowing exactly what had happened up there, and then I was hit by another nasty shock.

My gentle enquiry as to the address, No. 7 BPC. What did it stand for?

The orderly wrote it down. Base Psychiatry Centre. Psychiatry? PSYCHIATRY Centre, I asked! Have I, like so many before, gone mad as well?

That night I cried!

It was the first time in many months that self-control was lost, but in that cell of St Francis it was all very private.

The following day brought an interview, on request, with the M.O. He said that my reaction was normal and that time was a great healer etc., etc. and that 'You will not be sent back to a front line Unit again. In any case the war for you is over.'

That was some consolation I suppose but it wasn't what was wanted. Having come through the North African and Italian campaigns from the beginning to the very last battle and now *this*!

Life had to be lived I suppose, so great pains were taken in the endeavour to return to normality. Enormous relief was felt at being away from all the carnage of recent days, but the hearing problem was a continuing worry. Would I ever hear again?

After a few days the Orderly brought into the cell a wind up gramophone, obviously with the idea that, by playing it, I might somehow, help myself to hear.

There was one record only which I shall never forget to my dying day, Glen Miller *A String of Pearls* and on the other side *The Kerry Pipers,* neither of which could produce a sound I was capable of hearing.

During these days, friendship was sought from all and sundry who came into contact. One such chap, whose Christian name is forgotten was Bennett, a Marine Commando (Green Beret) who had been knocked about like myself and had been highly decorated as a consequence . We became firm friends and he went to great trouble to explain the things unheard by me, and for which I will be eternally grateful.

On the 15th day of rehabilitation, Bennett explained that news was coming through of a link up between the Allied and Russian forces in Europe.

That was good news indeed. Was the end in sight? From then on people were listening to hourly bulletins.

Two days later, 'Mussolini Shot by his own people' was the message.

Three days later on Thursday 3rd May 1945, FM Alexandra announced that, "All German land and air forces in Italy have surrendered unconditionally."

That news was really wonderful but during that evening the news was even better, I could *hear* with one ear!

At first things were deafening but after an hour of talking and listening to myself talk, I settled down to play *A String of Pearls* again and again until every note was learnt by heart. That record, no doubt whatsoever, played a big part in my 'rehabilitation'.

Tuesday 8th May 1945. The bulletin said, which I *heard,* "All German Forces surrendered to Gen. Eisenhower yesterday. The 'Cease Fire' sounded at 1 minute past midnight last night."

CHAPTER THIRTY NINE

THE CONCLUSION

It was some years after the war that, while on holiday on the south coast, I looked up Jim (he who had saved the tea and yet still managed to get under the table when 'Ted' was misbehaving). Now instructing carpentry at a boys' school, he told me of a reunion that the chaps in the Old Company held annually.

Needless to say, no time was lost in contacting the Hon. Sec., and from then on attending each year.

It is now a very sad gathering, I am sorry to say, because after fifty long years of peace there are only a half dozen or so of the original chaps left. To all of them I take my hat off and salute, for an excellent job, very well done!

Near my home in Wales, the 'Local Authority' have erected a Bailey Bridge, a very small one which is supposed to be temporary but, of course, has already been in position a number of years.

I can never cross, or see this bridge, without feeling emotional.

The 'Authority' have covered the main deck chesses with metal sheeting. These are loose and make considerable noise when traffic is crossing. It is not understood why 'Ted' doesn't lay down a 'stonk' on this noisy and important target.

It is then that I always turn over and go back to sleep.

By sheer coincidence the book opened at Chepstow and these closing words are being written during the week that the College closes for good. The final Passing Out Parade is Saturday 11th June 1994, just two days away, so marking 70 years of tears, toil and a million other feelings experienced by those boys 'who went through'. On looking back and asking was it worthwhile? the answer must always be yes! Chepstow educated me, and many thousands of other boys, on the way of life in a very short time and, additional to learning a trade, which formed the basis for the remainder of life, it brought friends and comradeship which could not have been gained in other places. Those friends still meet and enjoy each other's company more than 50 years later. Long live the spirit and memory of Chepstow!

Apologies for rattling on but the very last words must be these: –

When leaving the services in the 50s on Voluntary Redundancy, my current job then was as a Military Clerk of Works at Army Headquarters, Germany.

Thinking ahead for a future career, letters were written to two or three likely sources in the UK, but of course somewhere local to South Wales would have been preferred. One of the positions offered was just out of this world!

"A new bridge is going to be constructed over the River Severn at Beachley, Chepstow," said the letter, "and an old army Camp has to be demolished and rebuilt on more modern lines, will you accept the position of supervising the Contract?"

Would I accept the Contract? Would I accept the pleasure of putting a sledge hammer through the wall of the barrack room where daily, many hours were spent scraping and polishing floors? And get paid for it? You bet your boots I would, and did!

It was during the initial stages of that Contract that the Military Liaison Officer enquired of me, "Why did you volunteer to accept redundancy from the Army as a Warrant Officer? With your qualifications you could have stayed on and taken a commission!"

The reply given was different to the thoughts in mind: because, somewhere on my Record Sheets it says, 'He called his instructor a big bastard!'

Instead should I readily have answered, "Yes, Mr 'Bill', I *am* a little bastard, my parents were never married!" maybe promotion would have come much quicker then.

What about the O.C. Company, who in that other insane world insisted that two 'recce' ME109s were Spitfires, so putting the Company in danger of being Stuka'd. Was I right in asking him whether or not the Bofors Sgt. should be charged for firing at Spitfires?

There can be no choice. It is much preferred the way it is.

Now 72 years old I am still completely deaf in one ear and have only partial hearing in the other; but with the aid of the NHS, most things if beneficial to me, are heard.

Fifty years after the event the Ministry decided that I was entitled to a pension for 'loss of hearing whilst on active service'.

That is now drawn weekly and could pay for a pint or two of beer, but serious thought would have to be given before buying a round for the boys.

Rupert Brooke, 'The Soldier',

If I should die, think only this of me:
That there's some corner of a foreign field
That is forever England. There shall be
In that rich earth a richer dust concealed;
A dust whom England bore, shaped, made aware,
Gave, once, her flowers to love, her ways to roam,
A body of England's, breathing English air,
Washed by the rivers, blest by suns of home.